The actor makes up his personage. He borrows from his author, he borrows from stage tradition, he borrows from nature, he draws on his own stock of knowledge of men and things, on his own experience and imagination; in short, he sets himself a task. His task once set, he has his part; he sees it, grasps it; it does not belong to him, but he inhabits its body, is fairly it!

—*Benoît Constant Coquelin*

JAMES BROUGH

THE

FABULOUS
FONDAS

DAVID McKAY COMPANY, INC., NEW YORK

To all the company
of players that strut
and fret their hour
upon the stage . . .

ACKNOWLEDGMENTS AND THANKS

By far the best and most comprehensive account of the motion-picture and theatrical performances of Henry, Jane, and Peter Fonda is to be found in John Springer's lavishly illustrated book *The Fondas* (Citadel Press, 1970). The detailed history of the University Players Guild is related by Norris Houghton in his *But Not Forgotten* (William Sloane Associates, 1952). A fascinating insight into the thinking of Henry and Jane in the early 1960s is provided in *The Player* by Lillian Ross and Helen Ross (Simon & Schuster, 1962). William Gibson's *The Seesaw Log* (Alfred Knopf, 1965) tells the full story, as he saw it, of Henry's problems with *Two for the Seesaw*. To the collection of portraits comprising Roddy McDowall's *Double Exposure* (Dial Press, 1966), Joshua Logan contributed some penetrating words about Henry, and José Quintero about Jane. Each of those books proved to be a significant work of reference and is quoted from in this text. Among countless other research sources, the following were found to be of major value: "Jane Fonda Talks About . . . ," copyright 1970, *Mademoiselle*; "Playboy Interview: Peter Fonda," *Playboy*, September 1970; "Holden Caulfield at 27" by Rex Reed, *Esquire*, February 1968; *The New Army*, published by the United States Servicemen's Fund, November 1971.

Of the many people who contributed reminiscences or research to this book, special thanks are due to:

Christopher Allan	Alfred Aronowitz
Marc Connelly	J. Richard Early
Henry Ehrlich	Alfred Everett
Eileen and Jerry Ford	Dr. Seaver Gilcreast
Pegge Hlavacek	Arthur Laurents
Leo Lerman	Joshua Logan
Michael O'Neill	Sydney Pollack
John Sandilands	Stephen Shadegg
John Springer	Elaine Steinbeck
Mildred Stephenson	Helen Wallace
Donald Werner	

Contributions of equal significance were made by others under the promise of anonymity; they are offered equal gratitude.

Prologue

THE LIST of subjects that occupy the probing mind of Henry Fonda comes close to being endless. It extends from the techniques of applying pigments to canvas with the skill of a Dutch master painter to the simpler tricks of walking on one's hands or shinnying up ropes, two enduring abilities that consistently arouse the envy of his peers.

He is prepared to discuss the advantages of eating organic foods, to which he has been devoted for years; the principles of aerodynamics involved in assembling and flying aircraft models; the finer points of home handicrafts, which he practices as an addicted tinkerer.

Politics constantly engages his attention, occasionally to the level of violence. As a man who is prepared to stand up and voice opinions without risk of misinterpretation, he has been known to stride across a room and smash a television set in order to black out a despised face.

He is often happy, of course, to reminisce about the art and profession of acting, in which he has spent all his adult life, and even the particular roles he enjoyed playing. By no means all the roles, mind you, but at least Mister Roberts, Tom Joad in *The Grapes of Wrath*, and Emmett Kelly, the clown.

There is one subject, however, on which it is virtually

impossible to draw him into conversation, and that is himself. Persuading Fonda to talk about Fonda is akin to pulling teeth. When strangers or friends try it, the elegant, sophisticated superstar vanishes, and his eyes grow ice cold. "I want to hide," he says.

The reluctance disclosed itself nearly forty years ago, long before his name first registered on Broadway and in Hollywood. Something like two hundred stage, movie, and TV roles later, it shows no sign of changing. He has been the despair of press agents, who have usually tried in vain to coax him into muttering anything more than the time of day to any newspaper reporter, magazine writer, or tape recorder.

One perceptive public-relations hand, fancying that Hank might be more outgoing if he were left strictly alone to answer questions, broke all studio house rules for making sure that a star has a witness to anything he says. This sympathetic soul took to sitting outside Fonda's dressing-room door during every interview, secure in the knowledge that his vigil would be brief and that Hank would emerge smiling the moment the agony was over. In sheer gratitude, Hank accepted him as a friend for life.

In the days when Hank could control the situation, he stretched the veil of reticence over his family as well as himself. He was never one to rattle on in public about a wife or his children, yet surprisingly enough to Hank and every friend, there have been five wives, which is a constant amazement, because he doesn't seem, on the face of it, to be at all the kind of man that the score implies. In the entries he composed for standard biographical works like *Who's Who*, details of domesticity were minimized or just omitted. By sheer exercise of will, this very private man insisted that his not always unsensational life must not be sensationalized for public consumption.

Then, it seemed almost overnight, his son and daughter grew up, followed behind him in the long shadow cast by his career and his personality, and blew to smithereens his yearning to be virtually anonymous. First Jane and later Peter Fonda pulled faces at him across the generation gap, accusing him of having wrecked their past and damned their future.

Now the three of them have become the first family of show business, the fabulous, fascinating, fantastic, fighting Fondas, depending on which alliteration the headline writer is reaching for. Hank winces at every one of these descriptions, as he does at that other cliché that calls them "the royal family of Hollywood."

But, at the wholly unbelievable age of sixty-eight in 1973, Henry Fonda is a fact no more to be ignored than Mount Rushmore and still, all in all, the most sought-after actor in the business. The Fonda story in many ways is an archetypical image of our times, of lives molded and sometimes distorted by the pressures of changing circumstances, by choice and necessity, by the lightning flashes of success and the devastation of death.

This book was begun in 1970, when Jane was rapidly becoming the first lady of the New Left, second only perhaps to Angela Davis. Peter had emerged as an authentic idol of the Age of Aquarius and a millionaire at thirty. Hank's enormous army of admirers saw him as personifying the best of Middle America, with an aura of honesty and integrity like a carry-over from the past, when the West was young and the world more innocent.

Like his children, he didn't pay too much attention to hero worship. If anything, it embarrassed him.

He was young Mr. Lincoln, Wyatt Earp, and the President of the United States (in *Fail Safe*). He exemplified virtue, justice, and dependability. But as a working actor, he wasn't seduced by any of those. If any part, heavy or hero, was offered him at the right price, he would seriously consider it, so long as it promised him the chance to shape it to his talents.

The life-style of Henry Fonda dates back to the time of the titans. It is elegant, expensive, and the overhead is high. He had—and retains—a five-story Manhattan town house on East Seventy-fourth Street and a bigger hilltop house in Bel Air. The internal atmosphere in each of them is the same—deep carpets, lustrous antiques, the opulence of the days when radio and Hollywood provided the world with the only mass entertainment available.

Not to be seen in either house is a wing chair that had once been a favorite of his. With each new wife, it had been re-upholstered and re-covered. But the fifth Mrs. Fonda disposed of it at last.

There is another difference noticeable to his friends. He is visibly happier in this marriage than he has been for as long as they can remember. Shirlee Mae Adams was a former airline hostess when they were married in 1965, twenty-seven years younger than he. She has said, "I believe he's happy for the first time in his life." She has acknowledged only two things that she really hates, "and they are ex-wives and the label 'stepmother.' "

The past life of the family she would marry into was completely unknown to Shirlee Adams when she met Hank at a party given by friends. She didn't recognize the tall, slightly stooping man who came into the room, with the fresh-from-the-barber, clean-as-a-whistle look that used to be standard costume and appearance in the days when the big studios governed the motion-picture industry and wrote the rules for the way stars must behave off duty as well as during working hours. The story goes that Shirlee turned and gasped, "Now who's *that* gorgeous man?"

Later, when she knew him much better, she bubbled, "How he had so many wives, I don't know."

Friends who have known him for the better part of half a century detect little change in Hank over the decades. Physically, he is about as trim as when he was a settlement-house gym instructor in Omaha, Nebraska. He still has the easy, graceful, stallion stride that dominates the stage whenever he makes an entrance. Mentally, he remains a hard-driven perfectionist, demanding the most of himself as an actor and expecting the most from everyone who works with him.

Of course, he is still working: "I always need the money." He works in the theater, as he has for most of the past forty-five years. He also makes movies. In 1970 he was starring in a television series, playing, of all things, a cop. Talking stiffly, as he invariably does in interviews, he told one reporter, "I like the concept, the story of a plain-clothes cop and his family. I've researched the job. I spent a day at Parker Center, the police headquarters in downtown LA. I spent another day at the police academy. I rapped with detectives in a Hollywood precinct-house. I've had lunch with other cops.

"I've learned these are dedicated people. They're not sorry to be cops. They're proud. Now, I don't say there are no bad cops. I just haven't met them. These are nice guys, with a job to do, which is to have all sorts of things thrown at them, get hurt, get killed. I want to show that. Maybe it's because I haven't had bad experiences, as Peter has, or as Peter thinks he has. Or Jane."

He also stars in television commercials, for which he reportedly receives a fee of $250,000, though details of his income are another subject Henry Fonda prefers not to discuss.

Fonda had another project in mind, as well as his television series, more movies, and more plays. With a little outside help, he put together a one-man show, reading and performing passages that deal with a subject on which he might well rank as something of an expert—the generation gap. His title for it was *Fathers Against Sons Against Fathers.*

His selections included extracts from William Shakespeare, Benjamin Franklin, Arthur Miller, and Bob Dylan. His agent suggested that he ought to include a few minutes concerning his own life. That was difficult for a man as reticent as Hank Fonda.

"I'm a self-conscious person," he has acknowledged. "I'm an actor because I don't have to be myself."

Finally, he wrote a line or so that went as far as he thought fit. "Fathers are men who look eight feet tall and walk with giant steps. I knew my father was the best kite-flier that ever lived."

I

BEFORE GRAND ISLAND, Nebraska, gained a certain limited reputation as the birthplace of Henry Jaynes Fonda, the town was better known in the guidebooks as the home of Jake Eaton, "champion gum chewer of the world, said to be capable of chewing 300 sticks at a time."

When Fonda made his first appearance on May 16, 1905, old men sitting around the grain store could remember how the whole of Grand Island picked up and moved five miles north to its present location beside the Union Pacific Railroad, which otherwise would have passed it by. The new railroad was the town's making. Unlike other communities in the Cornhusker State, which run north to south and east to west, Grand Island streets were laid out parallel to the tracks, perhaps as a mark of respect for the whistling freight trains that hauled out corn and cattle and brought back gold.

You didn't have to be that old to remember the wars with the Pawnees, which lasted until 1890, when the Indian population had been devastated by cholera, tuberculosis, and smallpox brought by the white man. Or to recall riding the Oregon Trail, which stretched through the tall prairie grass and the vanishing buffalo herds, heading toward the riches of the Northwest.

Nebraska left many marks on Hank Fonda—the loping, Western walk, the spare, range-riding body, the point of view, and the voice. "Without that flat whine, that Nebraskan speech with which he portrays both humor and anger, without the tonelessness of the plainsman, where would our top symbol of the American be?" one of his closest friends once asked.

Home continues to mean Nebraska to Fonda. Whenever he can, on any coast-to-coast flight, he is sure to stop off there to visit and hash over the good old days with relatives and friends who go back to his boyhood.

He was the first child of Herberta Jaynes Fonda, who was a Christian Scientist, and William Brace Fonda, a commercial printer. At his christening he was named after his mother's father, Henry Jaynes.

The values and attitudes of small-town America were virtually built into his bones and his blood. From an up-state New York settlement named for them, a dot on the map labeled Fonda, both grandparents on his father's side had made the two-thousand-mile journey westward as pioneers when the land, once deemed unfit for cultivation, began to sprout farms and ranches.

Early times were tough for settlers. They had blizzards, droughts, and locusts to contend with. Cattlemen relentlessly fought farmers in ugly range wars until after the turn of the century, when the last unfenced land was handed over by law to the homesteaders. Only a comparatively few years separated Hank Fonda from living out the roles he'd play in movies—the rancher, the sodbuster, the sheriff.

The Eastern community where his grandfather and grandmother were born came as close as anything in the United States to being an ancestral home. Today, the town of Fonda, which numbers a shade more than one thousand people, stands, almost lost, just off the winding concrete ribbons of Interstate 90, due west of Amsterdam—a reminder that the Fondas came from a long, industrious line.

Some of the inborn pride of the man Fonda is traceable to his lineage, which, like his name, is originally Italian. There were Fondas living in the Apennine Valley near Genoa before that Mediterranean seaport's most famous citizen, Columbus, sailed on his voyages of discovery. The American branch of the family is descended from a nobleman who fled from Genoa to the Netherlands to escape political persecution in about 1400, when the city was warring with Venice for supremacy.

Around 1628, when New Amsterdam was no more than a precarious settlement of a few hundred souls huddled at the tip of Manhattan island, the first Fondas arrived from Holland. They made their way north, up through wilderness trails among the Mohawks, to found the settlement to which they gave their name. Hank doesn't stress the point, though the history is fascinating to him, but all this dates the family as being among the handful of true American patricians, like the Dutch patroons whose lands sprawled along the banks of the Hudson. There were no easy fortunes in farming, however, like those to be picked up in trading, which the Roosevelts, for example, found in the booming British colony after their ancestor, Claes Martinszen van Rosenvelt, arrived in the 1640s.

There is an enduring Fonda look, made up of smoke-blue eyes, strong teeth, hollow cheeks, and a long, melancholy face. Even now, when he catches sight of himself in a mirror, Hank's first reaction is: "That's my father."

When his son was six months old, Brace Fonda moved his family from Grand Island to the hustle and bustle of Omaha, about one hundred miles away and fast growing up as the biggest livestock and meat-packing center in the world. There he bought and operated the W. B. Fonda Printing Company, a quiet, introverted small-businessman who impressed strangers only with his unimpressiveness.

Two more children, both girls, were born there, Harriet and Jayne, named like her brother for her grandfather.

Harriet was considered to be the real beauty; the family sees a great likeness to her in her niece Jane. In the years ahead, Harriet would play a key role in holding the pieces of Hank's family together at a time when it was pulling apart.

"I had what I regard as a normal youth," Hank has said. On the surface it could scarcely have been more Middle American up to the time when he was a young schoolboy. If there was any visible indication of the kind of man he would become, all record of it has been forgotten.

Family albums show him as a contented, bald baby in beautifully laundered clothes, evidence of his mother's care —"an angelic woman," in his words. She was a handsome, forthright woman, busy in the Church of Christ, Scientist, where her mother-in-law was a Second Reader. Herberta loved to sing and play the upright piano, which stood in the parlor, for her children, while their father stretched out in his easy chair.

Life in the Fonda household was as conventional as a Norman Rockwell cover on the old *Saturday Evening Post.* Morality was preached, and morality was practiced. Standards of behavior were rigid. "I was never what is called a permissive parent," Hank said of himself later. "I don't believe in that. I was brought up as a disciplined person, and that's the only way I can be."

Most of his reminiscences of childhood are bland and unexceptional. He wanted to be a cowboy, a cop, a conductor on the street car he rode downtown to his father's office, where he'd be handed a nickel to go and watch Charlie Chaplin and William S. Hart at the nickelodeon. It is tempting to track his subsequent motion-picture career to the stirring up of ambition during long afternoons at the picture shows, but there is no justification for doing so.

He was a round-faced, chubby boy who grew into a skinny, stretched-out adolescent in his last year of high school. He was physically strong and long-muscled, a sprinter on the track team, a center in basketball. His memories include the friends he had then who continued to be his friends fifty years later: Bill Reed, who stayed in Omaha as an insurance salesman; Charles Dox, who went into banking in Chicago; Bill Johnson, who moved to California.

Together, they skinny-dipped in sand pits and built shanties out of planks and scrap lumber "borrowed" from building lots.

According to fond relatives, Hank impressed his nursery school teacher by reciting very nicely at the age of four. He made what by a stretch of the imagination can be called his stage debut one year later, overshadowed by the leading lady in a pageant produced by the Omaha Junior League. Of such minutiae are memoirs made.

Grandfather Jaynes was the one who most encouraged the artistic talents that started to show up when his grandson entered kindergarten. The boy undoubtedly had a knack for drawing, though he had no more formal lessons then or later than the usual school instruction. And he wanted, at the age of ten, to be a writer more than anything else he could think of.

By then, the Fondas had lived in several different houses in and around Omaha and were now installed in the suburb of Dundee. The local weekly newspaper was running a short-story contest. Hank wrote something called "The Mouse," told from the viewpoint of a cat's quarry, entered the contest, and won. The sight of his published by-line in the next week's issue fired the urge to succeed. When he grew up, he was going to be a newspaperman.

World War I brought prosperity to Nebraska. Hungry nations in Europe needed the corn that marched in limitless rows across the eastern half of the state and meat from the grazing lands of the western buttes and sand hills. The old song of the homesteaders was long since out of date: "Land of the bedbug, grasshopper, and flea . . . I'll tell of its fame, While starving to death on my government claim."

The W. B. Fonda Printing Company enjoyed its share of the good times, but it was contrary to family principles to take good times for granted. You had to work for anything and everything you wanted to achieve in life. "When I was going to high school, I always worked in the summers. It never occurred to me to question it. I just assumed I'd have to work."

Any newspaperman worth his salt could always use experience in a printing shop, learning how the words he put on paper were turned into hot type and then into the wonderful-smelling pages of tomorrow's first edition. His father took him on at the age of twelve during summer vacation and, because nobody should be compelled to work for nothing, paid him two dollars a week.

He graduated from Omaha Central High School in the year that Calvin Coolidge became the thirtieth President of the United States, to set about bringing income taxes down and pushing tariffs up. Hank entered the University of Minnesota, which had graduated its first students only a dozen years earlier, as a journalism major, trying hard to get down onto paper, as a serious writer, some of his impressions of a not altogether limited life. A few years later he had a trunkful of manuscripts, the first acts of plays, the beginnings of a novel, but, as always, he was the harshest critic of his performance. He was dissatisfied with his abilities as a creative writer. He had the ideas, the thoughts, but not the words to express them. He has often expressed this dissatisfaction: "I just couldn't communicate."

One of his professors came up with a suggestion that might help: "Why not turn to dramatics? It might be something better suited for you." Hank Fonda didn't take to the idea at all. He had decided to be a newspaperman, and Fondas don't easily change their minds.

Thanks to a soaring national economy, America's mood

was happy-go-lucky. The stock market was soaring. Prohibition was the law, but home-brew and bootleggers made a mockery of it. The Jazz Age had dawned and the generation of what the headlines described as "flaming youth" was allegedly coming into its own, sporting plus-fours and bugle beads. But Hank Fonda was no part of it. Work was what counted with him.

He held down two jobs to pay college expenses. First, he was a trouble-shooter for the Northwestern Bell Telephone Company. Then he moved into a settlement house five or six miles from the university as the staff director of physical education and an assortment of other activities that kept him on the hop until the pounds started to melt off his already bony frame.

He rode a trolley car from the campus to the settlement house, on the other side of town, in winter freezes that dipped to thirty below. He coached, and played on, the basketball team, and for this, he was paid thirty dollars a month, together with room and board. His father sent him an extra ten dollars a week.

Omaha in the 1920s was maturing. Less than a hundred years earlier, the youthful city had watched Missouri River steamboats dock almost every day, unloading emigrants and fortune-seekers to be fitted out at a price before they journeyed on west toward California and, maybe, gold. Gunfights in the streets were nothing unusual. Rough justice reached some kind of climax one day when two horse thieves were lynched at each end of a single rope tossed over the limb of a tree.

Now the city remained homey and casual in clothes and manners, but it was spreading outward to absorb small towns nearby and upward as new buildings rose on the flat prairie. The university had gone up at the corner of Sixtieth and Dodge. There was the symphony orchestra, made up of local residents, presenting winter concerts. The community playhouse had been organized in 1925 as part and parcel of a new emphasis on what could justifiably be called culture. Historically speaking, Hank Fonda was in luck.

One of the leading lights of the little theater was Dorothy Brando, the slim, attractive wife of Mr. Marlon Brando (whose French ancestors used to spell the name "Brandeau"); he was in the insecticides and chemical-food-products business. Dorothy was a close friend of Mrs. Fonda in the church and in social affairs outside. She had two small daughters, Frances and Jocelyn, at home, as well as a baby boy, Marlon Jr., but the playhouse was a real love of her life.

After two years of college, Hank was worn to a frazzle. His class work had fallen victim to the exhausting schedule at the settlement house. He went home for a rest; family finances, which had gone into a decline, never allowed him to return to study unless he could support himself.

At twenty, he was a lean and handsome youngster, still boyish-looking in spite of a dense, wiry hairiness of jowls that called for shaving twice a day to beat five-o'clock shadow. Dorothy Brando fancied he could be exactly right for a part in a new production the playhouse company was getting up for the forthcoming season. She telephoned Mrs. Fonda. Would she mind asking Hank to contact Gregory Foley, the Irish leprechaun who directed the group? The young man they had been counting on to play Ricky, the juvenile lead, in Philip Barry's *You and I* had turned down the role. Hank was the right age and physical type to step into his shoes, if he could be persuaded to.

In the embryo phase of development, almost any young actor or actress can use a stage mother. She serves as a kind of catalyst in the mysterious chemistry that transforms an outwardly ordinary human being into someone who can walk onto a stage and, by pretending to be a totally different kind of person, move an audience to laughter or tears.

Stage mothers are a sour joke in the theater. They are forever battling to curry special favors for their young:

larger typeface on the playbills, a chance to pause center stage for a moment or two longer so the audience can get to see and hopefully admire them that much more. Agents cringe at their approach. Directors would just as soon see the scenery collapse as have the average stage mother drop in on a rehearsal.

But the rare dosage of sheer gall and determination that an ambitious stage mother supplies works like a shot in the arm for many careers. The stage father is exceedingly rare. The stage mother has fathered a distinguished line of off-spring, from Mary Pickford to Elizabeth Taylor.

Do Brando was far from being an ordinary stage mother. She wasn't trying to find vicarious satisfaction for her own frustrated ambition. She was a first-rate amateur actress herself. One of her daughters, Jocelyn, went into the theater and ultimately appeared in the *Mister Roberts* company in which Fonda starred. The Brando baby, Marlon, who showed up in New York in 1944 and proceeded to set the Broadway theater on its ear, has often been rated the greatest living actor in America, though he has no great regard for his profession.

Fonda, whom the critics treat with almost equal respect, holds a much more respectful point of view. "Acting," he says, "is putting on a mask." Lack of a mask to put on is torture to him. He cherished a great esteem for Do Brando, who died in 1962. "She gave me the feeling I could do it."

Her telephone call to his mother found him at loose ends, a college dropout with no job in sight for the summer. Gregory Foley invited him over to talk about going into *You and I.* The little red-headed Irishman made his head-quarters in a studio with a skylight—"kind of bohemian for Omaha" was Fonda's immediate reaction. Hank was asked to read the part of Ricky. Foley straightaway cast him in the play. Hank could think of nothing better to do, so he agreed to join the playhouse company.

At first, he bitterly regretted what he had committed

himself to. As a physical education instructor, he could demonstrate headstands and handstands, perform forward rolls and somersaults without a tremor, because all that called for was good muscle tone and a few words of instruction. But on the stage he had to *talk*, mumbling his lines in front of a crowd of people he scarcely knew. Rehearsals were a nightmare. He wilted under the gaze of other people, suffering agonies of embarrassment. He had no ambition to be an actor.

However, he had given his promise, and Fondas were taught not to back away if the going got rough. Aside from rehearsing, he enjoyed many of the jobs the playhouse had to offer. He spent most of his time at the theater. Foley and Do Brando were delighted to find that his knack with a pencil and brush could be put to good use painting scenery. He could shinny up ropes, lend a hand with the props, help with the cleaning up.

Everything about the wonderful business of playing "Let's pretend"—except performing—appealed to him. He liked the sense of belonging to a group of people sharing the same goal. The unmistakable backstage odor of a theater, made up of grease paint, dust, and costumes in need of laundering got to him.

That tantalizing scent lingers nearly half a century later as his only memory of playing Ricky. "The idea of being on a stage where people could look at me seemed insane. I don't remember that first performance at all. I remember what it smelled like and what the makeup smelled like, and I remember the curtain going up, but I don't have any memories of playing the part."

He received no encouragement from either parent. Playacting didn't exactly fit into their definition of hard work and what it could achieve. But they reluctantly accepted the fact that he was enjoying himself. He hadn't been able to find any other steady employment. He'd tried to follow up his earlier ambition and land a job on a newspaper, but he had been turned down flat: no experience. He had gone from one thing to another, seeking at least to support himself. If he had written a resumé in those days it would not have been very impressive, when the only work he could find was as an iceman, a window dresser, a garage mechanic.

After the first season at the playhouse was over, the need to settle into some kind of employment, any kind, was acute again. He was twenty-one, poor in pocket yet never in spirit, with nothing resembling a career in sight. Then one day he saw an ad in the newspaper for the job of office boy at the Retail Credit Company. He applied and was taken on at eighteen dollars a week, more than he had ever earned.

He settled down to learn how to file and cross-file, which was his particular duty, and to pick up the routines of business life in the branch office of a national corporation. It was dull as ditch water, of course, but he set himself to put up with the monotony without complaining. His father was content, anyway, now that his only son had a job that looked as though it might have a future for him.

With the approach of fall, Gregory Foley was planning a new season's productions. The playhouse made a policy of restaging the best of what Broadway had done earlier. This time around, the director wanted to introduce Omaha to *Merton of the Movies*, written by George S. Kaufman and Marc Connelly, the story of a callow clerk in a small-town general store with daydreams of being a movie star in Hollywood. Glenn Hunter had triumphed in the title role on Broadway and then again when the play was made into a motion picture.

Foley called Fonda. "I want you for the lead. It can be a perfect part for you. Will you take it?"

Hank said yes. But when he came home to tell his parents, his reception was icy.

To his father it seemed that he was throwing away a

promising job for the sake of chasing rainbows, making the inexcusable error of putting pleasure ahead of responsibility. "Do you mean to say you're going to quit at Retail Credit?"

Yes, he meant just that.

The scene grew stormy. Where had Hank picked up the crazy notion that he could be an actor? What did he expect to live on? Did he know the kind of people he'd be mixing with? Was he looking forward to starving to death? Brace Fonda had all the arguments ready that a concerned parent uses to deter a son or daughter from going on the stage. Unemployment rates among actors and actresses make such advice as sound as a bell. The impulses that drive a young man or woman into the theater render such advice useless. Hank ignored it.

"I'm twenty-one years old, Dad, and I want to live my own life," he shouted.

"Not in my house, for sure."

"Then I'll leave home if I have to."

What had happened to change the shy introvert with his heart set on being a newspaperman into a budding actor, prepared to go hungry so long as he could put on grease paint and walk a stage? The alteration must have been as inexplicable to Brace Fonda as it was enraging. Hank could only be regarded as something close to a failure up until the time he had got the office-boy job. Now he apparently was hellbent on reverting to failure. How could it happen?

Because he had learned the security of wearing a mask. "I'm a self-conscious person," he once said. "I'm an actor because I don't have to be myself." Makeup and costume comprised a kind of armor against other people's intrusion into his private self. Each new role became a disguise for his own identity, enabling Fonda to remain unknown. He had felt this happen in a single session at the playhouse under Foley's direction and the prompting of Do Brando.

The need to communicate his own possibly revealing

thoughts and emotions had virtually ended. As an actor, he could make other men's lines sound incredibly like his own, while he kept his interior life a secret from all but a handful of intimates. Discovering that was what gave Fonda the wish to contest his father and an unrelenting will to succeed on the stage.

One of his long-term friends, Joshua Logan, has said, "Fonda was just as good the first day he went on the stage as he is now. He had an absolutely instinctual thing about himself and how he could behave."

Hank was as stubborn as his father; his mother was more diplomatic. No break with his parents ever came about. She patched up the quarrel and suggested a temporary truce. But Brace Fonda refused to speak to his son for a month. The uneasy peace depended on Hank doing both jobs simultaneously, getting into the Retail Credit Office at seven o'clock every morning, then rehearsing as Merton evenings and Sundays.

At this far distance in time, after the years have brought undreamed-of changes in him and his circumstances, Fonda is inclined to regard the opening of Merton as the most memorable event in his entire stage career. He lived the role, trembling with the excitement of discovery. The work he had put into it, sweating out every line and move until he had made them *his*, paid off in terms of psychology as well as glory. For the first time, he sensed what acting was all about. The idea of being *Merton*, not Fonda, opened up a new universe. He had fashioned his first mask, and the event is still fresh in his mind today.

His father, mother, and sisters were in the audience on opening night, the three women eager to see Hank shine, Brace Fonda skeptical about his son's chances. At the end of the performance, the whole house rose and cheered for Merton. The critic for the Omaha *World-Herald* went off to write a rave review, which appeared the next day headlined, "Who Needs Glenn Hunter? We Have Henry!"

By the time the newborn star of the show had got his makeup off and gone home, his family sat waiting in the living room. The girls and Mrs. Fonda were still excitedly gossiping about the play. Brace sat silent in his easy chair behind his evening newspaper.

One of his sisters, when the congratulations were over, had a word of criticism. "There was just one scene in which I thought you didn't quite—"

"Shut up," said Brace Fonda. "He was perfect."

For one wonderful week Hank played Merton. He went on doubling between the playhouse and the credit company until the following spring. Like every other big turn in his life, the breakout from the office came quietly and without drama.

If he had run true to his parents' desire for him, he would have stayed on at Retail Credit and, who knows, perhaps one day would have been promoted to branch manager. He could have satisfied his urge to act by making the playhouse his hobby, as a number of local people did. Harriet and Jayne, for instance, both became involved in useful, non-performing tasks like raising funds and selling tickets. Why couldn't Hank have the best of both worlds as a happy amateur?

Reason would have dictated that choice, but the desire to wear masks lies deeper than reason. It seems that Hank was only biding his time, looking for a chance to make the break. Just before Easter that chance came. The mother of an Omaha boy who was studying at Princeton, in New Jersey, had a proposition for Hank. Would he pick up her son and drive him home for the vacation? To make it worth his while, she'd treat Hank to a week in New York, so that he could see some shows on Broadway.

To any young man who, like Fonda, had never been east of the Mississippi, the offer would have been seductive. To Hank, wrapped up in a process of liberating himself with greasepaint, it was irresistible.

His boss at Retail Credit was dismayed at the prospect. "But I have big plans for you. You're the kind of man we need here. What do you say to going to the home office in Atlanta to train as a *supervisor?*"

But Hank's personal needs couldn't be met by any kind of promotion. He quit his job because for interior reasons he had to. During the next six years, before he began to start making any kind of money or reputation as an actor, he became well acquainted with hunger and chronic poverty, but not with despair. On the contrary, he was by all accounts as happy as a sand boy, behind his masks.

The dictionary defines a mask as "a covering for the face to conceal or disguise the identity." The wearing of them is as old as recorded history. Ancient Greeks donned them to worship the god of wine and vegetation, Dionysos. In the dawn of stylized drama, performers covered their heads with them to create tragic or comic character and to personify the most fundamental human emotions—fear, hate, joy, love, and sorrow. Savages and primitive tribesmen employ masks as a religious ritual, transforming themselves into animals or gods, or to frighten demons away. Actors, who constitute a special tribe of primitive people, disguised their faces with grease paint and false hair: *maskers* is what the civilized world consequently called them.

Herman Melville probed to another layer of meaning. "All visible objects, man," says Captain Ahab in *Moby Dick*, "are but as pasteboard masks. But in each event—in the living act, the undoubted deed—there, some unknown but still reasoning thing puts forth the moldings of its features from behind the unreasoning mask. If man will strike, strike through the mask!"

95091

II

IF THE OVERPOWERING need to mask himself from circumstance had not already been driving Fonda, the trip to New York would have clinched it. He looked at Broadway with awe in his marveling eyes.

He saw nine plays in six days, like a child in a toy store who has won a Christmas contest giving him a supermarket cart and five minutes to fill it. *The Front Page, The Constant Nymph, The Constant Wife, Rio Rita*—they were all part of a wonderland. He loved every one of them.

He had to convince himself that he had any hope at all of making a living in the work his psyche cried out to him to do. The only real encouragement came from Do Brando, Foley, and their colleagues at the playhouse. His family could not afford to support him indefinitely. In a week or so he was going to be twenty-two. He was virtually penniless, with no job in sight. There was nothing else for it but to drive back, as arranged, to Omaha.

Foley realized that Fonda had strong needs and limitless talents. He put the youngster on the payroll at the playhouse as assistant director, at a salary of five hundred dollars to cover the whole season. That forged one more link in the chain that bound Hank to the theater for richer, for poorer, in sickness and in health. He began to think he

pany consisting exclusively of college students, on Cape Cod that summer. The thought of Harvard men and Princeton men doing anything together was slightly revolutionary; the notorious fight that followed the 1926 football game had left many scars.

But this new intercollegiate enterprise was being put together by doves, not hawks. They called themselves the University Players Guild, and they set up in business with capital of four hundred dollars.

That was no more than pocket money to some of them. By and large, they came from families infinitely better off than the Fondas. The prime mover in the venture was Charlie Leatherbee, a much-traveled Harvard junior and president of the Dramatic Club there, whose stepfather was Jan Masaryk. His own father, Robert Leatherbee, owned a 110-foot yacht in Falmouth harbor that could be used as quarters for the new student company of players. His grandfather, Charles R. Crane, had been United States Minister to China after making a fortune in plumbing fixtures.

Charlie's companion in sparking UPG was Bretaigne Windust, known as "Windy," a Princetonian, brought up in Paris, who would go on to make his name as a top-flight director on Broadway. Johnny Swope, a classmate of Charlie's, was another founding member; he had his own sailboat in Falmouth harbor, and his father was president of General Electric. The Princeton side was in strength with Myron McCormick, a Phi Beta Kappa who wouldn't be caught dead wearing his key; Alfred Dalrymple; and Joshua Logan, a round-faced freshman from Louisiana, who became a self-made millionaire in the theater and in Hollywood. A leavening of girls from Radcliffe and elsewhere made up what his mother fondly called "Charlie's company."

When Bernie Hanighen dropped in at Dennis, Hank Fonda was not due to play any role that evening. He wasn't doing much at all except facing the prospect of having to retreat to Omaha. It was easy to persuade him to drive back with Bernie to Falmouth to see what the UPG, now in its third week of performances, was doing.

Madame Masaryk owned a summer mansion, "Whitecrest," at Falmouth, with a dazzling view of Buzzard's Bay. That made Falmouth the natural home for the UPG. Charlie had asked the owner of the local moviehouse, the Elizabeth Theater, to turn it over to the company during July and August on Monday and Tuesday nights, when no more than a handful of moviegoers usually showed up in its nine hundred seats. The owner agreed, in return for the better part of the bargain—55 percent of the price of all tickets sold. Rehearsals could be held in the Elizabeth on Sundays, when it was closed. On the other four week nights he continued to unreel such delights as Billie Dove in *The Yellow Lily* and Charlie Chaplin in *The Circus.*

Hank and Bernie Hanighen turned up on a Tuesday to catch the second and final performance of George Kelly's rollicking farce *The Torch-Bearers;* the previous evening's show had been a triumph for the student company, marred only by one accident when an actress tumbled over the footlights. They arrived too late to be seated together, and Fonda found himself tasting a new level of social life, alone in a rowful of perfumed matrons and their brilliantined escorts, golden-tanned debutantes, gilded young men in white flannels, summer people from Park Avenue and Brookline.

One member of the UPG has recalled a typical audience: "The ladies' white coats bore in their cut the stamp of Bonwit Teller, Bergdorf Goodman, or Carson, Pirie, Scott, and half of the men wore the new white linen dinner jackets which were coming into vogue."

Hank, by way of contrast, sported tight white knickerbockers. "It was the late twenties," Joshua Logan remembers, "the days of the plus-fours; and this Fonda guy was wearing minus-twos. His golf socks and sweater were black, which was either superb taste or Midwest ignorance."

But he made an indelible impression with the shriek of his laughter as well as his "minus-twos." It has been called an exploding, choking sob, a screech like a phonograph record played at too high a speed. According to the legends of that night, the actors could feel it in their bones, shaking the seats for rows around. When, in the middle of the performance, half of Johnny Swope's moustache came adrift, Fonda fell out of his seat.

Hanighen took him backstage afterward to meet the company. There were already signs of a love match. Anybody who laughed as he did at their gags and got the message of what they were doing had to be *simpatico*. When a smile broke on his sad face, the lights seemed to brighten. When he laughed again in the dressing room, plaster threatened to peel from the ceiling. One actor that night remembers, "He was three or four years older than most of us, even though he didn't look it. He had a handsome, boyish face and a slender body with that pressed-forward pelvis of his."

At the end of any performance the UPG's young men and women were in a mood for a party. As soon as the audience had gone home, they took off for Charlie's "camp," a large room built on a hillside some fifty yards from his mother's house, with a long screened porch, where rehearsals were held. Hank and Bernie were invited to join the midnight fun.

The company of twenty piled into the two available cars and drove off, squeezed tight in each other's laps, singing, arms and legs dangling. At the camp they got to work performing for each other. Josh Logan had discovered that the part he played in *The Torch-Bearers*, Mr. Huxley Hossefrosse, could serve very well as the model for a dead-pan monologue delivered by a pseudo-scientific lecturer, like a

Sid Caesar television character in later years. Someone else in the group, who had known Hank in Omaha, talked him into "doing Elmer."

"Elmer" was a brain child of Fonda's Omaha Community Theater days, a ten-year-old idiot child who had to be coaxed into performing animal imitations in dead-pan pantomime, such as wriggling his fingers to make a fish. "Elmer," combined with Hank's whinnying laughter, cemented him to the UPG and he was invited on the spot to join them. He was so taken with the whole atmosphere that he went back to Dennis the next morning only to pick up his bags.

The UPG operated on the sturdy principles of primitive communism, share and share alike. Each member of the company received room and board plus something in the neighborhood of $10 a week, depending on the state of the box-office till. A hastily staged subscription-ticket campaign had temporarily boosted the treasury to something close to $2,000, after it had dwindled to a perilous $168 and imminent bankruptcy. Qualified members—always males in that era preceding Women's Lib—took turns in acting and directing.

Room and board for the men meant eating and sleeping either at the camp or aboard the *Brae Burn*, the unused yacht of Charlie's grandfather, which they had scrubbed and painted for the purpose. The *Brae Burn*'s bunks were also shared by men and women alike for afternoon sessions of learning their lines. Then Charlie began to receive complaints from passers-by on the harbor road, who were shocked to see the company lying together two by two, boys and girls together.

"We do have our reputation to protect," Bretaigne Windust ruled, "so henceforth the bunks are not to be used during the day."

The girls were quartered in a rented cottage in Quissett, five miles away, so the roads around Falmouth were usually in use by one of the Guild's automobiles, raising the dust with a load of yelling college students aboard. Massachusetts morality was not what it came to be. Whispers of sex and sinning among the members of the company began to be heard.

The company's historian, Norris Houghton, later to teach drama as a university dean, reported: "It was also rumored about the community that the boys and girls occupied the same dressing room at the theater. This rumor was quite true, for the simple reason that there was only one dressing room there. When the company had its attention drawn to this—a situation that hadn't heretofore been given a thought—they retorted that nobody was ever seen in that dressing room wearing less than everyone on every beach on the Cape wore every day. Mr. Robbins, the theater's owner, was a little more respectful of public opinion than the company, however, and he built a second dressing room."

As soon as Hank enlisted, the Guild had a part ready and waiting for him: that of Tornaquinci, the aging Italian nobleman, with long white beard and cascading wig, in Sem Benelli's comedy *The Jest*; John and Lionel Barrymore had starred in it on Broadway. Josh had been going to play Tornaquinci in Act One as well as the headsman in Act Three, but he was happy enough to see the company recruit tackle the role in his place.

Fonda was an unqualified catastrophe. He was lost in false hair and heavy Renaissance robes. In his Nebraskan drawl, speeches written to ring out as poetry sounded like gossip around a livery stable. Windust's performance in the John Barrymore role of Giannetto drew a loving review from one woman newspaper critic: "His speech flows in lines of sound much as his body gives a constant plasticity of expression. It would seem that this slender form is always in some slight fluidity of indicated mood." Hank, by an act of charity, received not so much as a mention.

The Guild had no single leader, director, or maestro telling the young actors what they must do. Everybody learned by the method of sink or swim. You always had to judge and be judged by your peers. Everybody was equally involved and passionate about what they were involved in, that is, running what they dreamed would be one of the best repertory groups of the times. And everyone was young enough to say what he felt, no matter how damaging to someone else's pride. It was a terrifying experience to be a Guildsman. If you weren't any good, you were told so with no room for doubt.

At a morning-after rehash of *The Jest*, nobody was excited about Fonda's potential as an actor. He was fun to have around; he could always crack a joke or do Elmer. But what else had he got on the ball?

Windust, always businesslike, had a drastic remedy in mind, and he spoke for almost everybody. "Perhaps we made a mistake in inviting Hank on first sight to join the company. Shouldn't we tell him he ought to go back to Dennis?"

Charlie Leatherbee didn't agree. Hank was so very *likable*, which rated as an important qualification with the Guild. According to Hanighen, he'd earned a healthy reputation as an amateur in Omaha. He couldn't possibly be as terrible as he'd looked as Tornaquinci. Anyway, wasn't he supposed to be hot stuff at painting scenery?

Hank had no illusions about his performance. There seemingly never was a time when instinct failed to tell him the difference between a role he could handle and a role that would maul him. "Listen," he told his judges, "that was the only way I could get in. You'll just have to give me a part I can play."

With no great enthusiasm, Windust agreed to grant Fonda a reprieve. Building and painting the elaborate sets that were a hallmark of UPG productions became his principal occupation for a week or two. In that way he earned the uniform of a Guildsman, a French *matelot*'s blue-and-white striped T-shirt, one of a batch that Charlie had once picked up in Marseilles. To this he added dirty tennis shoes, decrepit dungarees, sometimes a smashed-in felt hat.

The part he could play came along in the seventh bill of the season, as Chick, the punchy prizefighter in *Is Zat So?* Hank got hold of a copy of the script in advance and decided he had to be Chick to prove to his new colleagues that he was good for better things than scene painting and ushering. Anybody could try for any part under the UPG's loose working rules. He read Chick for Charlie and Windy in the main cabin of the *Brae Burn,* got the role, and immediately submerged himself over the ears in it.

Chick goes through a fight onstage in the course of the play, but neither Hank nor Johnny Swope, who played his opponent, knew much about boxing. Once, as they rehearsed in an alley, the good people of Falmouth took it for the real thing and called the police.

"I think audiences like real people on the stage," Fonda once said. "An actor in some mysterious way can feel what the people out front are thinking. Of course, audiences vary. Sometimes you love them at first meeting not because they accept you immediately, but because you feel a friendship with them."

He played Chick in a fashion to minimize his own good looks, which embarrassed him, and with a realism that at both performances left him and Johnny with bloody noses after their scene in the prize ring. The woman critic who had fallen hard for Windust in *The Jest* found that "the fight, to feminine inexperience, was thrilling." Hank had passed the test. He was afloat in the uncertain sea of summer theater, prepared to weather any storm.

For the last production of the season, *The Thirteenth Chair,* he returned to painting scenery. The dominating feature of the set was a fireplace with a coat of arms over the mantel. Into the coat of arms Hank, the Guild's lettering artist and jester, introduced a motto he felt was a suitable answer to the accusations of immorality leveled against the UPG by peeping toms on the harbor road. *"In Turpitudine Felicitas,"* it read: freely translated, "It's fun to be sinful."

After the final curtain on the last night, Windy made a speech: "We shall be back next summer." Everybody else went back to college. Hank went to New York to look for some way of surviving the fall, winter, and spring until it was time to return to room and board in a bunk of the *Brae Burn* and a salary that might run as high as ten dollars a week.

"I was excited. I was nothing but optimistic. . . . It never occurred to me to be discouraged. I wasn't terribly smart. If I'd been smart, I would have given up and gone home."

His first season in New York added more iron in his soul. Four more winters just like it lay ahead, and of course he survived those, too, as he would have outlived any number of similar ordeals. "I was making myself a little dizzy. I was damn sure I was a good actor, and sure that eventually I was going to prove it."

He rented a ten-dollar-a-week room on 114th Street and taught himself to exist on virtually nothing, a matter of spending only a few cents a week. He went for one week without eating at all, subsisting on multiple glasses of water to fill his stomach before he left each morning to haunt the office of every theatrical agent in town. All his cigarettes had gone the first day, which was the best possible reason to quit smoking for a while. A package of rice, he discovered, goes a long way, boiled, fried and in a variety of other concoctions. He had no thought of asking his father for help.

"I figured I was on my own and perfectly capable of taking care of myself. If I did it so badly that I had to starve in the process, then that was no worry of the folks'."

What sustained him that harsh winter was nothing more nor less than the memory of being Merton in Omaha. He could remember the way he felt as Merton, a breathtaking feeling that seemed impossible to recapture. It was like being a ten-year-old child playing cowboys and Indians. The roots of a deep political radicalism began to grow in the bedrock of hardship. Norman Thomas was Fonda's man that November when the leader and perennial nominee of the Socialist Party ran against Herbert Hoover, and again four years later, when he polled close to a million votes against Franklin D. Roosevelt. Hank's outspoken approval of Thomas caused some domestic strife later with at least one of his wives.

At Christmastime, a companion showed up to share in his pursuit of rainbows. Kent Smith, an original member of the University Players, had just been bounced out of Harvard for overcutting classes.

"What are you going to do?" asked Fonda.

"Go on the stage like you," said Kent.

"If you call pounding the pavement of this Godforsaken town going on the stage."

Hank, who had joined Actors' Equity, showed Kent the thankless art of pavement pounding, taking him around on the calls at the agencies, introducing him to the Equity bulletin board listings of plays in production. Now, here was something: two men wanted by the National Junior Theater in Washington, D.C., for a production of *Twelfth Night*, specially arranged for children. Not only had Fonda never acted Shakespeare; he had never read the play. But the two Guildsmen applied, were accepted, and that night caught a train from Pennsylvania Station.

Henry Fonda's first bout with Sweet Will was playing Sir Andrew Aguecheek, the doddering, wise fool. He didn't feel that the part was exactly right for him. If he had thought otherwise, he might have been doomed to a career of swords and doublets. But he was good enough to please the producer and the children and to be asked, with Smith, to stay for the rest of the winter, as probably the most unlikely Shakespearean ever to walk an American stage.

In his social life, Hank lacked only one qualification for

becoming a lady-killer, if he had been so inclined. He had a sensitive, almost beautiful face. He kept himself in athletic trim, with the routine of a cold shower every morning. His love of laughter only deserted him now and then, when a mood of darkness descended around his head like a storm cloud. But he had not much more than a nickel of spending money to his name.

"Back in college," he said, "I developed a heavy crush, the way you do in college, and I got the same way a time or two while I was batting around in New York. But I never thought of marriage until I met Sullavan."

Margaret Sullavan, on the other hand, used to insist that she scarcely noticed him the first time around, except for the swat she gave him across his hollow jowls. Toward the end of the job in Washington, Bernie Hanighen telegraphed Fonda to come up to Cambridge, Massachusetts, and pass himself off as a Harvard man so that he could play in a musical comedy Hanighen and a classmate had written for production by the Dramatic Club in May. Only Hank would do, because the part consisted essentially of doing Elmer, which nobody but he could portray.

For the chorus of the show, called *Close Up*, a chorus of Radcliffe girls had been recruited, including one counterfeit, as Hank was among the males. Peggy Sullavan, at eighteen, was selling books at the Harvard Coop while she studied dramatics at the Copley Theater and dance at Denishawn in Boston, the school run by the gauze-draped Ruth St. Denis and her dashing partner, Ted Shawn. In one number of the musical the girls had to slap the boys. The "boy" Peggy belted with a strong right hand was Henry Fonda.

Nobody called her beautiful, but she had no need to be; she had an ineffable, magnetic charm. She stood only a couple of inches more than five feet tall, with shining gray eyes and what somebody once described as "hair-colored hair and skin-colored skin." Her accent gave away her origins—Norfolk, Virginia, where, as a well-to-do broker's daughter, she knew by the time she was six years old that she would be an actress.

Months before the start of its new season, the University Players Guild had run into fresh trouble. Mr. Robbins wanted to show movies six nights a week at his Elizabeth Theater, so the company was homeless. After checking the bank account ($1,200) and borrowing $20,000 from Charlie's grandfather Crane, the elders of UPG decided to build their own theater. A site in Falmouth was impossible to obtain, so they had found one at Old Silver Beach, across the railroad tracks in West Falmouth. There on the white sand stood a clapboard dance hall. Construction plans called for the theater to be connected to it, while the hall itself was to be converted into a combination of restaurant and nightclub. Here, customers could get a meal before the show and afterward enjoy dancing and maybe even a drink, which was a sure-fire attraction in those days.

Besides lacking a home, the Guild needed an ingenue. Charlie Leatherbee thought he had just the right girl in Peggy Sullavan. When he introduced her to Bretaigne Windust at the home of some friends, neither of them took the time to ask if she had acted before. She hadn't. But Windust remembered to raise the policy question of whether she had been to college, since that was a nominal requirement of the company. Thank God, she had, for a brief year or so at Sullins in Bristol, Virginia, which no-body had heard of, but it would do. One of the few stipula-tions about her joining the UPG, which Charlie made, was that she mustn't cut her long hair. (The hard bob and shingle were just coming into fashion.)

Leatherbee and Windust found her fiercely ambitious yet bewitching. "By the time I am thirty-five," she insisted, "I will have a million dollars, five children, and I will have starred on Broadway." Most of those dreams came true for her, together with some others she couldn't have counted on at eighteen.

When Hank got back to the Guild in June, the new

theater amounted to no more than stakes driven into the sand next to piles of wallboard and two-by-fours. He set to work lining out the murals that would help transform the dance hall into what was now known euphemistically as the "tearoom," with Kent Smith to help him. Three weeks later, three days before the flimsy, barnlike premises of the UPG were due to open with the first production of the season, carpenters were still nailing on the roof. Fonda spent a Saturday and Sunday with two or three other members of the cast, lying face down on the roof beams to install a massive grid from which the scenery and counterweights would be suspended.

Margaret Sullavan had shown up by now and had angrily given Leatherbee a taste of the temper that matched her Irish name. Contrary to his instructions she had bobbed her hair. He raged at her that if she refused to listen to direction she might as well quit then and there. "All right. If all you want is a head of hair," she snapped, "you can look elsewhere." Charlie at heart was a highly responsible man. She stayed. Sullavan—who was "Peggy" to her friends then, and "Maggie" only later on in life—usually got her way.

On Monday evening at five o'clock, with all the rest of the company, Hank was still laboring to get the theater in shape, with three hours to go before the announced curtain time. Then, with everyone else who was to act that night, he was sent off to clean up for his performance in the première production of 1929, something entitled *The Devil in the Cheese*.

In their first stage appearance together, Hank and Peggy were married and he became President of the United States. He was the juvenile lead, a ship's steward named Jimmy Chard, and she was the ingenue, Goldina Quigley, traveling with her parents on a European tour. The Quigleys arrive at a Greek monastery, where Jimmy crash-lands in a plane and, for reasons of the labyrinthine plot, Mr.

Quigley is talked into eating a piece of cheese, to conjure up an Egyptian god who will unveil to him the secret of youth. It was that kind of play. Norris Houghton has carefully chronicled the disasters that befell the company after the curtain finally rose, one hour late.

Act One called for the Quigleys to be delivered to the craggy Greek island in a basket. They emerged, spinning dizzily in it, from a trap in the basement and were dumped overboard onto the stage, where crumpled newspapers served as rocks.

Margaret Sullavan's opening line was delivered with cucumber calm: "Now, don't worry, Mother; everything's all right." "What an actress!" the backstage crew murmured admiringly.

"I must sit down," said Mrs. Quigley, who at this point was supposed to be offered a stool. But the stool had been forgotten, so Joshua Logan, as head monk, grabbed a grocery store carton from the wings to seat her on. Down went Mrs. Quigley, with the carton collapsing under her.

Hank's entrance as Jimmy Chard had to be preceded by the roar of a plane landing on the monastery rooftop. As that moment approached, somebody remembered belatedly that no such sound effect had been provided for. Windust, another cool head, had the company truck rapidly backed up to the stage door with its motor roaring. With that introduction, Fonda appeared from the wings, climbed a ladder while the audience watched in wonderment, then jumped down again to deliver his first explanatory line: "Here I am, Goldina."

The onlookers may well have been as relieved as the performers when the first act drew to its end. Worse was to come. The next scene was supposedly set aboard a yacht, in a daydream of Goldina's in which she was now Mrs. Chard on her honeymoon with Jimmy. She had a baby to fondle in the shape of a chiffon handkerchief knotted at one corner. When the curtain rose she was discovered preparing dinner over a stove. The stove was another prop that had been overlooked, so the genuine article had been hastily carried in from the tearoom kitchen.

This time, Hank's entrance was preceded by a totally unexpected gurgle of running water and muffled screams from the women's dressing room in the basement under the stage. The property department in this case had outdone itself by trucking in a live sea robin aswim in a twenty-gallon milk churn, filled with sea water from the Marine Biological Laboratory in Woods Hole, twenty miles away. Hank needed to carry the fish onstage in a net. Reaching in, he learned that a sea robin has built-in spikes that defy human handling. So he had a stagehand hold the net ready, while Hank upended the churn. Half the sea water cascaded between the planks of the still uncompleted stage floor onto the heads of the girls in the dressing room. The other half poured into the trough of the footlights.

Fonda didn't turn a hair but retrieved the net with his supposed catch and made his entrance. "Just caught him halfway up the mast," he explained.

"Good," said Goldina, completely unfazed. "Put him in the kettle, and we'll have him for dinner."

The fish refused to budge. Hank thereupon dumped the net into the pot, where its handle remained in full view for the rest of the scene. The bride and groom had a toast to drink to each other before they started their meal. Hank and Peggy raised the two glasses that stood, as required, on the table, clinked their rims together, took a swallow apiece —and turned pale. One of the prop men had filled the glasses with sea water from the milk churn.

The scene changes. Now young Mr. and Mrs. Chard were shipwrecked on a tropical island. Enter Fonda in grass pants, carrying a live turtle. "Speared in the bushes."

"Good," replied the imperturbable Goldina. "Pop him in the kettle and we'll have him for dinner."

While Peggy and Hank continued the scene, the turtle

clambered out of the caldron and toppled onto the floor. It paddled through the sea water that remained in the footlights trough, then fell off the front of the stage into the center aisle, where it crawled until it encountered the feet of Charlie's aged grandmother, Mrs. Charles B. Crane. She screamed as effectively as a heroine of old-time melodrama.

Until then, neither Hank nor Peggy had noticed that the turtle was running away with the show. They were too absorbed in their lines and other problems. For instance, Peggy had made an entrance wearing a grass skirt and a brassière of artificial flowers, with a borrowed pet monkey on her bare shoulder. Alarm, or possibly its critical opinions, prompted it to leave a warm trickle running down her arm into a puddle on the floor. Exit Goldina.

Jimmy Chard then supposedly checked on the island's flora: "Aha, some flowers for my wife!" and picked a handful. Flowers were something else that had slipped the mind of the property department. Josh Logan, in the wings with Peggy, tried to fill the gap by grabbing one of the blossoms that made up her brassière, with the thought of tossing it to Hank. But she knew that if he pulled out one bloom, the whole contraption would come apart. She fought him off in frantic silence. A straw bracelet she was wearing came off in his hand. Josh satisfied himself with that and threw it into Hank's hands.

Re-enter Goldina, with all traces of panic concealed. Supposedly an expert botanist, she was due to shout, "Drop that! It's the deadly camellia flower that brings on sleeping sickness." She switched the line to "It's the deadly camellia straw."

"I'm feeling sleepy," he murmured.

"Lie down," cooed Goldina, "and I'll just cover you with this grass mat." No grass mat in sight. Nothing that even a lightning ad-libber could make do with. "No," said Peggy, "I don't guess I will."

At approximately one o'clock on Tuesday morning, the

performance came to a close. The audience spared a few more minutes to applaud an unforgettable night, then laughed its way home to bed.

Laughter was the first bond between Fonda and Sullavan; a shared talent was the next, immediately identifiable in her, more slowly maturing in him. Before the summer ended, Hank had persuaded the Guild to present *Merton of the Movies* as another sure-fire role that he knew he could play. But he couldn't recapture the old feeling. With more seasoning as an actor, he was trying too consciously to re-create the character he had originally built instinctively from his own life experiences. The black cloud of depression started to settle around his head.

The Constant Nymph took care of that. The romantic tale of Tessa and her lover Lewis Dodd was the final production of the summer. Peggy and Hank were the leads, and their opening love scene in a Central Park setting seemed increasingly realistic at every performance that week. The final scene, with Tessa dying in Dodd's arms, held other members of the company as spellbound as it did the audience. Sullavan, the Guild recognized, had real magic. Fonda thought so, too.

Altogether, 1929 was a big year for him. Among other events important to his future that occurred in those twelve months, a disillusioned young woman named Clare Boothe Brokaw, after six years of marriage, took the train to Reno in Nevada to divorce her husband George, freeing him to remarry and leaving her to seek a job on *Vanity Fair.* One of her first assignments on that chic magazine was to write about Henry Luce, of Time, Inc.

At forty-nine, George Tuttle Brokaw of New York and Newport ranked as one of the greatest catches in the Social Register, with a fortune estimated variously at thirty to fifty million dollars. In their marriage, he had done his dull best to please his wife, in spite of the fact that his drinking kept him in an almost permanent alcoholic daze. The divorce was friendly, though a bitter legal battle developed later over custody of Ann Clare Brokaw, born in August 1924, their only child. The first Mrs. Brokaw, who in 1935 would become Clare Boothe Luce, accepted a cash settlement from her first husband of four hundred and twenty-five thousand dollars.

Elsewhere in the world, in Paris, where he was born of Russian parents, Roger Vadim Plemianannikow, who also figured in the Fonda future, passed his first birthday.

III

THERE WAS no doubt in anyone's mind that Fonda loved Sullavan with a youthful passion, but theirs was a long, long way from being a starry-eyed romance. If anything, she proved to be even more temperamental than he was, and his dark moods were notorious. "They fought so terribly," one Guild member recalls, "that you'd have to get out of the room."

But, like everyone in the company, they could work off some of their steam in the restaurant next door to the theater, where customers could get a meal and a drink after the show. The evening's entertainment started as soon as the final curtain fell on each stage performance. Actors like Hank, who doubled as nightclub performers, then had to hurry out of makeup to get ready for a different kind of show.

The supper club band, The Harvard Rhythm Kings, was made up of college students, led by Bernie Hanighen. Occasionally, the sweet scent of reefers drifted through the summer night and lingered in the rooming house where the males of the company now boarded; Falmouth harbor and the *Brae Burn* were too far away.

Jane and Peter Fonda both went through phases of singing the praises of marijuana but their father experimented with it once and only once, that summer. "I walked into my

rooming house and saw a group of people who lived there
—mostly musicians—sitting in a circle, drawing deeply on
a cigarette butt. I joined the circle and took a deep drag. I
felt a slowing of my senses, a strange feeling. I didn't particularly like it. But in those days, only musicians used it.
They seemed to think it made them play better. Probably
nobody else thought so. I didn't think it did. And I never
tried that stuff again."

He was a beer drinker, first and foremost, and the UPG
tried brewing its own. Some of the stock was bottled and
stored in the darkness of the theater's orchestra pit until,
in the middle of one performance of Karel Capek's sober
fantasy *The Makroupolus Secret,* Hank and Peggy were interrupted by an unrehearsed series of explosions. The amateur brewers had put too much yeast in the formula. The
hoard of beer blew up in a hail of shattered glass.

The brew was intended primarily for the actors. Something more potent was concocted for supper club customers, in addition to the bacon and peanut butter sandwiches,
ice cream sundaes, and setups for those who brought their
own precious booze. Charlie Leatherbee invented the orgeat cocktail. Orgeat is a syrup made from barley water
flavored with almonds, powerful enough to conceal the
taste even of bathtub gin. With egg whites and lemon juice
added, the formula called for vigorous shaking and Charlie,
a perfectionist, insisted that no less than eighty shakes were
required to produce a palatable drink. Since the demand
for orgeat cocktails skyrocketed, it became necessary to do
the shaking in a five-gallon milk churn, the same container
that had held the prickly sea robin for *The Devil in the Cheese.*

For Fonda, playing in the supper club was exhilarating
enough without need of orgeat. If the home-brewed beer
didn't improve with age, Elmer did; during all the years
Fonda performed as the idiot animal imitator, he could
always draw as many laughs from Guild people as from the
paying audience—and he can still play Elmer.

His closest companion and friend in the nightclub shows

was Logan, who in his portrayal of Professor Hossefrosse, barefoot and in a tailcoat, employed Hank as his stooge. Masquerading as an innocent member of the audience, Hank shuffled up to help out. For his services Josh handed him a large cake of ice, to be held onto while Hossefrosse orated on a dozen and more incoherent subjects. Fonda hadn't a word to say, but the agony on his face as his hands froze caused spasms among the patrons.

Of all the masks he has worn in his almost seventy years, the clown's lies as near as anything to his heart. "Another ability which is close to genius," in Logan's words. "Under the circumstances he could have earned his living and perhaps even more fame than he has in a circus or with the Mack Sennetts of his time. I believe that it is lucky for Charles Chaplin, Harry Langdon, Buster Keaton, and Emmett Kelly that he didn't join their game."

In the male-dominated UPG, the men had the fun as nightclub entertainers, while the girls did most of the menial jobs. They were waitresses from opening time until the 2 A.M. closing. They did most of the kitchen chores and washed most of the dishes. Because she hadn't many roles to play that season, Peggy Sullavan was stuck with more than her share of scullery maid's duties. The Irish in her, never deeper than just beneath the skin, surfaced again: "I'm an actress, not a kitchen maid."

A taste for resistance to anything that smacked of authoritarianism was something else she shared with Hank. Her temper was quick to flare up and simmer down again, while his anger burned for weeks on end. Eventually she was relieved of some of her waitress tasks. The outright battles with the management didn't start in earnest until the following season.

By the time the next spring brought the Guild veterans back to the Cape like pigeons fluttering to their coop, Peggy had been home to Virginia to face a very proper coming-out party as a Southern belle. She did this only to please

Mr. and Mrs. Cornelius H. Sullavan, her parents, who were dead set against a stage career for her, just as they'd been mystified at her choosing friends among the poor youngsters of Norfolk instead of from *good* families like her own.

Hank had weathered another winter of poverty in New York. Only two ill-paying jobs had come along. One was as a dance pantomimist, along with Kent Smith, joining with members of two professional dance companies in a performance with the Cleveland Symphony. Fonda's opinions of male dancers were inclined to be raucous, but the performance could be rated as experience. The other brief engagement was as a walk-on and understudy in the Theater Guild's production of *The Game of Love and Death*, which starred Claude Rains and Alice Brady.

Both engagements were due to the services of Charlie Leatherbee. He was out of Harvard now and working through the winter as an assistant stage manager at the Theater Guild. He owed his rapid start in the business to the help of Theresa Helburn, the lavender-haired little woman who had founded the Theater Guild and who chanced to be a good friend of his mother. Hank's social contacts with Broadway at that level amounted to zero. He had gone back to a steady diet of high hope and boiled rice.

Not surprisingly, he emerged in the summer of 1930 as what a colleague described as "the great leader of the unwashed" in the UPG group. With his friend Logan he was ready to make an issue of almost any decision management took. They always cast their votes against the two directors, Windy and Charlie. They were free souls, close to anarchy. Then Hank turned on Leatherbee with the usual passion that was endemic among this collection of talented hotheads.

The bone of contention was Ross Alexander, an engaging young actor with Broadway experience, who had traveled to West Falmouth to be with a girl in the company whom he adored. A lot of people thought he'd make a valuable addition to the Guild, but he lacked the standard qualification; he had never gone to college.

Leatherbee thought he should be admitted anyway. Ross was already sleeping in the men's boarding house and joining in the nightclub fun. He had a great sense of humor. Charlie wanted to make an exception in his case.

Windust put his foot down so firmly that it shook the Guild to its foundations. The whole purpose of the group, he said, was to provide experience in the theater for young men and women in college so that when they wanted to go into the professional theater they wouldn't be at a disadvantage compared with other people who had not gone to a university. If the basic rule was ignored, the spirit and meaning of the Guild would be lost.

Hank agreed with Windy completely and was perhaps more of a stickler for the rule. If Windy was going to split with Leatherbee over this question, then Hank would join him in setting up a breakaway group and leave "Charlie's company" to fend for itself. Half the Guild sided with Leatherbee, the rest with Windust and Hank. The quarreling grew vicious.

Josh was four weeks late returning to the Cape. He had fallen so far behind in work at Princeton that he'd been forced to take summer classes; he still had two more papers to deliver, which two girls in the company were glad to write for him. But he came fresh to the fight, and he was badly shaken at the idea that the Guild seemed doomed to be torn in two. Both Leatherbee and Windust attempted to win him over as an ally in the fight. As he saw it, the only sensible course was to patch up the quarrel and try somehow to cement the company together again.

"It would be ridiculous to break up," he said. "You wouldn't have as good a company. You'd have to go through all the pain of finding another theater. This season would be lost. Why not make a simple new rule? Take as many college people as possible, but if there's some outstanding noncollege man, take him in too."

Though Alexander, as it turned out, did not join the company, Windust and Leatherbee almost fell on Logan's neck in gratitude for his face-saving maneuver. They appointed him a director of the Guild for the first time; he had been a mere actor and supper club comic until then. That damned Josh as one of the Establishment, in Hank's view. As violently as he had opposed softening the rules, he turned against Logan. He taunted the new director by performing imitations of him to amuse the company. "You're pompous," he told his astonished friend. "You give answers without believing in what you say. You're trying to play the top." He looked on Logan, who had just turned twenty-one, as a babe in arms, scarcely worthy of attention, and often came close to not talking to him at all. The breach between them lasted for better than a year. Hank is slow to forgive.

The romance with Peggy had developed as many bumps as a washboard. Hank's unbending character was already molded; she was still, in many ways, a willful child, running barefoot around the place, wearing shoes only when required to on stage and in the supper club. She had another admirer in Charlie, and Hank's hostility to Leatherbee owed something to this. But she had the most fun with Hank.

"As we watched them," said one of the company, "they seemed to prove the truth of the adage: she couldn't stand to be with him, she couldn't stand to be without him."

He was certainly the better looking of her two suitors. In a long succession of roles, Hank was turning into a unique leading man. He could play romantic parts with a convincing sexiness, yet retain a kind of unawareness of himself as a sex symbol who stirred the women in the audience. They sometimes had to strain to hear what he said, because he despised "stagey" diction. He gave them

not so much as a grateful glance in response to their ap-
plause, except briefly after the curtain had been lowered
and his performance was over.

When an outbreak of matrimony affected the University
Players, Charlie abandoned any thought of making Peggy
his wife; later he married Logan's young sister, Mary Lee,
who joined the UPG as a recruit from Wells College.

Peggy and Hank originally planned to be man and wife
that winter, too. They had talked about it often enough as
the short, sweet days of a Cape Cod summer drew to another end. In New York they went so far as to get the
marriage license, but they thought it best not to use it.
Neither of them could imagine where the money was to
come from for starting a life together.

It looked as if the only discernible income would be
earned by Peggy, and he could safely be counted among the
last men in the world willing to live off a wife. She had
landed a job understudying in the Southern company of
Preston Sturges's hit play *Strictly Dishonorable*, directed by
Antoinette Perry, whose name endures in annual theatrical
awards. Miss Perry thought enough of Peggy's abilities to
release her to appear with the Princeton Theater Intime.
There, Peggy was spotted by a talent scout—he worked for
Lee and J. J. Shubert—the ritualistic first step that ranks in
importance, for an ambitious beginner in the theater, with
a saint's first communion.

She was signed for the lead in an easily forgettable drama
entitled *A Modern Virgin*, which opened on Boradway in
May, 1931. The critics disliked the play but they were en-
chanted with her confident style (what else after *The Devil
in the Cheese?*) and infectious laughter. She seemed destined,
one reviewer considered, "to cut a figure in the theater,
both Hollywood and Broadway." She read that heady forecast four days after her twenty-first birthday. She had
passed one more milestone on the road to her chosen desti-
nation.

Hank's progress in the same general direction seemed as long and dour as that of John Bunyan's pilgrim. The only opening he could find was back at the National Junior Theater in Washington, churning out productions for children. He left a special mark of his own multiple talents by taking *The Wizard of Oz*, adapting it as a musical, writing the music, designing the scenery, and finally directing it. After that, yielding to frustration, he took off for New York, where he would be closer to the Broadway agents, and even more frustration.

He cut down on expenses by moving into Leatherbee's Tudor City apartment, which, done up with Chinese prints and green velvet, was luxurious and ornate compared with any other place at which he'd ever stayed, Charlie was enjoying a pilgrimage of his own to Moscow to study under Stanislavsky. Grandfather Crane paid for the trip and stood treat for Josh, too, as a mark of appreciation for his work in keeping the Guild together.

Fonda fell back into the old pattern of eating rice and wearing out shoe leather to exist somehow until the spring, when he could go back to the comparative sanctuary and security of the Cape. In the meantime, his principal income was forty-five dollars he earned delivering flowers at Eastertime, a few weeks before his twenty-sixth birthday.

He was leaner and hungrier than Cassius when he turned up at Falmouth, wearing a thick black moustache. Logan was bursting to talk about what he and Charlie had seen and learned at the Moscow Art Theater. Charlie was working on Establishment plans, now that the founders had put their college days behind them, to convert the Guild into a year-round stock company to keep its members continually employed. Fonda had nothing to report, other than hard times. The gap between Elmer and Mr. Hossefrosse grew wider.

Hank had been among the first to come back from New York that spring, leaving Peggy starring in *A Modern Vir-*

gin. He was moodier than usual, with the preoccupied air of a man with much on his mind and on his shoulders. When her play fulfilled the critics' confident expectations and closed early, Peggy traveled to Falmouth with a run-of-the-play contract to return to *Virgin*, which was to reopen in August. Ahead of her arrival, Hank hid in the flies of the theater, eager to tease her, and stayed there while the girl he hoped to marry went the rounds of the company, deluged with congratulatory hugs and kisses for her Broadway success.

He stared down at her as she crossed the stage. "Hi," he said by way of greeting.

Peggy glanced up. "Fonda, shave off that damn fool moustache," was all she said. "Fonda" was what she usually called him. There was a certain affection in her manner of saying it, in a voice that was permanently husky; Lee Shubert once signed her for a role without an audition because, "You have a voice like Helen Morgan and Ethel Barrymore, and they are *stars.*"

Fonda and Sullavan appeared together that summer, in the Southern romance *Coquette.* They proved again that they had the power to move the company to tears of compassion; at dress rehearsal everybody wept. Then Peggy was recalled to *A Modern Virgin*, and Hank returned to Broadway, chewing on the stem of the pipe he had taken to smoking.

Establishment plans for moving onward and upward were starting to be fulfilled. They were going to present a winter season of repertory in Baltimore, a giant step beyond being a summer-stock company of amateurs. They signed a lease on the Maryland Theater there, a nineteenth-century downtown museum piece on Franklin Street, which seated fifteen hundred people. They made reservations at the Kernan Hotel next door, where rooms could be rented by the week, month, or hour, and which enjoyed its own separate entrance into the theater. They negotiated for the use of the hotel's sleazy basement nightclub, fragrant with odors of home-brew and bathtub gin, as rehearsal quarters. To give the company a more mature identity, they renamed it the University Repertory Theater.

First, they had to put six productions together and prepare scenery to fit a stage altogether different from their own. Overwhelmed by what they had seen in Moscow, Leatherbee and Logan laid down a rule that there would be no stars in Baltimore. Everybody, including stagehands, would be paid room and board plus fifteen dollars a week, starting on the date on which they opened with their first production.

That was more than the Establishment had ever shelled out before, but there was a snag: the two months that stretched between the end of the summer season on the Cape and the start-up in Baltimore. September and October meant room and board only, and Cape Cod got chilly after Labor Day. By mid-October, the company was rehearsing in gloves and overcoats. Fonda grew his first beard, like several other shivering males, either as an additional means of keeping warm or for lack of hot water.

Much of the time the company lived on frankfurters and beans—a novelty to some, but not to Fonda—supplemented by Wednesday evening dinner at "Whitecrest," which Charlie's mother kept open as a kind of five-star soup kitchen, with steaming showers and warm fires available for everybody.

Three new girls were enrolled to fill gaps in the company in its rough days of preparing for Baltimore. Accepting Logan's commonsense approach, the management hired a Smith College student as a character actress, found a leading lady who attended the Yale Drama School, and engaged Merna Pace, a beginner on Broadway, to take over Peggy's roles as the ingenue. Merna was no taller than Peggy. She had a similar sense of fun, though she giggled where Peggy's laughter was strong and throaty. His colleagues of that time recall that Hank found the two of them equally attractive. The fact that Merna's career had reached a point no higher than his may have added to her appeal for him, at least temporarily.

Toward the end of the first week at the Maryland Theater, the Establishment met in conference with the Maryland's manager, Leonard McLaughlin, on the sixth floor of the Kernan Hotel, which the company had taken over, room by room, to settle a thorny problem. Peggy had telephoned to say that *A Modern Virgin* was closing for the second and last time; she was available for Baltimore; did they want her?"

"As soon as she can get here," said McLaughlin. After opening night, box-office business had been slow. A Broadway name on the marquee would pull in bigger audiences.

The Establishment wasn't so sure. There never had been any stars as such in the old Guild, where everyone took turns playing major and minor parts. They didn't propose changing that tradition now, but what would Peggy's value be if she was not billed as "straight from Broadway"?

They decided to call in Fonda and ask what he thought about Peggy's return. "I'm against it. It wouldn't be fair to Merna."

She had rehearsed the roles that would go to Sullavan if she came back. Merna couldn't be blamed if she quit. Or maybe the idea was to fire her? The debate lasted all morning, until a compromise was reached that sat well enough with Fonda. Peggy would be invited back, but would not be starred; Merna would be kept on as second ingenue.

The compromise spared everyone's feelings but did virtually nothing to improve business at the box office, since Sullavan's arrival was not advertised. She went straight back rehearsing her old role of Tessa in *The Constant Nymph*, with Fonda again playing Lewis Dodd. Instead of presenting a different play each night in repertory, the University Theater turned to stock for the *Nymph*, which opened on the last day of November and ran for a week. In the interests of truth rather than sentiment, it has to be said that the Sullavan-Fonda combination made almost no impression on Baltimore. Audiences stayed away in droves even though the top ticket price had been dropped to one dollar. Not everybody in the company was sorry over that. A lot of people fancied that Merna, who was to have played Tessa, had been shabbily treated.

Three weeks later, with Christmas just forty-eight hours away, Fonda and Peggy slipped down to city hall one morning to buy their second marriage license. The next day, at breakfast in the hotel dining room, a reporter from the Baltimore *Post* walked in; he had seen the city hall list.

"What? Marry Fonda?" Peggy said in answer to his question. "Who'd ever want to marry *him?*" She skipped out of the room to avoid further probing.

On Friday, December 25, 1931, they were married. Later, most of their friends wondered why. Peggy and Hank were elated, but the country was in a state of chronic depression. Of all the depressed ways of making a living, the theater was perhaps the least promising. The setting for the wedding could not be considered romantic; the dining room of the Kernan Hotel, in spite of its marble pillars and fancy plasterwork ceiling, badly needed a fresh coat of paint. Behind a screen at one end of the room lunch was cooking, scenting the steam-heated air.

The bride was fifteen minutes late. "I refuse to go downstairs until that photographer gets out of the lobby," she said.

Horace Donegan, who had once acted with Charlie Leatherbee, performed the ceremony. He was now rector of Christ Episcopal Church in Baltimore, later serving as Bishop of the Episcopal Diocese of New York until he retired in May 1972.

Bretaigne Windust played the wedding march from *Lohengrin*, forgetting to take off the bandana he habitually

mother. Josh, who directed, considered it, in hindsight, to be one of the greatest performances either Fonda or Sullavan ever gave. The newspaper critics tended to agree with him; Baltimoreans did not. As real-life lovers portraying romance onstage, the Fondas drew autograph hunters to the stage door, but they couldn't get them into the box office, even at a dollar a head.

Financially *Mary Rose* was a loser. It seemed to establish a pattern of failure for the rest of the season. For all the skill of performance, audiences were skimpy. Gloom began to settle over the University Players. The festering quarrel between the Fondas and Logan flared up again. Windust was scheduled to direct S. N. Behrman's comedy, *The Second Man*, but the strain of weeks of pressure told on him. He was showing signs of tuberculosis and had to go into a hospital. Josh took over from him, though he had not so much as read the play up to that time.

Hank didn't need to look very hard to find reasons for hostility to Josh. He was tired of hearing about the genius of Stanislavsky and the wonderful way things were done in Moscow. He resented having been passed over in the management's choice of a new director, when he had piled up as much down-to-earth experience as anybody in the company—certainly more than Josh.

At the end of the first day's rehearsal, the atmosphere was tense. Hank convinced Kent Smith, the other actor in the four-character cast, of what had to be done. With the two girls, Peggy and Betty Fenner, watching, Hank grimly delivered an ultimatum to Josh.

"I want you to tell the people who run this company that we refuse to take your direction. Either they get a competent director from New York or we will quit. If you want to direct, go back to Louisiana."

Josh was shaken. "Don't you understand that I'm not trying to direct today? I'm just trying to learn the play. By tomorrow I'll have learned it and I'll know something and I'll help."

"You can't direct because you're not a director. We've got to have some *professional* help."

Logan accepted the situation as a challenge to show what he could do. He went back to his hotel room and worked on the play all night. The next day, he felt that he was at least competent. The rebels apparently agreed. Talk about replacing him petered out.

Logan gradually saw the cast start to cooperate. "Fonda even smiled," he reported. "But he sent in his resignation at the end of the season."

The end came slowly, like death by a thousand cuts. No production the University Players staged attracted more than a few hundred customers into the theater, whose rows of empty seats spelled financial disaster. By the middle of February it was all over. They had produced nineteen plays, built all the scenery, made all the costumes. They had run over their heads into thousands of dollars worth of debts, which Charles Crane was content enough to pay as the price of his grandson's experience.

"When they left," one admiring critic wrote, "they were like a regiment that has been through its first tough campaign."

In years to come, an almost unbelievable number of them went on to strike fame, fortune, or both in the theater and in motion pictures. The roll includes Joshua Logan, Myron McCormick, Kent Smith, Alfred Dalrymple, and Mildred Natwick, who joined them in Baltimore.

The most pressing problem the University Players faced was how to pay their way back to home base in Falmouth. They solved it by interrupting their journey to give four performances in Princeton. Then Charlie Leatherbee, acutely conscious of responsibility, ushered the survivors of the winter campaign to his mother's house, where they could be fed and sheltered until the spring and the beginning of yet another season at Old Silver Beach.

Hank said his farewells in Princeton. From there, he joined Peggy, who was already playing on Broadway in

Happy Landing, under contract with the Shuberts. She had left the University Players in Baltimore, the only one of them to make it so swiftly, a sure-fire success in everybody's judgment.

For what turned out to be the final season of the old UPG, the gap left by Fonda needed to be filled. Nobody had much confidence in the abilities of the gangly twenty-three-year-old, taller and even leaner than Hank, who applied at the suggestion of his Princeton friend Logan. The newcomer's father was in the hardware business in Indiana, Pennsylvania, but the son had gone to Princeton to study architecture. He had some other interests, too, far removed from drawing-board designs for office buildings and stylish residences. He liked to do conjuring tricks, he played the accordion, and he had appeared in Princeton Triangle Club shows.

The management hired him on the strength of those first two skills rather than his potential as an actor. Late-night patrons of the supper club enjoyed listening to Jimmy Stewart play and watching his magician's tricks. In a matter of months, after the final curtain fell on the concluding performance of the last season on Cape Cod, he followed in the footsteps of Fonda and joined his profession in pounding the pavements of New York.

By then, Fonda was on his own again. Marriage with Peggy had lasted less than two months. It was possibly foredoomed to failure. Their personalities were too similar —positive, perfectionist, supremely egotistical—for them to reach the kind of working compromise that is necessary between a steel-willed man and an equally steel-willed wife. She was the one with a career. His pride in himself, the certainty that he was good but overlooked, drove him away.

"When we found there was no show, we just talked it over and decided to call it quits," he said afterward. He did not talk about the nights when he paced the street outside their apartment in the company of Kent Smith, unable to keep his eyes off the windows of the living room, where he knew Peggy was entertaining Sam Harris, the producer, in the interests of her ambitions and her ego.

Hank and Peggy retained enormous respect, perhaps love, for each other. Some of his friends still believe that, if they could have stuck together, she might have been the one wife he needed. They tried reconciliation once, but it was impossible to make a go of it. Three years later she married William Wyler. She had made her first motion picture under a three-year contract signed with Universal, fighting all the way with the studio. She was the star in *Only Yesterday*, but, she complained "Acting in the movies is just like digging ditches." After seeing the first rushes, she tried, without succeeding, to buy out her contract for $2,500.

Now she was back in Hollywood to make *The Good Fairy* under William Wyler. She was so persistently hard to handle that he lectured her on the set one day in front of the cast and crew: "You have demoralized me, disrupted the company, and caused the picture to take up twelve weeks of shooting instead of the scheduled seven."

The uproar ended in a dinner date. One week later, Wyler and the former Mrs. Fonda were married in Yuma, Arizona. That marriage was over, too, before two years had passed.

In 1936 her agent, Leland Hayward, became her third husband in a ceremony at Newport, Rhode Island. Their first child, Brooke, was born the following year. That was also the year in which Jane Fonda was born, on December 21.

Jane, who regarded Brooke as the best friend she had in the world, once said to an intimate of the Fonda family: "I love Brooke so much I really think she's my sister. We *are* related in a way, aren't we?"

"In no way at all, my dear," was the reply, "though perhaps you might have been if things had worked out differently."

IV

THE PLACE could fairly be described as bachelors' quarters. Of the four tenants, only Fonda had been married and that for so little time that his friends sometimes found it hard to believe that he had once had a wife. The two miserable rooms in which he and his three companions starved together could also, with equal accuracy, be called a slum. Hank christened it "Casa Gangrene" and let it go at that.

The building stood on West Sixty-third Street in Manhattan, across from the Young Men's Christian Association. The flat bore the marks of neglect and roaches. The grimy bathroom reeked from the mildew on the shower curtain that none of them could afford to replace.

Under the windows, two-dollar prostitutes plied their trade under the eyes of their pimps. Gangsters and their gun molls paraded by. Jack "Legs" Diamond, racketeer and bootlegger, was gunned down on the street while Fonda, along with Jimmy Stewart, Josh Logan, and Myron McCormick, lived there.

Hank had gone briefly back to Omaha after the break with Peggy. Gregory Foley wanted him as a guest star at the Community Playhouse. Hank badly wanted to go home and, with a paid-for job to do, his marvelous pride allowed him to make the trip.

"Choose your own play," Foley said. Do Brando was no longer associated with the Playhouse. The family had moved to Evanston, Illinois, in 1930.

Fonda opted for *A Kiss for Cinderella*, a significant memento of his unforgettable years with the University Players. On the Cape he had been assigned to direct, design the scenery, and play the loving policeman in Barrie's tender-hearted comedy. Peggy had played the title role.

In Omaha, his leading lady was a fourteen-year-old local girl named Dorothy McGuire. Her career got on its way when the reviews gave her the same whoops of praise that Hank had received for *Merton of the Movies*, the praise that convinced him, against all logic, that he had to be an actor. Nothing had happened in six years to change his mind, though after *Cinderella* in Omaha he was reduced to working as a backstage helper at a summer theater in Maine, moving scenery and other actors' trunks, a failure as an actor and as a husband.

Then he went back to New York again, to the squalor of Casa Gangrene, one of the millions looking for work as the Great Depression deepened. If most of those millions were losing hope, Fonda certainly was not. He was sure that some day, somewhere, the doors would start to open for him. He staked his life on that.

The four tenants split the rent, whenever they could manage to pay it. Once again, Logan had struck it lucky. In the final season at West Falmouth, the Establishment had come to an agreement with a roly-poly young entrepreneur from Greenwich, Connecticut, Arthur J. Beckhard. In return for his paying the bills, the Old Silver Beach theater would try out any plays that interested him.

One of those plays was a comedy by Allan Scott and George Haight entitled *Goodbye Again*. When Beckhard brought it to Broadway, Josh was engaged to serve simultaneously as company manager, at twenty-five dollars a week, and box-office assistant, at another twenty-five. Myron McCormick kept the role of a bell captain, which he had played at Falmouth, and earned thirty dollars. Jimmy Stewart also repeated his Falmouth role of a supercilious chauffeur in the play and made his New York debut drawing thirty-five dollars.

Any bitterness in Hank's heart would have risen then to sour his nature. The critics on opening night singled out the former architectural student from Princeton. "It seems apropos to say a few words about James Stewart," one of them wrote, "player in this mad piece, who is on stage for exactly three minutes and speaks no more than eight lines. Yet before this gentleman exits he makes a definite impression on audiences because he makes them laugh so hard." Fonda, after five years of trying, hadn't made a dent yet on Broadway.

Absent from Falmouth, he had nothing to do with *Goodbye Again*. He was kept busy as the leading man with a stock company in Newark, New Jersey. His contract called for him to be paid 10 percent of the gross, on the face of it a sensational share, not exceeded by such hard-bargaining stars as Ethel Merman, who could earn as much as four thousand a week on percentages. But times were cruel and Newark customers stayed home to cut down on luxuries like going to the theater. Hank's take-home pay worked out to an average of seven dollars a week.

At the Casa Gangrene he did most of the cooking, which is another talent surviving in him today. Nowadays he is a Sunday-night barbecue chef at the Beverly Hills house; in that Depression period he specialized in Mexican rice and Swedish meatballs, made from ground veal, beef, and milk-soaked bread crusts, a recipe of his mother's. One of the housekeeping problems was the staggering appetite of Stewart, who, according to legend, once wrecked the budget by downing eighteen meatballs at a sitting.

None of them had money to waste on the pursuit of pleasure, but Fonda, forever inventive, came up with an idea for making a few extra dollars and, at the same time, enjoying themselves. He organized weekly beer parties. The first step was to club together and rent the cellar of a speakeasy on West Fortieth Street. The setting was crude, with an earth floor, but clubby. Young New Yorkers who couldn't afford nightclub entertainment might take a liking to the place.

On an old iron grill Hank packed salt into cheap cuts of steak, then with the help of Ross Alexander, the noncollege man who had sparked a crisis at the UPG, he baked the steaks for the customers. For a steak and all the beer you could drink, bought from the speakeasy upstairs, the charge was one dollar.

"I remember the food as being delicious," one old patron recalled. "The place got to be terribly popular, and the entertainment was great."

To amuse themselves as well as their clientele, Hank and Josh occasionally revived Elmer and Mr. Hossefrosse, while Jimmy Stewart played his accordion and performed his legerdemain. In that fashion, they celebrated their survival through another week.

The following summer Fonda reverted to another temporarily disused skill. One of his sterner judges, Bretaigne Windust, had long believed that Hank basically was only an indifferent actor. "Let's face it," he'd say, "you're a scenic designer." Designing scenery was Hank's principal job for the Westchester Players at their summer theater in Mount Kisco, New York. He knew he was better than good at that, too. "Any summer theater would have hired me as a scenic designer."

But he did get to play a role or two and was invited back for the next season. Fonda, always intuitive, sensed at this part of his life that the momentum was starting to quicken. The man who for many people became a piece of living Americana by playing every hero of the frontier introduced himself inauspiciously to Broadway as a comic. Leonard Sillman hired him as one of the cast of unknowns for the first edition of his revue series, *New Faces*, whose aim was to spread a little unpretentious, low-cost humor to lighten the darkness of the doleful 1930s. Elsie Janis supervised the production.

For thirty-five dollars a week, Fonda played in some skits with a wide-eyed comedienne named Imogene Coca, who was also making her start in this show, and delivered an unlikely burlesque of Max Gordon, the benign producer, who was utterly dissimilar to Hank in voice, shape, and nature. Imitations were not really Hank's *forte*, even if in some later roles he was accused of imitating himself. There is only one fantasy character that he can perform: the Fonda version of a London cockney with a slight lisp and trouble with his *W*s, which he can sustain for hours until you totally believe in him.

Max Gordon in person joined the list of characters in Hank's life that same year.

The reviewers, without singling out any performer for particular mention, sat through the opening night with mixed feelings. "Ardent and amateur" was one comment. "Filled to the eyelashes with pep and humor," said Burns Mantle in *The New York Times*. Dwight Deere Wiman, the producer, thought enough of Fonda's bits to offer him a contract at a hundred dollars a week, with the proviso that he'd have to learn to tap dance.

But there was hint enough of untapped talent in the undiscovered, sad-faced young man to attract Leland Hayward, a hot agent and shrewd wheeler-dealer, into signing Fonda as one of his stable of clients.

"If you listen to me," said Hayward, "I'll get you more a week in Hollywood than Wiman will pay you in a year."

Hayward was the smooth, sophisticated half of a partnership with Myron Selznick, David O.'s elder brother, who specialized in roughneck blasphemy in browbeating producers on behalf of the people he represented. When one of those clients, playwright Marc Connelly, objected to working on a screenplay for Metro-Goldwyn-Mayer because its theme seemed too trivial, Myron had some pungent advice for him. "Blow it out your nose," he said.

Myron and Leland were rare among agents in that they were solidly on the actor's side, not openly or secretly siding with the producers. In one classic encounter on behalf of another newcomer to the movies, Myron showed up with a monumental hangover at the producer's office, where he proceeded to prop himself up behind the desk of the boss. He seemed to be asleep as the producer paced the floor, outlining the contract he had in mind. Then he opened one bloodshot eye, grunted, "Go and fuck yourself," and dozed off again.

The producer, rocked on his heels, began to sweeten the proposition, but not enough for Myron, who at intervals repeated his blessing until he had obtained the concessions he wanted.

Though Hank enjoyed the services of high-powered management, when *New Faces* closed in July no new job appeared except at the Mount Kisco Theater again. The difference was that now he had star billing. He was to play leads, not design more scenery. The ache he sometimes had for Omaha took him home for a few days just at the moment when Hayward proved that he was worth his weight in gold cuff links. The two-page telegram he sent from Hollywood said, in essence, FLY OUT IMMEDIATELY TO SIGN WITH WALTER WANGER. Hank's reply consisted of one word: NO. Wanger made a point of having nearly half the young men of Hollywood under contract to him. When he had no pictures of his own for them, he simply farmed them out to other producers, taking a percentage of their earnings for his trouble.

Hank simply wasn't interested. He could count on a hundred dollars a week from Wiman as an actor in summer stock, a fortune of Arabian Nights proportions compared with the scrapings he'd lived on for years. The theater was his love. He could wear the masks so necessary for him.

But nobody could say no indefinitely when Hayward

and his partner had made up their minds. "I went out to Hollywood. Leland met me at the airport, took me to a hotel suite. Half an hour later, as I stepped out of a cold shower, there was Hayward with a man whose name I had heard often."

Fonda had stipulated a salary that he remembered as so astronomical that he was sure he'd scare any motion-picture producer away. He wanted to be his own man, steering his own course as an actor, not somebody's permanent hireling with little choice in choosing assignments. Wanger couldn't be deterred. "Dripping wet, I shook hands with Walter Wanger, and that's how I signed for two pictures a year, one thousand dollars a week."

This was 1934, the thirtieth year of Fonda's life. Breadlines stretched across the land. Soup kitchens served bitter coffee and watery porridge. The squalid collections of homemade shacks called "Hoovervilles" that sprang up on city dumps had disappeared, but happy days were here again only in the words of a campaign song. Hundreds of thousands still struggled to exist in shacks around the big cities. Prosperity was somewhere around the corner. But the motion-picture business flourished as never before. The Metro-Goldwyn Gothic and Paramount Byzantine palaces, where the double- and triple-features lasted half a day, had to hand out dishes and cut their ticket prices, but a seat inside promised escape into daydreams from the harsh reality of current history. Escape became a kind of national drug. Hollywood had never had it so good. From around the world, the nickels and two-bit pieces poured in, a flood tide that carried the industry into its own Never-Neverland, more fantastic than any movie plot.

The melancholy realist, Fonda, had seen to it that his contract with Wanger contained provisions allowing him to continue to work in the theater. The day after signing, Hank went straight back to Mount Kisco and the male lead in Ferenc Molnar's *The Swan*, the quiet tutor who transforms his pupil, a princess. Geoffrey Kerr played the prince.

Marc Connelly in New York was looking to cast a play he had written with a not-always-sober collaborator. They called it *The Farmer Takes a Wife*, the story of how the railroads rousted out the men who made their living on the Erie Canal in the 1860s, loosely based on a novel by Walter D. Edmonds, *Rome Haul*.

Connelly's concern for accuracy was punctilious. He traveled along the canal itself to absorb atmosphere and history. He persuaded Henry Ford to contribute two glass rolling pins of the period from the Dearborn Museum as stage props. The kerosene lamp used was an antique, donated by the Standard Oil Company. For his heroine, Molly Larkins, he wanted June Walker, the wife of Geoffrey Kerr.

She had seen and admired Fonda's performance in *The Swan*, so she recommended him to Connelly for *The Farmer*. The two men met in Connelly's suite in the Gotham Hotel, at the corner of Fifth Avenue and Fifty-fifth Street, the playwright cordial as usual, the actor customarily detached.

The script had been completed only three days earlier. Connelly read part of the first act to set the scene, then asked Fonda to read extracts from the role of Dan Harrow.

"He was patently ideal for the character, completely convincing, totally real," Connelly remembered. "He was the first to read the part. I knew nobody could be better. He's been playing the same part all his life. Somebody went around afterwards saying that I read him the whole play, but that was not true."

The legends had started to form, that touching up of the tame, whole truth, which is as important in the entertainment business as anesthesia is in major surgery. However, Hank had some sound financial advice from Connelly.

"You see Max Gordon tomorrow, and he'll sign you,"

Fonda was told. Gordon was the producer. "How much money do you want?"

"I don't know," Hank said, a novice at this kind of negotiating.

"Ask him for two hundred dollars a week, and don't take less."

When the play opened in October, he was praised to the skies for being Dan Harrow to the life. The critics reached for such adjectives as manly, modest, believable, captivating, strong, simple, lustrous, and everything else in the thesaurus along similar sympathetic lines. They have continued using much the same words to applaud most performances he has ever given since. He was close to being typecast at the moment of his first success. Audiences visualized him as American bedrock, as solidly dependable as Mount McKinley. The mask of Dan Harrow was a perfect fit.

The identification has sometimes bothered him in later years, and he has tried to explain that the man is different from the mask. "I'm not trying to suggest I'm a son of a bitch, but I wouldn't want the world to think I go around thinking I'm the kind of nice guy I portrayed in *Mister Roberts.*" But most of the world goes on believing just that, no matter what his son and his only-born daughter tried so hard to say when they were struggling to establish their own identities.

The Farmer's producer was Max Gordon, who made a modest effort to reduce the realism of the play in one respect. Dan Harrow has a fistfight with the bully of the canal, while the mob on the towpath eggs them on. "Kick him in the privates!" was one bit of advice delivered to Dan by an onlooker, but Fonda could never hear it. Marc Connelly also wondered why the line was always inaudible, until he learned that Max, a sensitive man, was paying the actor in the crowd five dollars a week from his own pocket to mumble the words, because the producer thought they were offensive.

Theatergoers liked life on the Erie Canal less than the critics. The play closed after 104 performances. Gordon, Connelly, and Fonda were disappointed, but less than heartbroken. Max and Marc had sold *The Farmer* to Fox Pictures, and Fonda went along with it as part of the deal, on loan from Wanger, who had no picture ready for his recent acquisition to start work in.

Hank was the third choice. Gary Cooper and Joel McCrea had been ahead of him on the list of desirables, but they had other commitments. It was a flying start for a man who six months earlier had been just another out-of-work actor. He was the male lead in his first movie, which had been bought for the biggest drawing name on the Fox lot, baby-faced Janet Gaynor, who five years earlier, in 1930, had won the very first Oscar in movie history for *Seventh Heaven.*

Fonda needed no more than a single day's shooting to appreciate the difference between "projecting" a role to a theater audience and keeping it in lower key for movie cameras. "You're hamming it," said the director, Victor Fleming, who stood no nonsense from anyone, actors, producers, or the New York money men who were always the real power behind the studios.

"And that's all it took," Hank has said. "I just pulled it down to reality."

The resultant picture focused mainly on Janet Gaynor, who couldn't come within a mile of repeating June Walker's portrayal of Molly Larkins. The movie disappointed Connelly and others, who considered that it lost the personality of the play. But, miraculously, it made Fonda a full-fledged star on his first appearance in Hollywood. The advertisements put his name right up there above the title, following Gaynor's. Lesser men have been transformed into human peacocks by such sudden blows. Not Hank.

The transition was easy for him as an actor. He had played Dan often enough to be able to pick up anywhere in the script and handle any scene out of sequence, according to the demands of the shooting schedule. The style he had evolved through grim determination was so deceptively simple that only those who knew the man and his motivations realized that he was acting at all. He was a natural for the movie business.

He slipped easily enough into high-flying social life from the night of the first party he was escorted to, on Wanger's behalf, at the house of madcap Carole Lombard. He exuded down-to-earth friendliness and good humor, and in short order he made a host of friends. Robert Montgomery, Tyrone Power, Hoagy Carmichael, the Gary Coopers were all on the list sooner or later.

In this new-found glory, he was an enigma to most laborers in the Hollywood vineyards. According to the rules of the big studios, a star had a long list of duties to perform, somewhat along the lines of the chores required of kings and queens in less demanding societies. A star had to make public appearances to promote his current picture, sign autographs, pose for publicity photographs, open his home and his heart for press and magazine interviews, attend motion-picture premières, and date other stars, especially those employed by the same studio. A star was equipped with a fanciful and colorful past by the public relations department, unless he happened to possess one of his own, and was expected to lead an equally glamorous present, with a house, wardrobe, and automobiles sufficiently impressive to give plausibility to the legend.

Fonda was reluctant to surrender his independence to do any of that. In the first place, publicity scared the daylights out of him. Without a mask to hide behind, he was as skittery as an unbroken colt. At press interviews, he could seldom think of anything to say that struck him as the least bit interesting. Only the money, he felt, "made it pretty attractive."

To supply the movie theaters with the four new pictures a week that they needed to keep their box offices jingling, the industry turned out its product—dreams in a can—on assembly-line schedules. The success of *The Farmer* was reason enough for Fox to push Hank into another movie with Janet Gaynor within a matter of weeks, though in point of fact she walked out of the remake of *Way Down East*, and another, less luminous actress, Rochelle Hudson, stepped into her part.

As soon as shooting on that was finished, Hayward rushed his brand-new romantic lead into another picture, this time for RKO Radio, with Lily Pons as co-star. Wanger hadn't yet come up with anything for Fonda, but, under usual contract terms, he was making money on him.

Hank cherished no illusions about what he was doing. "Some of my pictures aren't that good," he said retrospectively after the count of them ran into several dozen. "I could name you twenty pictures without drawing a breath that I'm ashamed of."

He itched to get back into the theater, but it was three years before he could find the time and a promising play to do. By then both his mother and father were dead. Neither of them had ever seen him on the screen. The only plays they had watched him perform in were at the Omaha playhouse and during one season on Cape Cod, when they drove in from Nebraska.

His domestic life reverted once again to bachelors' lodgings, a series of unspectacular rented houses that he later shared with two other immigrants to California from the University Players, Johnny Swope and Jimmy Stewart, who had been put under contract by Metro-Goldwyn-Mayer after being screen-tested and rejected by Fox.

One of the rented places became known tolerantly as the House of Cats. The description was innocent and truthful. Hank began with one cat named George, who was joined by a female, Cerisse, who had kittens. Neighborhood cats moved in with the family until cats sprawled in every room and up every tree in the yard, their eyes glowing after dark like jack-o'-lanterns in a haunted graveyard. For the sake of convenience, every one of them was called George.

Hank was in no hurry to marry again. The household had a distinct flavor of college dorm. At one time he lived next door to Jeanette MacDonald, the green-eyed singer from Philadelphia who was one of the reigning beauties of M-G-M, and he ventured to date her.

"At the beginning of the evening," he said, "I called her 'Miss MacDonald,' and by twelve o'clock Hollywood had us engaged." The so-called Iron Butterfly was only one of a dozen girls he intended to marry, if the public relations department were to be believed—but they were not. Shirley Ross, who also sang, was another. The newspaper copy on that brief encounter had Hank sounding as if he were inscribing a high school yearbook: "A lovely girl, and a good kid. We had a lot of fun."

The three men simultaneously took a fancy to Virginia Bruce and conducted some kind of contest to squire her. It resulted in a dead heat when all three escorted her to a preview of Fonda's fourth picture and the first he made with Wanger as producer, *The Trail of the Lonesome Pine*. The cartoonist Al Capp credits Hank's playing of Dave Tolliver, the square-cut Kentucky mountain boy, as being the inspiration for his comic strip Li'l Abner, the hillbilly square.

Swope waited ten more years before he was married—to Dorothy McGuire of Omaha, Nebraska. Stewart proved to be an even more reluctant bridegroom. Not long after he went on the M-G-M payroll, he began making pictures with Margaret Sullavan, who continually recommended him to her producers.

"I loved Fonda and I loved Jimmy," she once said. "Fonda was the man I was married to, but they were both my friends." The gossips insisted that Stewart remained a bachelor because he adored Peggy Sullavan. By the time he married a strikingly handsome society belle, Mrs. Gloria

Hatrich McLean in 1949, he was nearing his forty-third birthday.

Hank wasn't permanently successful in avoiding fan magazine writers. One of them, in *Photoplay*, carefully explained, "He wants, above everything else, to be part of an average American family with no fuss or publicity about it; he wants, if he married again, a wife and some kids and a good house." The second half of the wish came true in reasonably short order. But "an average American family"? He had traveled too far and too fast for that.

"The wife I'll have some day will be able to laugh," he promised. "But I'm not going around peering into the face of every woman I meet, asking myself, 'Can this be the one? Would she be a good mother and a fine wife?" The woman who was to be his second wife and mother his children was not yet in his orbit.

The year 1935, when Hank's father died, also saw the end of George Tuttle Brokaw. "Dawdie," as he was nicknamed after his childhood pronunciation of his name, had a taste for young women, with a long list of girls to provide his amusement. Clare Boothe was twenty at the time of their marriage; in the opinion of her friends, she married him for his money. After she divorced him, he did not wait long to find another bride. In January 1931, he married a girl two years younger than Clare, who was born in 1903.

The new Mrs. Brokaw ranked as a true beauty, with delicately molded features and lustrous brown eyes. Her reasons for marrying him were similar to Clare's. Frances Seymour's family boasted of its ancestors. Her mother, Sophie, was descended from a cousin of John Adams, second President of the United States. Her father, Eugene, twelve years older than his wife, claimed a longer, more illustrious descent—from Edward Seymour, Duke of Somerset, inextricably entangled in the matrimonial intrigues of King Henry VIII. Through her grandmother on her father's side, Frances was related to half the social register of old New York—the Stuyvesants, the Stoutenburghs, the Howards—as well as to the Biddles of Philadelphia.

The fortunes of her immediate family, however, didn't begin to match the bloodlines. Eugene Ford Seymour, his wife, and children enjoyed no more than the comfortable circumstances of the average residents of any small American town, in this case Fairhaven, Massachusetts, on Buzzard's Bay. Frances, the oldest of seven children, was the image of her handsome father. A cousin, Harry Rogers, with a Standard Oil fortune, offered to pay for a college education for her when she graduated from high school. She chose, instead, to take a course at Katharine Gibbs in Boston. "I want to go there," she said earnestly, "so I can go down to Wall Street and marry a millionaire."

Her first job was in a Fairhaven bank. Then she took the next step toward her goal by moving to New York and into a similar position with First National City. Her ambitions soared. She envied her cousins who had real money to spend, like the Rogers family. "I'm tired of being known as Millicent Rogers's poor cousin," Frances liked to say.

By the time she met Brokaw, the former millionaire playboy was showing sure signs of wear and tear. He had a law office, but he seldom went near it. He was gentlemanly enough when he was sober, but he was rarely in that condition. Hangovers brought remorse, and he would swear off drinking, ordering the staff of servants to lock up every bottle in the stone château, French-Renaissance-style, at the corner of Fifth Avenue and Seventy-ninth Street, which he had inherited from his doting mother. Even while he was ostensibly drying out, he had a secret hiding place. The golf trophies on the library shelves were filled to the brim with bootleg gin.

His stock portfolio had undoubtedly suffered somewhat in the Wall Street debacle beginning in October 1929, but he remained a multimillionaire. He kept standing accounts at Cartier's. He had paid $250,000 for Julius Fleischmann's six acres and private beach on Sands Point, Long Island, once a favorite weekend hideaway of the Duke of Windsor in his merrymaking, women-chasing days as the Prince of Wales.

There was a darker side to Brokaw's nature. He could be an ugly drunk prone to violence. According to her biographer, in the last four years of their marriage the first Mrs. Brokaw suffered four early miscarriages.

Like Clare, the second Mrs. Brokaw bore one child—in 1934. Her daughter was christened Frances; she inherited her mother's beauty and temperament. According to family intimates, she never met her half-sister, Ann, the child of Brokaw and Clare.

"Dawdie" died on May 28 in a Hartford, Connecticut, sanatorium where he had been committed as an alcoholic, leaving the bulk of his estate in trust for his widow Frances. It amounted to four or five healthy millions, but not the thirty or fifty it had once been guessed at. In cash she collected $750,000 in life insurance, which her never-forgotten bank training taught her to invest profitably and well. He left his two daughters nothing, since, as his will said, "they have been abundantly provided for in the will of my father, Isaac V. Brokaw [a clothing manufacturer], and my daughter Ann Clare Brokaw is provided for in a settlement made with her mother."

Eleven-year-old Ann was a serious, sensitive child, who had been badly buffeted in the aftermath of her parents' divorce. The terms of the original settlement had been fair enough in the lawyers' eyes: her mother and father would share her, with six months' custody for each. After George remarried, Clare wanted the full-time company of Ann. Brokaw would not hear of it. Instead, he sought the exclusive custody of their sad-faced daughter. Attorneys on both sides crossed swords for two years. True domestic peace was a rarity in Frances Seymour's first marriage.

Besides dazzling good looks, Frances had a sharp brain, which married life did nothing to dull. Whatever her feelings toward Ann, she realized that the legal squabble needed to be ended. She arranged a meeting with Clare when Brokaw was in the Hartford institution and made a clear-cut proposal. Clare should have year-round custody if she would agree to bear full financial responsibility for Ann's support. Clare, by this time a highly successful editor soon to be married to Henry Luce, agreed to accept.

After Brokaw's death from a heart attack, it took a while to clear up some details of his estate. Then his young widow, with several burdens lifted from her shoulders, went off on a trip to Europe with a girl who was engaged to one of her brothers, Ford de Villiers Seymour.

In California, Fonda remained single, but scarcely for lack of company of women with a mind to make a bridegroom of this steel spring of a man whose surface calm seemed like a disguise. He had lost the beanpole look as his standard of living rose high above a diet of boiled rice. He was filling out, watching his weight, working like a demon. New confidence showed in his walk, the stride that is a vital element of the Fonda persona. In relationships with women, he was far more often the pursued than the pursuer. That has been the case during most of his adult life, according to his long-term companions. He was *there*, like a mountain range, and women felt the urge to conquer him. None of them was ever to succeed.

The excitement he stirred in women audiences was whipped up when he and Peggy Sullavan—both clients, it must be remembered, of Leland Hayward—were cast together as the first brace of top-flight motion-picture performers who had once been husband and wife. Paramount's publicity department had a field day with *The Moon's Our Home*, which gave Peggy, playing a spoiled heiress and movie star, the chance to relive a bit of her immediate past by tossing lamps around the set in make-believe fury. It seemed like good, clean fun, but Hank was over-shadowed by her—zany comedy wasn't his meat.

The film industry was in the throes of a technical revolution that everyone felt certain would pile up even more gold, once the bugs could be ironed out. Technicolor had come to the screen, outdating almost overnight earlier, cruder tinting efforts that resulted in pictures looking like today's poorly tuned color television. The cumbersome Technicolor cameras proved they could handle outdoor shots for the first time in *The Trail of the Lonesome Pine*. Now Twentieth Century-Fox decided to try the same process in a story, to be shot in Ireland, England, and elsewhere, about a gypsy princess and her granddaughter who, for reasons of plot, must masquerade as a boy so that her horse can win the Derby. Fonda, whose blue eyes, fair, dimpled skin, and black hair showed up handsomely in color, was signed as the leading man.

His leading lady was a new screen sensation known simply as Annabella. She had knocked Hollywood in the eye as the star of French movies, which were being imported in serious quantities for the first time. Her disarmingly accented English could be counted as only a fraction of her charm. She was simultaneously a hobbledehoy, a *gamine*, a woman of the world. *Wings of the Morning* would be her first English-speaking role. To a man, the reviewers adored her as "enchanting" . . . "exquisite" . . . "delightful."

In the spring of 1936 Fonda sailed for Europe, "more because he wanted the trip and the experience of filming in Ireland and England than because he was interested in the routine leading-man role," according to his long-term friend and business associate John Springer.

His first taste of foreign travel delighted him. Working with the French girl couldn't have been better for him. Every day's shooting showed a completely believable and beguiling romance in celluloid. London and Fonda proved compatible. Here he was, a visiting Hollywood star, in a town with the taste and style to welcome him without undue fuss. He felt at home, a gentleman, getting to know how to read a first-class restaurant menu and developing a taste for good wine.

In England, in June, he was introduced to another charming American visitor who was enjoying herself every bit as much as he. Frances Seymour Brokaw had never been to a movie studio, so she arranged through a friend to pay a visit to Denham, just outside London, where *Wings of the Morning* was being shot. It is totally alien to Fonda's code to talk about his relationships with women, most particularly about the woman who was to mother his children. But the evidence is that Frances set her sights on him.

She was rich now and mercifully released from a marriage that had brought her nothing more than money. Here was an exciting motion-picture star who, miraculously, was available as a husband, a man as different from Brokaw as anyone could be in God's creation.

"Hank," an old friend told him not so long ago, "you have never married anybody—they all married you." That was true beyond a shadow of doubt the second time around.

When *Wings of the Morning* was completed at Denham studios, Frances went with Hank to Paris, then on to Munich, Berlin, and Budapest, in those days one of the most romantic cities in the world for touring Americans, renowned for *tzigane* music, candlelight, and Tokay.

Along the route of their travels they saw the ominous signs of Hitler's new armies on maneuvers. To Hank, much concerned as a good Democrat with the threat of fascism to America and the world, that spelled future war.

The conversation with Frances turned to the subject of getting married. After five years of bachelordom, he was willing. Frances could be the ideal partner for the life he hungered for, tranquil, sheltered, and cushioned by hard cash against adversity. She had beauty, brains, and style, and she was fascinated by him. She would be "the good mother and fine wife" he needed, different from the other girls he had been pursued by or occasionally pursued.

On August 24, 1936, Mr. and Mrs. Eugene Ford Seymour of 315 East 68th Street, New York City, announced the engagement of Hank and their daughter, Frances, of 646 Park Avenue. "Plans for their marriage have not yet been decided," said the formal announcement, headlined in all the society columns, which also carefully spelled out the lineage of the Seymours back to Henry VIII. It described George Tuttle Brokaw as having been "a retired lawyer and well-known sportsman."

Six days later, Frances and her brother's fiancée sailed for New York from Le Havre. The wedding plans were not allowed to hang fire for long. On September 16, three months after their first meeting and less than two weeks after their return to New York, Hank and Frances were married in quiet style by the Reverend Ralph Sockman in Christ Episcopal Church, at Park Avenue and Sixtieth Street, which is as fashionable as any church can be. The ceremony would have been held four days sooner, but it took that long to find an Episcopal minister willing to marry the divorced actor and his widowed bride.

Four or five hundred cheering women waited outside the church. In the chapel, a comparatively small group of thirty guests watched Hank arrive in a top hat and morning coat with Joshua Logan as his best man, attended by Leland Hayward and one of the bride's brothers, Roger. Both of Hank's sisters made the trip from Omaha to be there.

For the three o'clock ceremony, Frances wore powder-blue tulle and an off-the-face hat, carrying pink roses and blue delphiniums. Her brother Ford escorted her. Her sister Mary was her only attendant. Her cousin, Henry Huddleston Rogers, was among the guests. Five-year-old

Frances de Villiers Brokaw, a beautiful fair-haired child in a little French frock of blue organza with a matching bonnet, sat in one of the pews.

The reception was held for one hundred and fifty guests in the stylish Roof Garden of the Hotel Pierre. Frances wore bouffant black velvet for that. On the following day, Mr. and Mrs. Henry Fonda flew to Hollywood, where he had to start another Walter Wanger production, *You Only Live Once*, directed by the German master Fritz Lang. Hank was still a working man, though his pay checks were getting to be impressive.

When he had stepped off the boat onto the Hudson River pier, he had been bubbling over with talk of the marvelous time he'd enjoyed in London. He went on talking about it for hours later.

"Well, what's she like?" he was asked by one of the friends he ran into who had read the wedding announcement but had not met Frances; none of Hank's friends knew her.

"She's the most wonderful thing you ever saw," Fonda replied. "We'd go for long rides on the buses, then get off and wander into some old English inn. We went dancing and looking into shop windows like a couple of kids."

"Isn't it wonderful to find a girl like that to marry?"

"Marry?" said Hank.

"Aren't you talking about Frances?"

"No. I'm talking about Annabella."

V

SO FAR as their friends could judge, they lived on parallel tracks that only occasionally converged. By the standards that movie fan magazines led every outsider to believe were typical of Hollywood, the Fondas were quiet stay-at-homes most of the time. Except for the company of dear friends—Jimmy Stewart, Johnny Swope, Josh Logan, and a handful of others—Hank developed something close to horror about going out to other people's parties, though Fonda wingdings around his own swimming pool gained a lively reputation among those friends.

Theater was all he really liked to talk about. He regarded the business of making talk as silly and refused to attempt it. He liked to sit and watch, not to join in chitchat.

Frances had different ideas. She delighted in company, aware of her beauty, admired by women as much as by men in the society of talkative talents that made up most of the motion-picture business. The theater did not really interest her, so she rarely spoke about it. If she had anything much to say, it wouldn't have helped to pull their parallel paths closer.

"Hank wouldn't dream of listening to her opinions," someone who knew them has said. Yet Frances was very much a man's woman, with little interest in talking with women, seldom listening when they talked to her.

Hank's older companions were slow to warm to the woman who had been a stranger when he introduced her. They used to joke maliciously among themselves that getting along with Frances was easy if you were prepared to talk about the five subjects that absorbed her. They listed those as sex, children, jewelry, the rise and fall of the stock market, and surgical operations, which fascinated her in general, as well as in specific, gory detail.

Fonda was never an easy man to live with. He found it impossible to pretend, except in the roles he played, and he accepted most of those as a continuing challenge to his special abilities. He worried endlessly over them, searching for a way to make them come "true" to an audience so that they would accept the fictional character of the screenplay as a living man.

With few exceptions, he took whatever pictures were offered to him—Westerns, farce, drawing-room comedy—many of them totally unsuited to his particular, intense style. But those he remembers invariably cast him at the down end of the social scale from that which Frances regarded as her own. He liked to portray troubled, earthy people—an ex-convict in *You Only Live Once*, a telephone lineman in *Slim*, a guerrilla fighter in *Blockade* (not so much for the merits of the movie but because the sentiments appealed to his highly political nature; the screenplay, concerning the Spanish War between the Loyalists and Generalissimo Franco, was written by John Howard Lawson, later pilloried and described as a suspected Communist and one of the "Hollywood Ten," but it became heavily diluted in Walter Wanger's production.)

Politics was another subject on which Hank and Frances could not see eye to eye. In those days, the big money men behind most of the studios insisted that movie stars be romantic, glamorous, and politically neutered. A majority of stars accepted that dictum. At the House Un-American Activities Committee hearings on the Hollywood Ten,

Louis B. Mayer, boss of M-G-M, appeared as a voluntary witness to call for federal supervision of the industry. One of his employees, Robert Taylor, urged that all Communists be shipped to Russia.

Fonda risked his career by joining liberal causes that sometimes veered way left of center; the blacklist was a favorite weapon of the witch hunters. In 1938 he was one of a group that petitioned Franklin D. Roosevelt to cut off American trade with Hitler. Later, his sympathies carried him into active campaigning for Adlai Stevenson, John F. Kennedy, Eugene McCarthy, Edmund Muskie, and George McGovern. Nevertheless, he could maintain friendly relations with a man like John Wayne, whose opinions were poles apart from his, out of sheer respect and liking for him as an individual, or real friendship with Jimmy Stewart, another rock-ribbed Republican.

"Henry Fonda," an intimate of his has said, "is a man so dedicated to everything honest that if he can't do it onstage, he can't do it offstage. He can't exaggerate. He can't lie." In the widening gap between his personality and his wife's, he couldn't compromise either.

Together, they had more than enough money to live in high Hollywood style. At the time of their marriage, he was earning $56,000 a year, under the terms of his contract with Wanger. The figure had tripled within a year or so as he went from one picture straight into another, grinding them out at an average rate of one every thirteen weeks. Into every assignment he put the same grueling analysis and self-doubt.

One of the subjects that husband and wife did agree upon was the desire to build a house. "Home" was an important word to Fonda, who had been a creature of hotel suites and rented places too long to satisfy his deepest instincts. He chose a remote nine-acre lot on a hillside off Tigertail Road in Brentwood, California, and there they built a New England-style farmhouse, a deliberate anachronism of split shingles, with a long, covered porch running along its length. They saw it as a haven from the artificiality of work in dreamland. Then they toured half the antique shops in New England on furniture-buying trips, picking up hand-hewn furniture, braided rugs, a cobbler's bench, lamps made from butter churns.

The result satisfied something in both of them. Early American was virtually unknown in the motion-picture colony, where tastes in interior decorating more often ran to plaster cupids and tigerskins. "You're going to be considered very chic," a friend told them, "because nobody in California knows what it is."

Children were another important subject to Hank and Frances. His stepdaughter, called "Pan" to distinguish her name from her mother's, worshiped him, and he returned her affection. A home needed children to be complete, in his Middle American view.

Their first child, born in New York on December 21, 1937, but taken back to Hollywood when she was a few weeks old, was christened Jane Seymour Fonda, because Frances had just been reading about Lady Jane Seymour, the distant relative, mother of Edward VI of England, who lasted one year as the third wife of Henry VIII. Their new daughter was called Lady Jane for years by those in the family. When she first went to school, the tapes on her clothing read "Lady Fonda," which probably had rather more social-aspiring significance than a mere mother's joke. The child herself developed an early dislike of the label, which was just as inevitable, perhaps, as her jealousy of Pan.

Two years and two months after the arrival of Jane, Frances bore a son, also in New York, Peter Henry Fonda flew home with his father and a nurse when he was fourteen weeks old, leaving his mother to visit friends and relatives. Like Jane, he had three godfathers, the same three —Jimmy Stewart, Johnny Swope, and Joshua Logan. When Hank made a friendship, it stuck.

In their looks, both children were unmistakably Fonda babies. Though a delicate handsomeness inherited from Frances shows up in Peter's face now, more appealing to audiences of his generation than his father's ruggedness, he was Henry Fonda in miniature when he was born.

Logan remembers vividly his first sight of him. Frances, who had driven him to the house, had some errand to do, so she dropped Logan off at the front door. "Don't wait for me," she said. "Just go upstairs and see the baby." The maid let him in and he climbed to the third-floor nursery. He stood in the doorway for a moment, fascinated by the sight of the playpen with the child in it.

"Peter was looking out, and I started laughing. It was as though Henry Fonda were inside this tiny child, looking out and saying, 'Save me!' The eyes were identical, but there was this *baby* around them."

The childhood home that both Jane and Peter remember is the farm that once stood on Tigertail Road. Neighbors were far removed. The two children grew up in the closed company of each other, along with three dogs, a cat, rabbits, and chickens. In the hills beyond the fields lived bobcats, coyotes, and rattlesnakes. This was in a different age, before smog blotted out the sunlight, before development houses, replete with redwood siding and giant picture windows, crept up the canyons and over the landscape.

The children ran around in levis most of the time, like their father, who felt more comfortable in work clothes than in anything else in his wardrobe. Jane has no memory of owning a dress until she was eight years old, but family pictures prove she was mistaken in this.

Being a dirt farmer was another mask for Hank, another specialized form of escape. This was no make-believe gentleman's property where hired hands sweat out the work and the owner watches them contentedly. Fonda often plowed his own fields with his own tractor, relishing the outdoors, going in out of the hot sun and the scent of upturned soil only when the pealing of the big bell on the house roof announced that it was time to eat.

He believed firmly in organic farming thirty years before chemical-free food blossomed into a national fad. A compost heap supplied the only fertilizer he chose for feeding his crops. Under his forty or so fruit trees, his allies the earthworms kept the ground sweet and the yield healthy. Faith in the virtues of an organic diet was something he passed on to Jane. When she was arrested in Cleveland in 1970 for alleged pill-smuggling, the police seized three vials labeled "B," "L," and "D" from her handbag and proclaimed that here was the evidence that would be used against her. Each of the vials, as a matter of fact, contained the particular vitamin pills she was taking as part of that diet, at breakfast, lunch, and dinner.

The children played around the swimming pool, which was not the conventional tiled model surrounded by striped umbrellas and chaises for sunning, but a body of water disguised by Hank to look like a farmhouse pond. They borrowed his two mules to ride bareback out into the hills and explore among the bobcats, coyotes and rattlesnakes that lived there. They dreamed of contests in which they'd lasso buffalo.

Their father kept his two lives, as an actor and a farmer, completely separate. On Tigertail Road he was no more able, or willing, to talk about himself and what interested him than anywhere else, except in the tight circle of close friends. His motivations were his secret. Jane wondered why he sometimes grew a beard and then shaved it off. She asked her mother why and learned for the first time that he was a motion-picture star.

The distinction between pretending and actuality blurred in her mind. Up in the hills away from the house, she acted out with Peter the adventuring life she thought her father lived in the few movies of his that they had been allowed to see. They were cowboys, frontiersmen, Indian fighters, with Jane keeping a watchful eye on her brother,

Fonda made his film debut in 1935, appearing with Janet Gaynor in *The Farmer Takes A Wife.—UPI*

Hank Fonda wanted the role of Tom Joad in Steinbeck's *Grapes of Wrath* so much that he signed a seven-year contract with Fox to get it. *—UPI*

Fonda and his second wife, Frances Seymour Brokaw, in 1941. Frances was the mother of Jane and Peter.—*Acme–UPI*

(below) Henry Fonda and his first wife, actress Margaret Sullavan, in 1935. The marriage was shortlived. —*Acme–UPI*

(above) Fonda married Susan Blanchard shortly after his second wife committed suicide. They are shown here at the west coast opening of *Mister Roberts.*—*Globe*

(right) Fonda met Countess Afdera Franchetti in Rome, while shooting King Vidor's production of *War and Peace*. They were married in March, 1957.—*UPI*

Fonda and Shirlee Adams were married December 2, 1965.—*UPI*

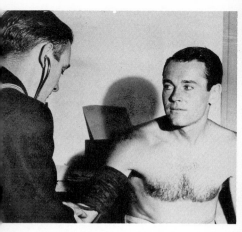

(above) In 1942, Fonda interrupted his career to enlist in the navy as an apprentice seaman. Always a superstar, he received the bronze star and a presidential citation for his service.—*UPI*

(right) In 1958, Fonda played opposite Anne Bancroft in *Two For The Seesaw*. After struggling with the role, Fonda, on opening night, gave what Brooks Atkinson called "his most limpid and moving performance."—*UPI*

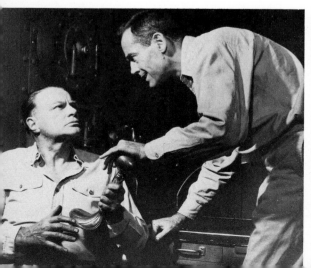

Fonda returned to the stage in 1950, after an eleven-year absence, to star in the landmark hit *Mister Roberts*. He is shown here with William Harrington.—*Acme–UPI*

(on facing page) Margaret Leighton, Henry Fonda, and Ann Sothern in the 1964 movie *The Best Man*, which was an uncanny forecast of the 1972 presidential election. —*UPI*

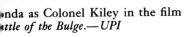
...nda as Colonel Kiley in the film *...ttle of the Bulge.—UPI*

Young Henry Fonda romps with daughter Jane.— *John Springer Film and Theater Collection of the Bettman Archives–UPI*

The Fondas arrive in Rome, 1955. It was during this trip that he met Countess Afdera Franchetti.—*UPI*

(above) Jane and Vanessa Vadim. Jane said that having Vanessa was one of the two most "violently important" things in her life, the other being her decision to become an actress.—*Pat York–Globe*

(right) Jane as *Barbarella*. Husband Roger Vadim directed her in the movie, which was publicized as a sort of sexual *Alice in Wonderland*.—*Pat McCallum–Globe*

1964—Peter shortly after a tennis accident and before the personality change that culminated in movies like *Easy Rider.* —*Max Miller–Globe*

Henry Fonda with one of his own paintings (1966)—*UPI*

The three acting Fondas meet in New York. Jane was making *Sunday in New York*, Henry was filming *Fail-Safe*, and Peter was doing *Lilith*.—*Don Ornitz–Globe*

because she felt that was her duty. She was always very possessive and protective of Peter.

They were terrified by Hank's apparent ordeal in *Drums Along the Mohawk*. This was his second movie under John Ford's tightly reined direction, following *Young Mr. Lincoln*. They watched *Drums* some years after it was released in 1939. For two days, on the screen, Fonda ran for his life from marauding Indians as they massacred settlers along the Mohawk Valley in the Revolutionary War. The two children couldn't stand the thought of seeing their father die; happily for their sake, he really didn't.

"It was the longest movie of my life," said Jane.

Not all of the childhood memories were accurate. Her imagination would take a single incident and, like any child's, expand it into something permanent and universal. In her twenties, one such example lingered in her mind.

"The way I was affected by the movies was that my father brought it home with him—not the business talk, not the movie-star bit, not the glamour, none of that, because he separated it very well. But he did look the way he looked in the movies. And he brought home the people that he was in pictures with. John Wayne, John Ford, Ward Bond, Jimmy Stewart—they were company at the house.

"They would play a game called pitch. And they would sit around this big table, with a chandelier above it that had great big covered-wagon wheels with lights hanging on them. And they wore cowboy hats with holsters, and they would take the guns out and put them on the table, and they'd all sit around and play cards, and it was right out of any of the movies. We didn't need to see the movies."

Fonda, with adult accuracy, remembers that all of this actually happened once. "It was a benefit party and someone took photographs and I still have a picture. It was a single event, not a way of living. When a legend grows up around a man there is often no means of pruning it, even within his family."

Jane modeled herself on Hank. She spent half of her

young life wanting to be a boy because she wanted to be like her father. "I didn't start wanting to be a girl until I was in my early teens. I was embarrassed. I was shy of boys."

At one point, after the family's days in California came to an end, she hacked off the long, light-brown hair that hung to her shoulders. "And someone came up and said, 'Are you a boy or a girl?' I was so pleased."

The sister and brother made up a closed company of two, each idolizing the father who, in return, idolized them. Jimmy Stewart, at one dinner party, looked around the table, where Jane and Peter usually sat with the guests, and said sentimentally, "That's just what I want in life, a family like that." However, he had a few more years of bachelorhood left in him.

His son and daughter regarded Hank as being close to perfect, not only because he was their father, but because that was the way he was presented in any of the movies they were allowed to see. Their half-sister, Pan, was a distant, almost grown-up being, aloof from their games and fancies, an heiress in her own right, under the terms of George Brokaw's will.

Jane could not feel close to her. Sometimes she would watch her through a window "when she gave what I thought were wild parties." Pan seemed to be the favorite of their mother. Of Frances, Jane recalls her "great beauty" and her "great head for finance." Though she was never close to her, she felt that she knew how loving and generous she was. "If you lose your mother before you're old enough to get close to her, you almost never understand her as an individual in her own right, and that's what happened to me."

A tangible token of Frances's generosity was the little house she bought in Brentwood for her mother, Sophie Seymour, a calm, loving woman, strong but not aggressively so, who became increasingly important to the family when a desperate need arose. She knew her daughter inside and out. In her eighties, she still lived in the house, a widow.

Jane and Peter had few companions. Among the few, and probably the closest, were the Haywards' children, whose ages fitted well with theirs. Margaret Sullavan and Leland Hayward had three now. After Brooke, Bridget was born in 1939 and William Leland in 1941. The two families encouraged the friendship. The faithful trio of Stewart, Logan, and Swope had been assigned as godfathers to the Hayward children, too.

Some people, looking in from the outside, felt that there was a certain piquancy in the relationship between the five playmates who might have been brothers and sisters if Fonda had had less intractable pride and Sullavan's temper had been a shade or two cooler. The children could scarcely care less about events that had taken place before the beginning of time, so far as they were concerned. Brooke was the girl Jane would have wanted as a sister, if she had had the choice. Little Billy was okay as a baby brother. Bridget became a shining light in Peter's eyes—and the working out of her life contributed to almost wrecking his. But that was only one of the things that waited for all of them down the dark corridors.

Marriage with Hayward appeared to agree with the first Mrs. Fonda. She was known to him as Maggie. On the surface, at least, her nature, like her name, had changed. She was calmer, gentler, even domesticated, but her magnetism hadn't diminished an iota. In the theater, she still ran ahead of Hank. *Stage Door* for her had outmatched *The Farmer Takes a Wife*, though, sharing his brand of honesty, she had refused to be starred in it.

"I haven't earned that, yet," she said.

Between the births of her children she continued making pictures, not at the same furious pace as Fonda, but adding one on top of another to her credit as a unique, highly respected talent in *The Shopworn Angel*, *Three Comrades*, *Shop Around the Corner*, *The Mortal Storm*, *Back Street*, *Cry Havoc*.

Hollywood's respect for her found no response in her feelings about the movie business. Her ambition was still to star on Broadway and make a million dollars.

Fonda's love for the theater languished unrequited. During a dozen years after he had arrived in California, he had one disappointing respite from shooting pictures during the summer when Frances was pregnant with Jane. *Blow Ye Winds*, scorned by the critics, was a comedy whose run of five weeks on Broadway scarcely justified his time and trouble. His performance as a college-boy boatman impressed one reviewer as an intriguing mixture of casualness and assurance, an effect that Fonda struggled mightily to achieve.

His life as a loner in Hollywood depended largely on his being a freelance actor. He had no binding, annual contract with a major studio such as Clark Gable had with M-G-M, Tyrone Power had with Twentieth Century-Fox, Errol Flynn had with Warner Brothers, or Fred Astaire had at RKO. That worked as much against him as for him. The film-producing assembly lines favored their contract employees in matters of pay and billing over actors signed up picture by picture. Fonda was, accordingly, a star but not yet a superstar. The arrangement exactly suited his hunger for independence. Then, in order to satisfy his eternal urge to make something perfect, he had to sell his freedom.

One movie he was itching to play in was *The Grapes of Wrath*. To get the part of Tom Joad he had to sign a seven-year contract with Fox. He regretted it, but he signed. He had no alternative.

Darryl F. Zanuck, the rambunctious studio boss at Twentieth Century-Fox, was another Nebraskan. He came from Wahoo, population 3,610, a farming town 30 miles west of Omaha. He is a stocky dynamo of a man—Fonda tops him by 8 inches—with a will even steelier than

Hank's. He reigned supreme over the 100-odd acres that made up Fox Movietone City, reading, casting, cutting and putting together pictures whose only real purpose, as he saw it, was to guarantee profits.

He had paid $100,000 for the screen rights to John Steinbeck's classic story of the 1930s migration of the "Okies" from the dust bowl of the Midwest into economic slavery in California. He pictured it not so much as harsh social commentary as a telling human story of a family facing challenge.

His biographer, Mel Gussow, tells of Zanuck's first meeting with Steinbeck, who was highly suspicious of the little cigar-smoking tornado sitting in his office behind an imitation George Washington desk that had once been a prop in one of his movies. He was talking about changing the ending of the book for the movie when his secretary buzzed him.

"Mr. Zanuck, there's been an accident on one of our sets! Shirley Temple has lost her tooth, and . . . "

"Her front tooth?" said Zanuck. Yes, it was. "For God sakes, tell 'em to do something," he snapped.

"They feel it's such an important event, you should come to the set."

Steinbeck had listened in silence. "Don't bother about me," he said coolly. "*The Grapes of Wrath* is unimportant compared to Shirley Temple's tooth."

Fonda wouldn't have agreed with him. The proposed movie had everything in it to appeal to him: a fine acting role in Tom Joad, who in the final reel leaves his family to become a political activist and organizer fighting oppression; a director he knew and respected in peppery John Ford; dialogue to fit his tongue; an urgent social problem that stirred his heart.

Ford wanted him. Steinbeck felt he was perfect for the part. Zanuck had conflicting ideas. This had to be a colossal picture, a cannon fired in his studio's running battle with its bigger competitors, notably Metro-Goldwyn-Mayer. That called for a superstar to sell to the public.

"What we need on the payroll," he believed, "is a combination of P. T. Barnum and Buffalo Bill Cody."

His first choice, as always, was Tyrone Power, the soft-faced, violet-eyed Irishman who was Zanuck's favorite, principally because his gentle personality never clashed with his boss's. Power starred in everything from romances to musicals; but as an actor, Fonda had wiped the floor with him in *The Return of Jesse James*. If not Power, then Don Ameche, said Zanuck. Ameche habitually played the best friend, the rival, the brother, Jonathan to Power's David.

Steinbeck still thought Fonda was the man. Ultimately, Zanuck approved the choice, but he saw the opportunity to bargain. Hank wasn't tied to any studio, and Zanuck had plans for him in all kinds of pictures, much as he had for his faithful standbys, Power and Ameche. The price Hank paid to play Tom Joad was to go into bondage on a long-term contract. That decision caused him years of grief.

The end product was an acknowledged masterpiece, as a film and as a performance. The man and the role "fuse into the performance of art," in the words of *Time* magazine thirty years later. Fonda *was* resolute, quick-tempered, saturnine Tom Joad. Embittered Tom Joad *was* Fonda, on his way to being a superstar, a reluctant, chained oarsman in the Fox galley. But the movie added another stalwart to his tight circle of friends. Steinbeck and Fonda had much in common, including a kind of inspiration for each other.

"It is strange but perhaps explainable that I find myself very often with a picture of you in front of my mind, when I am working on a book," Steinbeck wrote nearly twenty years after the movie was released. "I think I know the reason for this. Recently I ran a 16mm print of *The Grapes of Wrath* that Kazan had stolen from Twentieth Century-Fox. And I think that's the reason.

"It's a wonderful picture, just as good as it ever was. It

doesn't look dated, and very few people have ever made a better one—and I think that's where you put your mark on me."

Steinbeck possessed a penetrating insight that enabled him to peer into Hank's nature and describe what he had seen during those years before his death in 1968. He had written a matter of weeks earlier: "I suppose one human never really knows much about another. My impressions of Hank are of a man reaching but unreachable, gentle but capable of sudden wild and dangerous violence, sharply critical of others but equally self-critical, caged and fighting the bars but timid of the light, viciously opposed to external restraint, imposing an iron slavery on himself. His face is a picture of opposites in conflict."

A classmate of Jane at the Brentwood Town and Country School, reminiscing about the Fondas' home life on Tigertail Road, was more specific when she talked not long ago with a magazine reporter. "We were all afraid of Jane's father in those days. We always felt he was a time bomb ready to explode. But it was years later when we actually saw him lose his temper over some forgotten trivia. He was booming, purple-faced, with veins sticking out on his temples. It was the only time I was ever privileged to see what may have been a constant for Lady Jane."

It could hardly have been a "constant"; he wasn't around that much. Fox drew its blood by the pint and, immediately after Tom Joad, pushed him straight into the cardboard-cutout role of Alexander Moore, one of the many admirers of Lillian Russell, the principal houri of New York's gaslight era, who was portrayed by Alice Faye in a movie named for her. Don Ameche played the hero, while Hank waded through it like a man under water.

That piece of Technicolor treacle and two more Fox pictures added to *The Grapes of Wrath* made a total of four Fonda films released in 1940. His performance as Tom Joad made him the odds-on choice to win an Oscar. After the nominations were in, the handicappers privately listed Fonda as first favorite among the male contenders, followed in order by Charles Chaplin *(The Great Dictator)*, Raymond Massey *(Abe Lincoln in Illinois)*, Laurence Olivier *(Rebecca)*, with James Stewart *(The Philadelphia Story)* trailing badly.

And the winner, voted by the Academy of Motion Picture Arts and Sciences, certified by Price Waterhouse and Company, was James Stewart, who admitted that he personally had voted for Fonda. If Hank had felt certain of winning, or was crushed when he lost, he said nothing about it in public. Only the steadily growing band of his solid admirers protested, "He was robbed." He simply went on working, his bitterness for Fox increasing, suffering most of the time in roles so flimsy and remote from the core of his feeling that his professional reputation jerked along like a car whose clutch is slipping. He could not escape from the contract, which committed him to all kinds of movies that he despised. His anger still burns at the thought of them.

That was the temper of their father when Jane and Peter were very young. A career that kept him in well-paid bondage, frustration in his longing to be a serious actor, a marriage that seemed to intensify his loneliness—and the two children, looking back, took years even as adults to begin to comprehend why he seldom talked with them.

When Zanuck and the other Fox bosses couldn't find a picture for him, they lent him to other studios, a common practice in the flesh markets of the movies, permissible under contract terms that gave the lending studio the right to negotiate the terms of their loan. Fonda had no complaint, since his loan-out jobs often resulted in better pictures for him, like *Lady Eve* for Paramount and *The Male Animal* for Warner Brothers.

Then along came another script at Fox that he ached to do and another violent series of rows with Zanuck before he was allowed the role. *The Ox-Bow Incident* was based on Walter VanTilburg Clark's novel about mob rule in the Old West and the lynching of three innocent men. It dealt with blood-lust, misery, and sadism, with a grim regard for truth that totally shattered the myths of the standard horse opera of those times.

Fonda set his heart on making it. Here, once again, was the irresistible combination. He knew the kind of characters involved in the locale—Nevada, only twenty years before he was born. He admired the uncompromising story of conflict between justice and cruel power, with its unsugared ending. He liked the laconic detachment of his role as a stranger in town, watching the mob take over. He approved the idea of acting in a brilliant group of players, all of whom would receive equal handling by the director William Wellman before the cameras, with no special focus on himself.

Zanuck prided himself, justifiably, on being an expert in prejudging box-office reaction, even as he exclaimed, "God, how I hate audiences!" He anticipated that the lynching theme would turn *The Ox-Bow Incident* into poison on the balance sheet. He had already spelled out the consequences of the war that was devastating Europe—and movie-theater receipts: "Star power is valueless, no matter how big the personalities or even if they are Clark Gable and Joan Crawford combined, unless the subject matter in the story stands the test."

He had shut down work on several new properties. As a shrewd economy measure, he was grinding out remakes to older pictures. *Love Is News*, with Tyrone Power and Loretta Young, emerged six years later as *Sweet Rosie O'-Grady*, with Robert Young and Betty Grable. *The Bowery* of 1933 became *Coney Island* in 1943. *Folies Bergères*, starring Maurice Chevalier, was transformed into *That Night in Rio*, with the ever-popular Don Ameche, Carmen Miranda, and Alice Faye.

Fonda could not be deterred. The running battle lasted for days. It would have been exceptional for Hank to keep his temper that long. It would have been unusual for Zanuck not to toy with the thought of suspending him or interrupting with one of his classic lines, "God damn it to hell, don't threaten me! People don't threaten me. I threaten them."

In the end, he drove another bargain. All right, he would reluctantly agree to *The Ox-Bow Incident.* But only on condition that he'd get no argument from Hank about doing *The Magnificent Dope,* a favorite, recycled Zanuck theme, having to do with the hayseed who comes to town and makes fools of the city slickers. He'd used it in *Thanks for Everything,* with Jack Haley, in 1938. It owed something to Gary Cooper's 1936 success in *Mr. Deeds Goes to Town.* It had recently shown up in a hunk of hokum in which Jimmy Stewart, for M-G-M, had been "Mr. Smith" going to Washington. And Hank's co-star this time around would be none other than Don Ameche.

Zanuck turned out to be right about the audience reaction to *The Ox-Bow Incident;* it flopped like a stranded mackerel. In 1942, when the picture was shot, the Philippines surrendered; the massed fleets of the United States and Japan were fighting it out in the battles of the Coral Sea and Midway Island; Rommel's Afrika Corps drove the British back into Egypt; the Russian southern front was in a state of collapse. Moviegoers wanted to goggle at the charms of Rita Hayworth and enjoy vicarious victories over evil Japanese and jack-booted Nazis, not watch American pioneers string up three innocents in Nevada in 1885.

Fonda wasn't around to read the reviews, which were strongly in favor of the movie and his performance in it. Stewart had already enlisted in the United States Air Force after being rejected on his first application because, six-feet three-inches tall, he weighed only one hundred and thirty-nine pounds. Hank made one wartime quickie, *The Immor-*

tal Sergeant, about war in the African desert, for Zanuck, who had turned his company to war production on an assembly-line schedule. Then, one bright morning, Fonda enlisted in the Navy as an ordinary seaman. There wasn't much to hold him back, except his age. He was thirty-seven.

He was a sailor for more than three years, starting with the modest rank of quartermaster third class when he graduated nine months later from Naval Training School in San Diego, posted to a destroyer that was sailing for the Pacific. Later, the ship's executive officer recommended him for a commission. Quartermaster Fonda was flown to headquarters at 90 Church Street, New York, for discharge and immediately commissioned as a lieutenant, junior grade. He was scheduled for Washington, to make training films, but he requested sea duty. For the rest of the war, he was an assistant operations officer and air combat intelligence officer on the staff of Admiral John Koover in the Marianas, and was awarded a Bronze Star and a presidential citation for his service. Before he was finally out of uniform in October 1945, he had been promoted to the rank of senior lieutenant and served as master of ceremonies on a Navy radio show.

Jane and Peter went through a prolonged period when, in interviews, they habitually complained that their father shared too few of their childhood days. At that time, Fonda, with some justification, snapped back.

"It gets boring to hear them say they missed Daddy when they were young. So I should apologize because a world war came along and I had to go away or because I had to work while the kids were in a beautiful farmhouse out in Brentwood with their friends and horses? That's all .a crock."

Jane's need for him was more clearly spelled out in her mind because of her age. Peter's was so deep and hidden because he was too young to recognize it. Nevertheless, they yearned for his company. A lot happened while their father was gone. He was unsuccessfully sued for child support by a girl who claimed they had met during the filming of *The Immortal Sergeant* in El Centro, California. He had never met her.

"Of course, I believe him," said Frances. She was handling all his business affairs, as usual, since his enlistment. She added, with a touch of the mettle in her, "This girl will have to settle with *me.*"

While Hank was away at the war, the first of the seemingly unending series of violent deaths involving the family in one way or another occurred on the far perimeter of their lives. Frances's stepdaughter, Ann Clare Brokaw, a serious-minded, sensitive student due to graduate from Stanford University three months before her twentieth birthday, died when the open convertible in which she was riding was hit from behind by another car and she was thrown out against a tree. That was in 1943. The event was too distant in time and feeling from Frances's first marriage for it to have much impact on the family on Tigertail Road.

Margaret Sullavan had come within an ace of realizing her ambitions, though not exactly as simply as she once imagined. She had gone back to Broadway to play in John Van Druten's *The Voice of the Turtle* as its acknowledged star, now that she felt she deserved such billing. To make the million dollars she always sought as a target, she invested a modest three thousand dollars in the production.

No one was better pleased than Fonda at the result. In the opening night audience Howard Barnes of the New York *Herald Tribune* called her "the finest actress of our day in the theater." Van Druten detected some characteristics she shared with Hank in spite of the years that had passed since they acted, loved, and quarreled together. "She has a simplicity," he wrote, "an almost embarrassing directness and a friendliness that have nothing of the theater gush about her." Except for the friendliness, this held true for her first husband.

The play made more than three million dollars. After staying in it for one year she left the cast on the recommendation of her doctor. Back in Hollywood, she divorced Hayward, insisting that custody of the three children should be hers, while he promptly married Nancy Hawks, universally known as "Slim," ex-wife of Howard, who directed for Fox and played croquet with Zanuck. That marriage, incidentally, lasted until 1959, when "Slim" divorced Leland, keeping custody of the daughter she had borne him. Hollywood, in the days of its prime, was a tight little society.

Its children, almost without exception, paid a price for their parents' peccadilloes: they were chronically insecure. They lived in a kind of gold-plated commune, the product of marriages that weren't expected to last, with husbands and wives changing partners as casually as in a square dance. Who was a half-brother or a stepsister? What happened to last year's father? Guess who Mother's going to marry next? In the exclusive day schools and the expensive boarding establishments, the children gathered to gossip and speculate.

The Fonda children weren't like that, because Hank wasn't "social," though they accepted what they saw around them as normal behavior on the part of everyone. "If you have glamorous parents," Jane commented later, "you just have to live a special way."

She impressed her teachers at the Brentwood school as a sweet-natured little girl, inclined to be shy, with her long light-brown hair usually tied with a ribbon. She was sturdier than her brother, who was a skinny kid with exactly the same hesitant smile. Her classmates came from a similar stratum of the community—a son of Laurence Olivier, a daughter of Gary Cooper, a daughter of Claude Rains.

The most memorable subject on the curriculum was how to treat rattlesnake bites.

Her social life was contained within limits similar to her father's. She would be taken to birthday parties given for other stars' children, crushed to discover how different their lives were. They would be decked out in frilly dresses, miniature models of deportment. She usually ended in tears, and the nurse would whisk her home.

She was much more comfortable at home with Pete, the tame rabbits, the chickens whose eggs it was her job to collect, and particularly the horses kept at a riding stable not far from the farmhouse. A wide-brimmed Stetson and spurred boots were added to the blue jeans to make a riding habit; she rode from the age of five, but never in the jodhpurs, hacking jacket, and caps that were fashionable among the sons and daughters of the Hollywood rich.

The only hero was her father. What he did, she had to do. In the movies she saw, the bad guys usually felt his fists, so she had to beat up people, too. She picked fights with boys at the local riding stables, a hellion who kicked and bit them.

She didn't escape unscathed in the cause of emulating Hank. She broke an arm in one fight, suffered another break when she fell from a horse, fractured a wrist roller-skating in the hall.

She was nine when she suffered her first serious case of puppy love. At the start, it was fine, because the boy didn't notice her, so she could just stand around, adoring him. When the day came for him to ask her to a dance, she responded like an Amazon, hitting him as hard as she knew how. It seemed that she never would catch on to the idea of how civilized people behaved toward each other.

Out of the Navy, Hank felt that he was at loose ends. His contract at Twentieth Century-Fox still had to be served out. He wasn't eager to go back into moviemaking. He wanted to walk a theater stage again, but he couldn't get enthused about any play scripts that were submitted to him. He had no alternative but to return to "doing those bits and pieces for a movie."

Colonel Zanuck was back behind his imitation George Washington desk after wartime service in the Signal Corps that won him the Legion of Merit for "exceptional bravery under fire." John Ford had returned, too; as a commander in the Navy, he had been assigned part of the time to Zanuck, shooting film in North Africa.

Hank grew a beard, saddled up, and went to do a stint as Wyatt Earp under John Ford's direction in *My Darling Clementine*. The future looked as if it were going to be pretty much the same at home and at work as when he left it to join the Navy, but appearances could not have been more deceiving. His second marriage could be rated a casualty of war.

VI

FOR THOSE who sail Long Island Sound, the spindly white spire of the Second Congregational Church at the top of Put's Hill marks the town of Greenwich, standing just barely on the Connecticut side of the New York State border. To every appearance, it is a green, smog-free haven from the turmoil of Manhattan, stretching down from gentle hills to sandy beaches, a place of quiet back roads, lawns, and secluded estates, one of the precious handful of satellite suburbs favored by rich commuters that ring the moneyed megalopolises of America.

Jane remembers the years she spent there only in dark colors. Greenwich, in retrospect, was "a racist community" in her words. She went to school there, and once, coming back from a visit with some friends, she remarked airily to Hank that "The Jews are moving in and spoiling it." He realized that she must have heard this from prejudiced neighbors. The line of Oscar Hammerstein's ran through his mind: *"You've got to be taught to hate and fear. . . . "*

"We don't talk like that in our family," he told her gently. They hadn't lived in the town very long, but he knew they would have to put their house up for sale and get out.

For all its apparent calm and Republican self-possession, the town has a raffish past. The Byram River, which marks the western border, was named "buy rum" in pre-Revolutionary days for the fact that farmers came there to peddle illegal liquor to the tame native Indians, who were later massacred at the foot of Put's Hill. William Tweed, the porcine boss of Tammany Hall, built a waterfront clubhouse for himself and his boozy cronies. Behind the fieldstone walls of at least one piece of wooded, sprawling estate, bootleggers ran a wholesale Prohibition business. Marriages could be arranged with only an hour's notice given to a long line of judges who lingered around the town hall. Coupling and uncoupling among the back-country crowd led to a fast turnover of title to the handsome houses, where the hired help gossiped freely among themselves about what went on in the upstairs bedrooms. There was at least a modicum of truth in an old accusation that Greenwich cared about dogs, trees, and children—in that order.

Peter Fonda's memories are painted in the same somber tones as Jane's. "Greenwich is one of the most prejudiced towns in the world," he told an interviewer from *Playboy* magazine. "I remember one time we were going to meet David O. Selznick, who was coming to pick us up and go sailing on the biggest yacht that ever hit Greenwich. There was David O., with his full crew and everything, approaching Greenwich Harbor to pick us up, and Margaret Sullavan and Jennifer Jones, among others. This fucking boat was as big as the Empire State building and there was plenty of room for it in Greenwich Harbor, but they wouldn't let him dock because he was Jewish. That's a minor example of the many insipid and deceitful things that happened to us in Greenwich."

The Fondas moved to Connecticut because Hank was enjoying himself in the theater more than ever in his memory. The painfully created pieces of his chosen life had suddenly fallen into a pattern called *Mister Roberts.* Nothing could top his joy over this. The taste it left later was bittersweet, like the red berries of that vine, which are poison to eat. He could have echoed the lines from *A Tale of Two Cities*—Dickens was possibly his favorite author among all the others whose books filled the big library in the Brentwood farmhouse: "It was the best of times, it was the worst of times, it was the age of wisdom, it was the age of foolishness . . . it was the season of light, it was the season of darkness, it was the spring of hope, it was the winter of despair." The family never recovered from the consequences of that period.

He had at last ground his way through the Fox contract. As an actor, he was free again. His farewell picture was as lusterless as most of those he did for Zanuck. To complement Joan Crawford's usual coloratura performance in *Daisy Kenyon,* he portrayed her bland young husband as a passive backdrop. The role was all the more galling because it followed on the heels of *The Fugitive,* made on loan-out. In that film, he played an agonized whiskey priest on the run in Mexico, the protagonist in Graham Greene's *The Power and the Glory,* on which the somewhat laundered film version was based. John Ford, who directed it, said he could think of no actor he had ever known who could equal Fonda's performance.

From *Daisy Kenyon,* Hank went into a vignette written by John O'Hara, with Jimmy Stewart as his colleague in a completely dispensable bit of frizz entitled *On Our Merry Way.* Though the years they had each spent in the business added up to nearly twenty-five, it was the first time the alumni of Casa Gangrene had managed to work together.

Hank was looking forward to playing in a much more important creation of O'Hara's, the 1934 best-seller *Appointment in Samarra.* Its anti-hero, Julian English, was a man after Hank's heart—"from the wrong side of the tracks," in O'Hara's words, "and never wore a buttoned-down collar in his tragic life." But the book's climax demanded Julian's suicide under cumulative pressure. Like horizontal kissing, belly buttons, and such uttered blasphemies as "Hell!," suicide was anathema to the censors of the Hays Office, to whom the producers tamely submitted every screenplay for blue-penciling in advance of shooting. There seemed to be simply no way to get *Appointment in Samarra* onto the screen.

Hank turned for advice to Josh Logan, whose career as a director in the theater and in movies was in high gear. The kinship between them was ostensibly firm now. All their quarrels had long since been patched up, possibly because they met only as friends, not as workmates.

With Thomas Heggen, the author of the best-selling book, Logan had just finished writing the play of *Mister Roberts*, having to do with the wartime tribulations of Lieutenant JG Douglas Roberts, the frustrated cargo officer aboard the U.S. Navy Supply Ship *Reluctant*, wallowing around the Pacific. Though neither of them had mentioned it to the other in the course of getting the script down on paper, both Heggen and Logan had Fonda in mind as they shaped the part.

He met them in a hotel room, where they read the play aloud to him. That was the only persuasion he needed. O'Hara and Hollywood meant nothing compared to this. He yearned to be Roberts more than he had fought to be Tom Joad.

"I'm going to do it," he said immediately.

"But Hank," said Logan, "we only read it to you because we knew you couldn't."

"I'm going to do it," he repeated. "I'll call my agent to get me out of the other picture." His agent now was Lew Wasserman, who succeeded in carrying out Hank's instruction. It meant a considerable salary cut. And it meant that Fonda once again would be in a play under the direction of Logan, as he hadn't been since the battles they fought on Cape Cod and in Baltimore.

"I'd directed so many hits in the meantime that I didn't have any fear of anybody," Logan recalls. "But I should have."

Hank flew to New York to start rehearsing. After a day or so of that, Logan broke in at one point to say to Hank, "I think maybe here you might get up and walk around the table." Lieutenant Roberts, on the bare stage, took not the slightest notice of him.

"Hank, did you hear what I said? Don't you think it would be a good idea to walk around the table?"

Fonda turned his ice-cold eyes on Logan. "Josh," he drawled, "this isn't the Princeton Triangle Club. This is Broadway."

In both of them the old, not entirely fond antagonisms were rising fast. "What do you mean?" asked Logan softly.

"That's the most amateurish piece of direction I've ever heard in my entire life."

Logan was no martinet. His method, fundamentally similar to Stanislavsky's in Moscow, was to evoke from an actor a performance based on deep-down identification with the character portrayed.

"Well," he said, "I don't know that it's amateurish. It's not definite. It's just *maybe*. If it's a good idea—"

Hank broke in. "Do you *understand* the character of Mister Roberts?"

"Understand it, you son of a bitch? I *wrote* it."

The tension rose. "Well, you certainly don't behave as though you understand it."

"Do *you* understand the character of Mister Roberts?"

"Of course I do."

"I think you need a little instruction. Come and have dinner with me tonight, and let me explain something to you."

"I certainly will."

They sat down to a room-service dinner in Logan's rooms at the Lombardy Hotel on Lexington Avenue. Logan, with the experience of the months he'd spent working on the play, talked until four o'clock the next morning, uninterrupted because he gave Hank no chance to break in, explaining Roberts's every motivation, thought, and stage movement.

He said on a later occasion, "I think that for the first time in my whole life Fonda respected me. He said, 'Understand; thanks very much.' He shook my hand, left, and never gave me another moment's trouble."

Hank worked as he always does, closing in inch by inch on his personal discovery of the soul of the character, a process that he calls "babying up." Whatever he does on stage must be true in terms of his evocation of the man he is portraying. "Babying up" renders him querulous, belligerent, impossible to exist with until he has made the mask fit him like skin. He says, "I'm suspicious of anything that happens too fast or too soon." His family missed nothing in the nature of a whirl in Fun City by staying in California.

But Fonda, in whom pleasure and pain are inextricably mixed as the result of his experience with them, was having the time of his life just then. Once he had fitted himself into the Roberts role or, perhaps more accurately, had fitted the Roberts role into himself, he even agreed to publicity interviews in advance of the company's Broadway opening at the Alvin Theater. Four days before the event, a *New York Times* feature writer, who somehow forgot to mention the names of Jane and Peter, reported glowingly in that newspaper's Sunday entertainment section, "He says that his London assignment (in *Wings of the Morning*) was the luckiest thing that ever happened to him. For while he was there, he met a young American girl, whom he married. . . ."

In fact, Frances by this time had already left home on one occasion, impelled by doubt about the compatibility of their marriage and about her health; she had also undergone surgery for suspected cancer. It was accepted at the time she went into the hospital that she had no more than five years to live. Neither Jane nor Peter nor anyone but the closest friends and relatives was told about that.

After eleven years away from the theater, Fonda had no fear or feelings about having grown rusty. So far as he was concerned, he hadn't really been absent at all, only biding his time until the dead-right play came along, and here it was.

"*Mister Roberts* was a love story backstage. We were all just crazy about the play. If anybody let down, he had thirty other guys on him. It really was like being in love. You had this good feeling in the guts practically all the time. I love to act, and in this play I always knew everything I was going to do, but could make it look like not acting at all."

The only physical problem he ran into before the Philadelphia tryout at the Walnut Street Theater was in projecting his voice again across the orchestra and into the balcony. Speaking movie lines for the benefit of microphones had softened his speech almost to inaudibility. Otherwise, *The Times* noted, "Hollywood has left no detectable mark upon him." His friends, however, could spot one difference. His old diffidence had disappeared. The stage presence, the posture of command, the backstage confidence of *knowing*—these had replaced it. The superstar aspect of Fonda was coming into clear view.

He was a rich man who had already made all the money he needed, the newspapers said. He owned a movie theater in Westwood, another Los Angeles suburb. He was a big stockholder in Southwestern Airlines, which Leland Hayward had been instrumental in starting at Thunderbird Field, near Phoenix, Arizona, with planes to train U.S. airmen.

With a contract signed to stay with the play at least through the following year, Fonda opened in Philadelphia on the day after Christmas. He had a temperature of one hundred and three degrees and was shot full of of penicillin to tackle a virus infection. Between matinees and evening performances, he took to a hospital bed. In his dressing room he underwent a certain amount of extra therapy under a sunlamp—the entire cast depended on ultraviolet rays in lieu of makeup for their tanned hides in the cause of realism.

From the moment the first-night curtain fell there wasn't a shred of doubt that *Mister Roberts* was going to be a landmark wherever it played. Advance bookings swamped the Alvin box-office. The Broadway debut only justified all the excitement, with half the cheering audience of first-night notables standing on the seats to yell for the players to take another dozen curtain calls.

As public relations man John Springer remembers it, Fonda was induced to say a few, rare words: "This is all Tom and Josh wrote for us. If you want us, we can start all over again." The late John Chapman, gruff old critic of *The New York News*, wrote that night, "I hung around awhile, hoping they would." There is a footnote to the success story. The bitch-goddess Success exacted a high price from Tom Heggen. Increasingly timid and afraid that he would never be able to write another *Mister Roberts*, he took to dosing himself with sleeping pills. Under the influence of too many of them, he was found drowned in a bathtub.

Around the corner of West Fifty-second Street, Broadway moviehouse marquees flashed Hank's name as a star in the other way of life that he had turned his back on, spelling out his appearances in *On Our Merry Way* and in *Fort Apache*, the last picture he made in Hollywood for the next seven years.

In his exuberance he talked in public of his California days in the past tense, as though this pilgrim's progress had brought him to his goal at last. "Just think of those poor kids who have never seen a snowstorm. They have never enjoyed the bracing effect of winter winds. Of course they had a good time in California. We all did. We have a nice home, in which I have a darkroom and a laboratory, and I have made a complete movie history of these kids when each of them was a few hours old."

His family's move East waited for half a year, until the Brentwood school was out that summer. A furnished house had been found for them to rent meantime in Greenwich, which would be an easy, forty-five-minute ride aboard a New Haven express from Grand Central after his performance each night. The choice of location was not accidental. Frances already had a married sister and brother-in-law living in the town, which had some other, indirect links with her life.

George Brokaw had married Clare Booth in the town's elegantly Gothic Christ Church, and the reception had been held afterward in the rambling Pickwick Arms Hotel. Clare first lived in Greenwich as a girl in a pretty white frame house near the secluded public beach ("Residents Only," said the sign) after her widowed mother married Dr. Albert Elmer Austin, chief of staff of the local hospital; then in splendor in a pillared mansion set in a sixty-acre estate when Clare married Henry Luce. Greenwich and Frances seemed to be well matched in matters of taste and style.

Living in Manhattan didn't hold much appeal for Hank. The contrast between sooty sidewalks and the sunny fields of the farm was too sharp for mental comfort. Besides, New York was no place to bring up children. He looked forward to living in Greenwich, too.

Before his family arrived, he stayed with the Logans in their discreetly sumptuous apartment on the top of River House on East Fifty-fourth Street with its views looking over the East River. A good means of filling in the waiting time was to paint. Fonda does not believe in letting any skill go to waste or die of neglect. He could paint ceilings, walls, or scenery. His charcoal portraits of his University Players Guild companions, done during the lean months before they went to Baltimore, were professional enough to be hung in the lobby of the Maryland Theater.

Now he set to work again, first experimentally with a box of pastels that someone had given him, then as his skill increased, on to watercolors and oils. There was an important difference in subject matter this time around. He painted still lifes, not portraits. As in everything else he tackled, he was self-driven and self-taught, taking lessons from nobody while he evolved a personal style of superb competence.

The painters he most admired were Andrew Wyeth, Thomas Hart Benton, and the classical Dutch masters like Vermeer. Fonda painted scenes of utter tranquility with the fine brushwork that artists call a satin finish. He worked with his customary dedication and concealed passion, in his dressing room at the theater, in a room set aside for the purpose at the Logans'. His first canvases he gave away to friends—his host and hostess, the John Swopes, Jimmy Stewart, John Springer. Later, his paintings began to fetch prices in the thousands of dollars, and he took on commissions to paint for Hallmark cards and advertisements.

One of his early works, a laquered Mexican fruit bowl reflecting the stripes of a crumpled white tablecloth on which it stands, was finished overnight. Painting from life with real fruit in front of him, Fonda had been running into difficulty hitting the right tones for a banana in the bowl, which seemed to change color every time he turned his back. He couldn't understand why, until Logan's cook explained, "Bananas ripen fast, Mr. Fonda, unless you keep them in the icebox."

He sat up most of the night to finish painting a speckled banana at its peak of perfection. Then Logan asked him, for the sake of effect, to add a conch shell to the design. Hank obligingly added the shell, together with a silent comment of his own, a small red and yellow crab apple.

But portraits were something he could never finish. He could paint the backgrounds, the props, and the figures, with the folds and creases of clothing expertly detailed, but the faces were left blank, totally anonymous, lacking all identity. Without a mask, there was nothing.

"I enjoyed having been born with a platinum spoon up my ass," Peter has said, "but I remember being very down on my father for not speaking to me. He was a busy man, and I was a hypersensitive kid who needed somebody to talk to; so I reacted quite bitterly to him."

In Greenwich, as in Brentwood, a platinum-spoon unbringing meant going to a private school. There was only one such place for him, if he was to live at home. Brunswick School is both a landmark and a tradition in Greenwich, a neat, red-brick building that has a reputation for providing almost a parent's care for its students, some of whom get precious little of it from the natural source. Its motto is, "Courage, Honor, Truth." The uniform consisted of brown wool jerseys over long corduroys in warmer weather, suits and ties in winter months.

Judging by the odd jackets, slacks, and Western boots Peter habitually wore after he was entered to join the hundred or so boys of the Lower School, he hadn't a suit to his name. The whole idea of such formality seemed to bewilder him. But this was the East, unknown territory to him, and he regarded himself as a Westerner, visiting only temporarily from California, where people and customs were different.

The frail, eager-to-please, soft-spoken newcomer was amazed to find that Easterners apparently worked schoolboys harder than was done in the West. He was shy but outgoing, eager to make friends as fast as possible, anxious to be accepted and liked.

"In a way, there was a sadness about him," one of his woman teachers remembers. "He was more at ease with adults than with his classmates. He was *different* from them, and we ascribed this to his having come from a different background."

As usual in a dormitory suburb where mothers take over most of the absentee fathers' roles, Frances was the key parent, the one who conscientiously and frequently dropped in on his classes to see how her son was progressing. Probably from her side of the family he had inherited left-handedness; she liked to amuse the class by deftly chalking mirror writing on the blackboard.

The headmaster of those days, Alfred Everett, enjoyed talking with her. "She was strikingly beautiful, sincere, and genuine, unlike some other parents. She wanted to join in our school life." She gave no sign of illness of any kind.

Hank made a similar effort, but more painfully. Except for the headmaster, he found himself the only man in a roomful of women at the first parent-staff meeting that fall. He sat at the back near the door until all the turning, coiffured heads and fluttering glances grew too much to be endured. Then he left to watch two boys' teams at football practice in the field outside before he went home.

He returned, none too eagerly, but dutifully, for Fathers' Visiting Day, an annual event designed by the school to establish contact with the rarely seen male parents so they could be given an idea of how their sons spent most of their days. He left Peter's fourth grade teacher convinced that where education was concerned, he was a die-hard, admiring older, stricter methods of teaching over the more relaxed approach of Brunswick.

"Sitting there with a long face in the classroom, he seemed impatient if some of the less talented boys had a problem with a lesson," the teacher said afterward. "I'm sure that he's a stickler for discipline at home, expecting a lot of himself and just as much from everyone around him."

The reports that the Fondas received on Peter were reassuring. Schoolboys practice cruelty on each other, but Peter was never known to commit a single act of meanness. He was basically bright, even if his school work didn't reflect that. He had a real talent for drawing, usually cartoons. "He gives a lot of himself," was one typical comment.

He also liked to fantasize, dream, and act out roles. A favorite trick was to recite, with hammy pathos, a poem, "Aladdin," beginning, "When I was a beggarly boy and lived in a cellar damp . . ." He longed to be in the school play when this other annual rite came along. His mother discussed the subject at school.

"If he's going to be in it, be sure he isn't given a girl's part," she said. "To please his father, make sure he has a male role to play."

Pete finished up as an Indian, with feathers stuck in his headband and watercolor war paint on his thin ribs and gentle face. He was disappointed with the whole performance. "I didn't get the chance to *lurk*," he told his mother.

A sizable proportion of the boys, as in every private school in Greenwich, came from broken marriages. The impact of divorce was less powerful in Hollywood, but its consequences were as mystifying to the children. One of Peter's new friends lived with his divorced mother. When the fourth-graders heard about Noah's Ark, the small boy reported that his mother had a friend who had a yacht, and he'd like to bring in some color slides of the boat for an upcoming show-and-tell session because, "This is the man my mother's going to marry."

Peter was amazed at the news. "Isn't your mother married yet? *My* mother was married years before I was born."

One block away from Brunswick stood Greenwich Academy, headquartered in a stately old building that looked as if it had been transported from nineteenth-century England. This all-girls school was stricter and more cloistered than Brunswick. *"Ad ingenium faciendum"* said the motto of the crest embroidered on the top pocket of the green blazers that were part of the uniform. The shoes were stipulated as brown oxfords. The length of the pleated tunic was carefully spelled out: it must touch the floor when a girl knelt. Perfume, makeup, and jewelry were banned in all grades, which started with nursery school at the age of three, and finished with girls close to nineteen. Twice a week, on Mondays and Thursdays, all girls assembled to chorus the school song:

> What gifts are these that thou dost impart
> To those who ask, of thee?
> A joyous mind, an eager heart,
> A spirit fair and free.

In her teacher's eyes Jane came close to being a model pupil. The stocky little girl with the disarming blue eyes was a hard worker, more docile and therefore somewhat less interesting to outsiders than her brother, who, in a way, appeared to be older than she was. They enjoyed each other's companionship, even at the age where brothers and sisters mostly pull apart from each other.

At eleven, she had shaken off the "Lady Jane" joke at long last, simply by refusing to answer to the name. The labels in her new uniforms identified her only as Jane Fonda. That was about the extent of her rebelliousness. She accepted her uprooting from West to East where Peter kicked against it.

"I wrote 'I HATE THE EAST' on the walls of the houses we moved into," he says, "and then my father would make me go around and erase it all."

She used to depict herself, in later years, as having been something of a hellion at the academy, entertaining her friends by telling a schoolgirl's smutty jokes behind an outbuilding on the grounds. But if this was sinful in her eyes, it could only be taken as the sign of a moralistic upbringing and a mark of her ignorance about customary behavior among her peers.

As the squeakier wheel, her brother got more attention, especially from Grandmother Seymour. "Peter was always rebellious," Hank recalls. "We overworried about him, I think."

"I was shy, difficult, and lied a lot," Peter has said; and one childhood friend was once quoted as remembering him as "a weird kid, relegated to purgatory." Those are not the memories of the Fondas' friends and acquaintances when they first went to Greenwich. If family life was unmitigated hell, only Hank gave a fleeting, unspoken hint of it in his melancholy face. Yet he had worn much the same look most of his adult life.

The few neighbors with whom the Fondas had regular contact thought Frances was "a terrific woman," a high-style dresser, almost embarrassingly eager to make friends, a high-strung personality. On the first Thanksgiving Day that the family spent in Greenwich, she called on her closest neighbors with a turkey Hank had won in a shoot after Frances had already bought one. She would stop by to borrow a loaf of bread or a thermos bottle so Hank could take the children swimming at the town beach.

Fighting hard to keep a marriage of two incompatible people intact, he planned days of sunning and swimming with Peter, teaching him to dive and jump off his shoulders into the calm water of the Sound. They went in to Manhattan together occasionally to such standard father-and-son attractions as the Museum of Natural History, usually with a new playmate of Peter's, Donnie Neilsen, whose father was the superintendent of an adjoining estate.

Donnie thought of Jane as a tomboy, much superior to the average girl, and fondly called her brother "You skinny nut." Looking back on them as an adult, the Fondas struck him as being solid, down-to-earth people who fitted neatly into the local scene. Their Dalmatian dog Buzz gave them the right credentials in a decidedly doggy community. Their Japanese houseman was a bit exotic by local standards, but they were in the swim of things when their new car was stolen in one of the series of robberies that were endemic in the secluded back roads. They lost a point in their choice of car, however: backcountry Greenwich is Cadillac country, and they had bought nothing fancier than a Mercury.

They were nonconformists in another respect. *Mister Roberts* had made Hank a star on Broadway as well as in motion pictures; there is nothing whatever in the world to compare with the feeling. New York lay at his feet like Cleopatra beguiling Anthony. Restaurant crowds, autograph hunters, passers-by in the street all paid him the tribute he'd won by his terrifying, single-minded determination to be an actor. Audiences worshiped him as the epitome of a decent young American holding the crew of the gut-bucket together in face of a tyrannical captain and the dreadful monotony of war.

This was pleasure undiluted, the most fun he'd ever had. Before every performance, he would sit in his dressing room, feeling his skin tingle with anticipation. A special joy was for Josh Logan to come to a performance and say, "Fonda, you son of a *bitch!*" "The pitfall you get into in most long runs is you stop listening," Fonda says. "It never happened in *Mister Roberts.*"

With Logan, there was also a constant game of mental Indian wrestling. At one point, toward the end of the long run, he concluded that Fonda's understated acting style was contagious; the rest of the cast were all trying to underplay him, which made for an overall thin performance. Logan called a rehearsal in an attempt to set things right. When it was over, Hank telephoned him. "I don't feel it's my play any more," he complained.

"No, you superior bastard," said the coauthor and director, "but it's *mine.*"

The good ladies of Greenwich couldn't understand why
the Fondas didn't mix more in society. Why didn't they
join one of the country clubs? Why did Hank sit alone in
a corner, fending off attention, on the rare occasions when
he went with Frances to a party? Why didn't he *conform?*

They began to get the idea that he didn't much care for
the town. Frances, on the other hand, was different. Greenwich attracted her as a pond in which she was going to
swim like a fish. Tired of living in other people's rented
homes on Pecksland Road and then on Sherwood Lane, she
began to dream of building another place of their own.
Frances enjoyed owning real estate—on the St. Lawrence
River she had bought a little hideaway and named it Fonda
Isle. In her own right she was a comparatively rich woman,
with a well-balanced stock portfolio, heavily invested in oil.
In Greenwich she picked up two more pieces of property,
ultimately building on a quiet street called Martindale a
handsome house that the Fondas were never to live in.

Her older daughter's future was much on her mind. Pan
had grown to be a beautiful seventeen-year-old, taught
mostly by governesses rather than in school. To her stepfather she was "Dreamboat." She was an accomplished artist,
a gifted pianist, but lazy, in the opinion of those who sensed
her potential.

Jane, who had never sought out her company, had less
need of it now. Her best friend Brooke was in town, entered at Greenwich Academy. "Lady Jane!" screamed
Brooke, greeting her old schoolmate. "My name is Jane,"
was the reply. "You spell it J-A-N-E."

Margaret Sullavan had moved in from California, putting the maximum distance between her children and Leland Hayward. Billy Hayward followed Pete into Brunswick, one grade lower, "a cute little fellow," as one of his
teachers said, "who seemed to miss his father."

Bridget had a rival for Pete's affections. An older woman,
aged twelve, had come into his dreams, the only sister of

Donnie Neilsen. "I'm going to sell my new English bike," he promised her, "and buy you diamonds, furs, and jewels." Peter, like Jane, was settling in quite satisfactorily, enjoying his friends and hanging around Ted Wall's Round Hill Stables nearby.

Toward the end of the fourth grade he was bought what he said was his first suit, a conservative Eastern check, of which he was inordinately proud. The occasion was the June wedding of Pan, who was being married to a young man to whom Peter could raise no objection, since he was an older brother, Charles, of one of his New Brunswick friends, Tony Abry. From almost anybody's point of view the couple were well matched; Charles and Tony were grandsons of Rush H. Kress, retired from S. H. Kress & Company chain stores.

In the second year of the run of *Mister Roberts* and the Fondas' residence in town, the gap between Hank and Frances widened. He spent less time in Greenwich. The tensions in Frances grew more obvious. For their second Thanksgiving Hank was away, confined briefly in a New York hospital for an operation on a knee. Eugene Seymour lived in New Jersey, separated from Sophie, whom he only rejoined in California in his final years, after he had begged her to let him spend them with her. He took the opportunity of Hank's hospitalization to visit his wife and renew contact with his grandchildren. He had no wish to see his son-in-law.

Over that holiday, Frances spoke calmly and deliberately of ending her life. She warned an intimate woman friend, who was planning a trip to Europe, that if she went, she would kill herself. The woman realized that this was no empty threat. Talking together in that friend's Manhattan apartment, Frances deliberated, "If I go insane, he won't be able to marry her." Pretended madness and the blotting out of her own life were the only two weapons left for her use to punish her husband.

In a hospital in Scranton, Pennsylvania, Pan Abry, after less than a year of marriage, gave birth to a premature daughter, who lived for only two hours. As soon as she was well enough, Frances hurried her off to Europe, where her marriage to Abry was ended. When Frances returned, her own marriage to Hank was over in everything but the legal fact.

The newspaper stories said that a divorce was "being arranged." Mr. and Mrs. Fonda, in the words of the one or two stilted paragraphs, "had made several futile attempts at reconciliation for the sake of their children." Hank remained permanently in an apartment on East Sixty-fourth Street. The gossip was that he planned to marry a girl only ten years older than Jane.

At twenty-one, Susan Blanchard, born Levine, had glowing good looks and a pensive, generous-hearted way about her. She was the child of the first marriage of an Australian actress, Dorothy Blanchard, whose name she had taken; Dorothy was now the second wife of Oscar Hammerstein II. Susan had originally come backstage at the Alvin Theater because her stepbrother, Billy Hammerstein, was assistant stage manager. Then she had quietly haunted Hank's dressing room, one of the endless crowd who came to applaud him and share in a little rubbed-off glory.

At first he thought that, frankly, she was something of a pest. He preferred to relax in solitude from intolerable domestic pressure, tinkering with the model planes that he was constantly in the throes of building, with wing and motor assemblies strung around the room. He seriously considered asking a friend to drop her a hint that she wasn't welcome. But that had changed. They had taken to showing up at the Hammersteins' parties and elsewhere, as bedazzled with each other as Pyramus and Thisbe.

The amount of money in the settlement under arrangement with her attorneys became an obsession with Frances. They encouraged her to strip Hank down to his last inconsequential endowment policy. "Well, she's got everything else, so why not?" was his response.

The need to talk about her despair drove her to follow a friend's suggestion and see a psychiatrist in New York. She went to him exactly once. She told her friend, after the only session with him, "I know you're right, and I know he's right, but I can't make it work for me. I spent that twenty-five dollars for nothing."

Money can be the most costly commodity in the world. Without the reflected adulation of being Mrs. Henry Fonda, Frances found her ego, her essential being, destroyed. She had to have money. She had to have tangible, living evidence that she was desirable to men. Her smile grew more intense, her speech more rapid, her eyes remote and dreamy. She arrived for no particular reason at Peter's school one day and in a staff office began pouring out an explicit account of her troubles. When she spoke of going into his classroom, the sympathetic woman teacher steered her away and into her car, suspicious that she had it in mind to let Peter's class hear the same story.

Not long after, she was admitted to a rest home in Stockbridge, Massachusetts; on a different occasion Margaret Sullavan, too, was a patient there. In the toils of a pretended breakdown, Frances Fonda symbolically erased the memory of her second marriage by throwing her wedding ring out of the window of her guarded room.

At this time she received from a friend, Eulalia Chapin, a copy of the prayer from Saint Francis of Assisi. The words were intended to help break the tightening chains of her anguish and old ambitions, which had lost whatever meaning they ever had.

> Lord, make me an instrument of your peace.
> Where there is hatred, let me sow love,
> Where there is injury, pardon,
> Where there is doubt, faith. . . .

> For it is in giving that we receive.
> It is in pardoning that we are pardoned.

The words were irrelevant to her, she thought. She ignored them, as she ignored other people's comforting. She was out of Stockbridge only briefly when she committed herself into Craig House Sanitarium at Beacon, New York, on the banks of the Hudson River. Ten weeks passed, and she appeared to be bright and cheerful enough to have the run of the grounds.

"She was making a wonderful recovery, as we thought, and her discharge was expected soon," said a nurse. It was Frances Fonda's turn to wear a mask. She waited for the return from an out-of-town trip of her favorite doctor, so that she could play a last game of bridge with him one evening.

She retired to her room, and sometime in the very early morning of Friday, April 14, 1950, she wrote two notes. One she addressed to Amy Gray, her night nurse. It said, "Mrs. Gray—do not enter the bathroom, but call Dr. Bennett." She taped it to the bathroom door, which had no lock. The other note she wrote to the doctor. It said, in part, "Very sorry, but this is the best way out."

When Nurse Gray went into the room at 6:30 A.M. with a glass of wake-up orange juice, she found the bed empty. She read the note, which was intended as a final kindness to spare her, and she did as she was told. Dr. Courtney Bennett brought another doctor with him in response to her alarmed call. They opened the bathroom door. On the tiled floor lay Frances Fonda, her throat slashed with a razor blade, as calculated a suicide as the doctors had ever known. Some newspapers hinted that hers was a case of terminal cancer. There was no basis in truth for that.

VII

THAT FRIDAY morning on the roads that wind between Greenwich and Beacon, Hank had to concentrate on hard, cross-country driving. Beside him in the car, Sophie Seymour asked the question she would repeat for weeks to come: "How could Frances do anything like this?" There was a second thought that kept recurring in her conversation: "We should never have moved here; we've had nothing but trouble."

Even those close to Frances hadn't guessed how much it hurt her to be shunned by Hank. Except in the past few months, she had not complained. She was no crybaby. She appeared to be content to run things in her usual busily efficient way—the household, the children's schooling, plans for building the new house, which was something of a drain on family cash. She was always there waiting, it seemed, ready to accept whatever Hank wanted to give her.

"He has had ups and downs in his life," said someone who knew both man and wife. "Marriage with Frances was a down, but he loved that house in California, and he loved those kids."

Arrangements for the funeral were quickly made. Frances was taken to a crematorium, as her will directed, the ashes to go with the remains of other Seymours in the family cemetery at Ogdensburg, New York. Sophie returned to Greenwich, to serve as an anchor and guardian for her grandchildren. Hank went on to New York, to play that night in *Mister Roberts*. It was the best thing he could think of to do. The performance he gave was indistinguishable from all the rest in his three-year run. The troubled man disappeared behind the face and soul of the cargo officer.

"I don't think that was so remarkable," said someone who watched him. "It's easier to do something you're used to than to sit down and tell people how awful it was. I don't think there was anything cold-blooded about it. It was a thorough escape, trying to carry on in the 'show must go on' department."

The next morning, the most important and most hazardous task remained undone. Jane and Peter had not been told what had happened to their mother. Hank could not accept the responsibility of telling them. Neither could their grandmother. The instinct of this kind, competent woman was to cover up the unthinkable fact. So far as the children were concerned, Frances had died a natural death. Sophie sent a penciled note by hand to Donnie's mother: "Dear Mrs. Neilsen," she wrote, "To protect the children we are telling them that it was a heart attack. I hope they will never know."

"It seemed easier on the kids not to tell the whole truth," Hank says regretfully now. "But the bottom line of it all is: I wasn't telling the truth." His innate, consuming honesty made the decision to pretend hurt like a thrust that leaves a scarcely noticeable cut in the skin but stabs deep into the body tissue.

Years later, Peter said, "Nobody told me the truth about my mother, man. I was ten years old and I didn't understand." He knew she was dead and he felt that he was alone. He was fifteen before he learned how she died. He was in Rome with Hank, where his father was making *War and Peace*. In a barber's chair he picked up a magazine and read about her suicide. "It blew my mind, man. And nobody to this day has ever told me anything." That was late in 1967, when he was talking to a tape recorder.

But Jane knew the truth a few months after the event. She was told the truth by someone else in the house. This is how it happened. She was the special joy of a very proper Bostonian governess, Helen Wallace, who had been enrolled as an intimate of the family. The girl and the woman entered into a rapid friendship. Jane went into Miss Wallace's bedroom late one night to talk with her because she couldn't sleep. In school that day a girl had handed her a movie magazine that said her mother had taken her own life.

The governess went downstairs to the kitchen to bring up a glass of warm milk and a few cookies. Back in her bedroom she gently and calmly told Jane exactly how the life of Frances Fonda had ended. The girl heard it all in silence. Then she paused for a few moments. "Don't let Grandma know that I know," she asked. Miss Wallace, another stickler for truth, kept the secret.

The following morning, Jane slept late. Her grandmother, as usual more worried about Peter, who also was still in bed, encountered the governess at the foot of the stairs, taking Jane's breakfast up to her room. "Ah, Miss Wallace, you do spoil her," she said lightly. Sophie was a calm, stern woman, with a rousing sense of humor. She used to joke about her own marriage. "My husband saw to it that I had five children, one after the other, to make sure I stayed at home." But she needed help in deciding what her grandchildren might do now. Should they continue going to school in Greenwich or perhaps be sent elsewhere? Ought they to be kept home until the hammer blows of the headlines—FONDA'S WIFE, ILL, COMMITS SUICIDE—had been softened by the passage of time? So she did what Frances would have done—held a conference with the teachers.

Members of the school staff were no strangers at the

Fondas. When one of his teachers came to dinner, Pete would be up extra early, dusting his room with a washcloth in case she dropped in to inspect it. One morning soon after Frances's death, the Brunswick headmaster and the fifth-grade teacher, Edna Hale, arrived at the house on Sherwood Avenue one morning for the crucial talk. Mr. Everett sat with Hank and Peter in one room, while Sophie talked with Miss Hale in another.

Conversation between the two men faded out within seconds. To make small talk to break the thickening ice, the headmaster chatted with the boy on a subject that obviously interested him: pistols. Guns fascinated Peter Fonda. Then Everett, seeing a painting on the wall that had all the marks of a Thomas Hartnett, turned to Hank and discovered that it was he who had painted it. The thaw set in. The master took the opportunity to offer some advice.

"I think it might be best for Peter if he came back to school in the morning." Hank agreed. Both the children picked up their classes the next day. They lived at home, Pete more taken up with such attractions as guns than with lessons, cajoling Kate the cook into doing his arithmetic homework. Jane was learning to wear a mask of assumed ignorance at school and at home.

People around her thought of her as a healthy child, grown up for her years, but she insists that she was in no way mature. Her shy smiles deceived everyone, she has said. Her real feelings were invariably concealed. Within her family, all she saw was surface calm. "I grew up not knowing how to show hatred, anger, or grudges." Her habit of storing up emotion turned out to be a serious handicap in her early years as an actress.

She came home one afternoon from the academy with another question for the governess. Some of her classmates had been talking to her, jeeringly, about Susan Blanchard. "Is it true what they say, that she's a sex fiend?"

Helen Wallace calmed her, as she was often able to do. "That's a silly thing for anyone to say. Don't you think that your father, who loves you, has the ability to choose another wife?"

He went around like a man under water, his face marked by a deeper melancholy than it had shown before. "In the company of others, Susan appeared unable to lift the burden from his mind, and they sat together like a couple of old owls, watching, saying nothing, remote from the rest," as a friend remarked. "And this was Hank Fonda, who used to get up at parties and put on all those silly acts. He had lost all the comedy, all the everything."

The odd repetitions of pattern that showed up in his life and in Peggy Sullavan's developed again that summer. At a party in London, where she was playing in *The Voice of the Turtle*, she was introduced to a little Englishman, who stood not much taller than her five feet two inches. Kenneth Wagg had four sons—Timothy, Jeremy, Anthony, and David—by a previous marriage but that was no obstacle to Peggy's making him her fourth husband.

"Imagine being on a honeymoon with all these children," said the new Mrs. Wagg, whose humor still bubbled, in a letter addressed to the Fonda household. The Waggs moved into a house a mile or so away from the household that was now run by Sophie.

The Fondas and the Waggs remained friends. There was one day when Hank and Peggy turned up together at Brunswick, where Jeremy had gone into the fourth grade along with Billy Hayward, who struggled with lessons that his new stepbrother could sail through. Peggy and Hank had nothing to say to each other, but the teaching staff, pretending not to watch, put that down to a passing tiff.

Another rip had been torn in the curtain he had tried to keep drawn around himself and his family. The Fondas made news again when Frances's will was published. She had drawn it six months before she died. She had managed her money competently, but not quite as brilliantly as her friends had imagined.

Sophie was given life occupancy of the house bought for

her in Los Angeles, which was ultimately to go to Jane and Peter. Sophie received most of her daughter's personal possessions, including the grand piano on which Pan had played. Sophie was to draw 60 percent of the income of a trust fund while she lived, with Jane and Peter sharing the other 40 percent until each reached the age of twenty-five, when they would inherit close to $100,000 apiece. Fonda Isle was willed to Peter.

Of the $650,615 estate, Frances left her husband nothing. Under Connecticut law, however, he had the right to one-third, no matter what her desires were. He waived that right early in the throes of probate by the court, which lasted for years and saw the principal sum eroded by lawyers' fees. All that Hank got was half the cash balance in a joint bank account of $75,086, an unusually large sum "maintained for convenience" and for financing the new house, which had already been sold when the marriage was breaking up. There was one more rub. Hank was forced to petition a Los Angeles court before he was designated the guardian of his son's estate. Frances had excluded him in favor of her mother.

As the year dragged along toward a welcome end, newspaper gossip columns began to titillate their readers with hints of what the next Mrs. Fonda would wear at her wedding. If any reader expected a showy celebration to match her elaborate gown, he was disappointed. Only close relatives of the bride saw Dr. Everett Clinchy, president of the National Conference of Christians and Jews, make Hank and Susan man and wife at the Hammersteins' home in New Hope, Pennsylvania, on December 28.

The parents of the bride had another wedding to go to that day. John Steinbeck took as his third wife Elaine Scott, formerly married to Zachary Scott, the Hollywood actor. The ties between the Steinbecks and Hank drew closer when they moved into East Seventy-second Street and he settled into a town house around the corner on East Seventy-Fourth.

Immediately after their wedding, the Fondas left for what in those days of limited air travel constituted something close to an end of the earth. To honeymoon in Virgin Islands sun, out of reach of reporters and telephones, called for flying to St. Thomas, then finishing the journey by boat to St. John's. They were there for a little more than a week, out of touch with his family, before their honeymoon ran headlong into disaster. Their hopes for a permanent, solid marriage may have ended at the same time.

On January 8, Tony Abry, younger brother of Charles, invited his friend Pete to go with him and another boy, Reed Armstrong, to visit his grandfather. Rush Kress owned an estate, Rock Hill, in Ossining, New York, about a forty-five-minute drive from Greenwich. The Kress chauffeur, John Reed, was sent to collect the three boys.

On a cold Sunday morning the boys went out to play on the shooting range, which was one of the luxuries of Rock Hill. Peter picked up a long Civil War pistol, which everyone believed to be unloaded. Holding the barrel against his stomach with his right hand, the ten-year-old boy tried to break open the weapon with his left. A round had been left in the chamber. The act of breaking the pistol pulled the trigger. The bullet exploded into Peter's stomach, pierced his liver and ripped into a kidney.

In the days when he was determined to register himself as a renegade and outcast to the family, Peter chose to drop broad hints that this was a try at suicide. There was only his word for it. Medical history records few attempts by ten-year-olds to end their life in front of a group of people, which in this case included the chauffeur.

Subsequently, Peter amended his account. "I'm not sure if I was really trying to kill myself or not," he told *Playboy*, but I do recall that after I shot myself I didn't want to die. I was conscious after I shot myself; I was also very scared. . . ."

Only a little blood seeped from the wound, but internal hemorrhages were severe. The boy was dying when big, black John Reed, sensing that there was no time to call a doctor, drove him straight to Ossining Hospital. Peter credits the chauffeur with saving his life.

"They were giving me shots for gangrene and shock and pain and I was beginning to get a little dopey, but I remember that they didn't know what to do. There was just one doctor around who knew how to operate on bullet wounds and they finally got him on the phone. I remember looking down at the floor and seeing all these legs walking by all the time, different legs belonging to doctors and nurses, and then suddenly there was a set of legs with mud-covered hunting boots on. That was the man."

Ossining was the home of Sing Sing Prison, and Charles Sweet was the prison doctor, well up on the treatment of wounds. He had been contacted when he returned home from duck-hunting in the marshes along the Hudson River. He scrubbed up and prepared to operate.

It was much harder to reach Fonda on an island without telephones. The only solution was to ask for the Coast Guard to take him off St. John's, so that he and Susan could fly home. The news he received was that his son was close to death. Their plane was grounded temporarily in Bermuda on its return flight. The hours inched by into another day.

Icy rain was beating on the windshield as he drove up out of New York on Route 9 to Ossining. Peter's condition was critical. The bullet had to be removed, as it was, without waiting for Hank to arrive.

At the hospital bedside, the only conclusion Hank could reach was that his son was going to die. Surgery was long and delicate, leaving a four-inch welt across the boy's abdomen. Three transfusions needed to be carried out to replace the blood he had lost. He was wheeled from the operating theater into an intensive care unit. Accident or deliberate flirtation with dying? It was too early then to resolve the facts. For whatever cause, the loss of Peter would write a final period to the past nine months that would compare with anything the Greeks had performed, wearing the masks of tragedy.

A friend of Fonda says, "I think Hank must have felt, 'I let my children down. I let her commit suicide. Now Peter.' "

The boy fought to live. "A remarkable recovery," said Dr. Sweet.

The place of Hank's children in his new marriage changed. If he wasn't a model husband, he became something close to a model father, as some of his children's teachers were to believe, so far as the circumstances of his livelihood allowed. Yet neither Jane nor Peter saw it like that at all.

People around the family came together to help the Fondas. For the four weeks that Peter was in the hospital, Margaret Sullavan volunteered to chauffeur members of the household to and from Ossining. Anything to do with medicine held a fascination for her. She could joke about a doctor's mistake in diagnosing her as a diabetic after switching urine samples. But she had turned to a steady intake of prescribed pills to calm her worries about her children, her increasing deafness, and her resentment at growing old.

When the new term began at Brunswick, Peter was a celebrity. Every morning in assembly the headmaster had read a medical bulletin on the boy's condition. There were cheers when he was pronounced out of danger and louder cheers the day he arrived back for classes. After four weeks in the hospital he looked paler and skinnier than ever, but he wore a grin of pleasure a mile wide at his reception.

"He gave us no problems when he was here," said the headmaster. "The school seemed to be his world."

His grandmother refused to fuss over the shooting. She set the tone for making light of it by fondly nicknaming him "Old Leadbelly." She did not say to the children what she sometimes told other adults: "I'm so lonely with Frances gone."

Jane accepted her father's marriage easily enough. She and Peter went to live in New York with Hank and Susan; Sophie returned to California later. Jane found no serious problems in making the adjustment to her new stepmother. "She was just great," she said. "It was like having a family again." Young Mrs. Fonda, in turn, thoroughly admired Jane. They went out and about together; a woman who knew she was good-looking and dressed the part, and a schoolgirl who was certain she was as plain and lumpy as a suet dumpling.

When the Broadway run of *Roberts* ended and the company took to the road, Hank stayed on for a total of more than eleven thousand performances, lasting over three years. Wherever he was—Washington, Chicago, San Francisco—he faithfully telephoned to keep in touch with his two families, pushing himself to take some part in the essential trivialities of their days.

He was intrigued, typically, to hear that in Greenwich Sophie's bedroom had been invaded through the upstairs porch by a rare flying squirrel from the woods outside. It had made a nest among her gloves in a drawer, where she fed it nuts sent up from the grocery store. It exercised by leaping from the finials of her four-poster bed. The squirrel figured in Hank's telephone calls, but Sophie had to set it free to save furniture before he could get back to see it.

But in Greenwich there were more serious questions to talk about, notably what was to be done for Jane and Peter's education and, equally important, wasn't it time for the Greenwich days to end? Hank's sister Harriet visited from Omaha. Frances' sister and brother-in-law joined in the debate. Conferences were not always cordial.

"After a while," Susan remembered, "Peter asked if he could call me mother, and Jane said she was going to call me mother, too. The Seymour side of the family got very angry."

Part of the solution lay in sending both children off to boarding school, Jane to Emma Willard in Troy, New York, Peter to Fay in Southborough, Massachusetts. The disintegration of the family life took a further step.

Once again Jane proved to be a good student though she prefers only the memories of trouble, of being a chronic nonconformist. She has told of laying a trail of lighter fuel down a corridor from her room to the room of a girl she disliked, then setting fire to it, in the knowledge that the flames would go out before any damage was done but that her chosen enemy would get the message.

She made no lasting friendships in that era of her life. She found herself, in the first year, communing with the caged white mouse in the biology laboratory. She felt as dowdy and insecure as the average thirteen-year-old, resentful of all efforts to teach her the social graces of how to sit, how to walk, how to gesture gracefully. Friends were lacking for her in New York, too.

With Susan, she was a frequent visitor at Fay, which prided itself on being the oldest elementary boarding school in America, "dedicated," as parents were informed, "to the development of the whole boy to assume the mantle of responsibility which will be his as a leader of tomorrow."

Susan impressed the male teaching staff as a genuine charmer. "She showed a real desire to care for Peter," one of them recalls. The little, frail boy made a less favorable impression. He was egotistical, his master concluded, something of an exhibitionist and sadly insecure, but he had a sense of humor that helped to compensate for his shortcomings.

As a scholar he was judged to be "extremely average," but among his few achievements in English he wrote love letters for other boys. "Fay's Own Shakespeare" was the description he earned in the school newspaper, *The Pioneer*, a lively four-page tabloid produced with a minimum of adult supervision. He turned his hand to a dozen and one fitful activities—chess, the camera club, basketball, the band, cheerleading—without making any special mark. As a sign that the recent past was being buried in his memory, he took up riflery as a hobby, too.

Whenever he could take time from the new play he was appearing in, Fonda went to see his son. *Point of No Return*, which was based on John P. Marquand's novel of the same name, held no attraction for Hank. He regretted having gone into it with his own peculiar intensity, though the producer was his old agent, Hayward. The critics returned to praising Fonda to the skies ("Our most ingratiating male star" . . . "tremendous honesty" . . . "convincing, amusing, and moving") but when he moved back into his familiar dressing room at the Alvin Theater, he responded as sourly as a quince.

He decided that he hated his role as Charles Gray, the young bank executive struggling for success in a career that he doesn't really enjoy. Instead of refusing to talk about it, Hank almost welcomed press interviews. "Listen," he'd tell bewildered reporters, "don't ask me about this play. It's terrible. I can't talk about the character because there is no character. Just write down something to tell people, 'Don't come to see it.' "

No matter what he said, the audiences kept coming. *Point of No Return* was a hit. "He's quite marvelous even when he thinks he's terrible," says one of his directors, "but when Fonda gets a hate on, I don't know what you can do. You can either give up or try to win him over, and that's quite difficult."

Perhaps more than in any other business, the theater takes inordinate pride in seeing children follow in their fathers' footsteps. Entertainers in general are an exuberant lot, both by nature and by the necessities of their trade. They delight in introducing their young to the crowds who applaud them. Alphabetically, the endless list of family businesses begins with three generations of Barrymores and runs through the Crosbys, the Dean Martins, and the Sinatras, to the Waynes. The children who make it in the shadow of the parent—and they are in a minority—"always wanted to act," according to the customary press handout. But in this respect the Fondas, as usual, were totally different.

Hank, who had done his best to shelter Jane and Peter from contamination by Hollywood, had no particular desire to see them follow him. He did not stand in their way, but they had no irrepressible urge to be led. At Emma Willard, in the habit of boarding schools, the girls put on plays under the direction of the English department. In her second year Jane joined the drama class and did her first acting in Christopher Fry's *The Boy With a Cart*, produced for Thanksgiving and performed in the chapel. She played the male lead, a plump schoolgirl in green tights and a green hat with a feather attached.

She experienced none of the legendary tingling in the bones to tell her that this was *it*. She simply enjoyed doing it, liked the costumes and putting on makeup and getting attention. It was exciting, but had nothing to do with serious acting. Acting was more fun than math. That was all there was to it.

At Fay there was a similar tradition, calling for three productions every school year—Gilbert and Sullivan in February, Shakespeare in May, and something more contemporary in-between times. In this highly conservative school, where the heavy emphasis was on Latin and mathematics, play-acting was regarded more as a form of therapy than as career training.

"We figured it was a boost for a boy's ego to do something on the stage," explained Dr. G. H. Gilcrest, who was the debonair head of the English department. "It would sometimes make a boy blossom, when he had done nothing until then."

Peter fell into that category. At Fay, he ran into various

kinds of trouble of a inconsequential kind. He insisted on reading aloud from a mildly risqué book on a group outing by train to New York and was reprimanded for it. He was caught with cigarettes in his pocket; he was reprimanded again. His class work was mediocre, so he temporarily lost the weekly privilege, highly valued in an otherwise cloistered existence, of going downtown to eat ice cream at what in Massachusetts is known as a "spa."

Gilbert and Sullivan coincided with Winter Weekend, when parents and guests came up for such ritualistic pleasures as basketball in the gym, a tug of war, and skating on the frozen football field, followed by hot cocoa and marshmallows as a treat for the boys. The staff enjoyed the experience because, as one of them said, "It gave us a chance to talk with the parents and see why the kids were so queer."

Hank was a silent participant. He saw Pete one year perform a modest role in *The Pirates of Penzance* as a cute little girl in the chorus. Mothers in the audience were sometimes stricken at the resemblance between their sons, dressed as girls with lipstick and makeup, and themselves. If Hank had any comment, nobody remembers it.

The climax of a Winter Weekend was a dance, conducted under arrangements that discouraged any youthful romance. The girls all came by invitation from Dana Hall in Wellesley. Boys and girls alike were lined up in rows according to their height, to be paired off by the staff in charge. Pete, still lacking inches, came close to the end of the line.

The following year, growing slowly, he was promoted to playing Sir Andrew Aguecheek, a performance as forgettable as his father's had been in the same role long ago during a hard-luck winter in Washington, D.C. Either inspired or repelled by his brush with Shakespeare, Pete then wrote, produced, and directed a take-off on a Broadway hit of the season, a prison-camp comedy called *Stalag 17*. His version, *Stalag 17½*, was given one performance in the gym. "It was rather dreary," one master recalls, "but it was good for his ego."

To keep contact with his children and to stay close to the Broadway theater, Hank made New York his home. Movies were always something he could go back to, if he must, but even *Point of No Return* was more rewarding to his soul than, say, *The Magnificent Dope*. He found a little relief from the tedium by going to work for Adlai Stevenson in his run against Dwight D. Eisenhower. Steinbeck wrote the speeches for Hank to deliver.

Elaine Steinbeck, with experience in the Theatre Guild's production department, served as coordinator for the speakers, while her husband churned out the words in response to her telephoned instructions: "We need a five-minute speech for Hank, and two minutes for a twenty-five-year-old blonde who'll appear at a rally in Cleveland."

Steinbeck, whose first drafts tended to be flowery, improved with this daily practice. The closeness between the two men advanced a notch tighter. "Hank became the personification of what my husband stood for," says Elaine.

An atmosphere of controlled calm had returned to the Fondas. The divided family was running much more smoothly. Many of the internal wounds seemed to be healing. Though Peter was the chief cause for concern, he was scarcely distinguishable from the rest of his peers at Fay. Jane was hardly a misfit at Emma Willard, and her later comments ("It was ghastly—all girls, and that's unhealthy") represent a kind of distorted hindsight.

In November 1953, the Henry Fondas adopted a newborn baby, whom they named Amy. The process of reintegration was well under way. There were no violent outbursts from Fay or Emma Willard. And Hank had found a new play that looked like it would become another landmark in the American theater.

He brought to the part of Lieutenant Barney Greenwald in rehearsals of *The Caine Mutiny Court-Martial* his inevita-

ble snarling, nitpicking method of closing in on the character, making it his own. "You feel your way in every instance," he has explained. "You close in on your lines, then
ways of doing them begin to come to you. I always know
when it starts to feel real."

He had never been more "real" than in this courtroom
battle, extracted from Herman Wouk's best-selling novel,
over the fate of the rebellious Lieutenant Maryk, United
States Navy. At every performance, seven times a week, he
wound up audience emotions to cracking point with his
climactic scene, weaving drunkenly after a slew of whiskey
sours, denouncing facile patriotism, which he happened
personally to deplore.

Another Navy officer, Lieutenant Douglas Roberts, was
meantime setting several varieties of longevity records. In
road companies and overseas companies, a sizable selection
of Hollywood's foremost leading men, with gallant Tyrone
Power at the top of the list, had played the Logan-Heggen
character. Now the time had come to make the movie, and
the sweepstakes for winning the role rivaled the jostling
that had gone on over playing Rhett Butler in David O.
Selznick's version of *Gone With the Wind*. (Fonda had been
one of the legion of movie males with ambitions to sign on
as Margaret Mitchell's pulsating hero.)

Warner Brothers bought screen rights to *Mister Roberts*,
with the services of Logan penciled in as director. He also
wrote the screenplay, together with Frank Nugent, whose
career as movie critic of *The New York Times* ended when
Zanuck hired him away—some people said simply to silence his disdainful comments about Zanuck as a producer
—at $750 a week. Leland Hayward negotiated himself in to
produce *Roberts*.

But relations between Fonda and Logan had suffered
another pendulum swing. They were at odds with each
other once more. Logan felt that the movie demanded a
younger cast than the man he had seen growing older dur-

ing the phenomenal run of the stage productions. Memories of his last run-in with Hank—"I don't feel it's my play any more," and, "No, you superior bastard, but it's *mine*" —still rankled.

The word spread in the industry that Hank had been out of pictures too long. After seven years away from Hollywood, he had lost his attraction as what the trade calls "a screen name," meaning someone that audiences would line up in the rain to see. William Holden was rumored to be under consideration in Hank's place, but Holden, an aloof actor with almost as much pride as Fonda, let it be known that he wouldn't do a picture that rightfully belonged to Hank. The in-fighting started.

Logan had a definite idea about whom he wanted: Marlon Brando. "I didn't want to go through that domineering stuff with Fonda again," Josh said. Brando, the long-displaced Nebraskan, liked the idea. Logan wanted to settle a score or two with Hank, so he let it be known that so far as he was concerned, Fonda might be given the role of Doc, the aging philosopher aboard the sweltering *Reluctant*. "I couldn't think of anything else to do to let him know how I felt."

When Hank heard about that, his boilers blew. He raged into Hayward's office: "If that son of a bitch directs the picture, I won't play it."

Hayward, shrewd as he was, was in danger of getting scalded. He wanted Fonda in the role. He wanted Logan to direct it. The solution was one that seldom fails in the motion-picture business: money. Logan's agent served as the go-between.

He told his receptive client, "You can either direct it, the way you were planning, or you can step aside and let John Ford do it, who's the best director of men there is. If Ford does it, you'll have a very much bigger percentage of the picture."

Logan was persuaded. "Rather than cause any more

problems, I'll take the money and let them do it," he said.

Hank was satisfied. He was in. Ford had been a comrade, of a nonpolitical nature, on a dozen previous pictures. The fact that he hadn't sat through a stage performance of *Mister Roberts* seemed to be unimportant. That might make it all the easier to ensure that "Roberts" was Fonda to the hilt. With Susan and Jane along to share in some of the pleasure he expected in converting what had been a love story backstage, he set off for California. From there he joined the company on Midway Island, where most of the movie was to be shot.

Ford, a brilliant and arrogant director, was something of an idol of Hank's. He looked forward to watching his old companion at work on the deck of the *Reluctant* in the first day on location. What he saw astounded him. Ford was discarding the play, which Hank knew backward after three years of starring in it, and making up something quite different. Laughs were being lost, subtleties cast aside, points and purposes destroyed.

That evening the cast and crew went ashore to the Navy accommodations where they were staying. Over a drink, Ford asked Fonda, "Well, how do you think our first day went?"

"It stank," said Hank, no waster of words.

Ford, a man of action, knocked him halfway across the room. Hank was up in an instant, but others in the group grabbed him before he could continue the fight. Somehow, the two of them applied a very frail patch over their quarrel. The next morning they resumed work. But Hank watched every move Ford made now with the hard, cold Fonda stare, silently pressing his will on him.

Before many more days had passed, Ford began to wilt. He was reaching the point where he could no longer direct the picture. When Ford, on grounds of illness, was relieved of his responsibility on their return from location, *Mister Roberts* was close to being a fiasco.

A new director was appointed, Mervyn Leroy, whose regard for the play was so high that he simply had the cast speak the lines of the script. When shooting was completed, Hayward realized that what he had in the cans was a film unfit for release. He asked Logan's emergency aid.

All that could be accomplished in three extra days of shooting in the studio by way of close-ups, extra dialogue, and voices imposed through the ship's loudspeaker system was done. When the picture was released, audiences packed in to see it. Fonda, a "screen name" again, was regarded as an ideal Roberts, Jack Lemmon's reputation soared with his portrayal as the lecherous Ensign Pulver.

According to a long-term intimate of Hank's, "Fonda and Ford still speak of each other with affection and respect, but there has been no reconciliation."

For Fonda, two great pleasures, a role and the companionship of a man, had self-destructed.

VIII

CAPTAIN AMERICA, his blue eyes cool behind spind-ly-framed sun glasses, rides his chromium-plated chopper across the walls of most of the students' rooms these days. The cocaine-sniffing hero of *Easy Rider* is the pre-eminent pin-up idol of Westminster School, where Peter Fonda spent more than two years at the bottom of a well of despair. His instructors still speculate over what went wrong.

They used to wonder what prompted his father to send him there, to Simsbury, a cultivated little town of no more than a few thousand people in the Farmington valley of northwestern Connecticut, where exclusive boarding schools like Miss Porter's and Ethel Walker flourish, along with the local broad-leaf tobacco crop.

His teachers thought that perhaps the reason was Westminster's old reputation as the place where successful Broadway actors almost automatically enrolled their sons. In the 1920s, classes would be suspended for days at a time, while highly glossed play productions drew audiences of parents and guests. A special New Haven train would run up from New York, with such celebrities as Cole Porter aboard to see the shows. Three of the plays, written and directed by the grown-up son of the headmaster, who also conducted the English department, were staged at Westminster before they struck oil on Broadway.

But when Pete started in as a new boy, that tradition had languished. In his eighteen years as head, old "Prof" Milliken had established different customs, stern enough to satisfy Hank. The school was then a Calvinistic society, oriented toward athletics and rough-and-tumble masculinity. A less likely environment would be hard to imagine for the lean, sensitive adolescent who remained inches smaller than most of his classmates.

Discipline was strict and sometimes arbitrary, not completely different from the rigors of schooldays under Mr. Creakle at Salem House in nineteenth-century England. Serious offenders against the rules were not so humiliated as to be forced to wear a placard like David Copperfield's "Take care of him; he bites." But they were sentenced to carry a log of cordwood or a brick around with them everywhere except into chapel until their offenses had been expiated.

Twelfth-grade boys, known in English fashion as sixthformers, had the power of tyrants over their juniors. Enforcement of the code was left largely in their hands. To exercise that authority they had privileged use of the sixthform paddle. A prescribed number of swats on the backside was a junior's punishment for being caught smoking cigarettes, talking back to one of his overlords, or a variety of other crimes. A sixth-former in charge of a corridor had the right to walk into any junior room along it to search for transgressions.

Peter got paddled in his first year. It was probably inevitable under the standards set in his years there. It could have been for smoking or impudence or chronic sloppiness in his work and his form of dressing—he was guilty of all of them. When he was reprimanded or punished, he invariably wept. "Highly immature," the school records observed.

He was not left alone to suffer through Hank's indifference. As a parent, Hank scored "A-plus" with the staff. He wrote constantly to the school, much concerned with

Pete's health, behavior, and progress in classes. On paper, he could express himself fluently and with considerable, unforced literacy.

"Without being fussy or motherly, those letters were a model of what a parent should rightfully concern himself with," said one staff member. "The faculty thought Henry Fonda was just great."

Talking with him, though, was a different experience. On his visits to see his son, Hank was tongue-tied as ever. On the first Parents' Day, driving up the hairpin curves to Cushing Hall, he sat down for dinner at a group table in the dining room presided over by the prefect who swatted Pete.

Throughout the meal, listening but never joining in the conversation, he spoke precisely one word. "Would you care for seconds, sir?" asked the prefect.

"No," said Hank.

The end of Peter's first year coincided with Jane's last at Emma Willard. That summer of 1955, Hank had a movie to make in Rome—the Dino De Laurentiis production of Tolstoy's *War and Peace*. Jane and Peter accompanied their father. From later versions of their reactions, each of the three of them might have been inhabiting a different planet.

By Jane's account, she was utterly bored. "We lived on an estate outside the city, and I had nothing to do except eat figs and get fat and watch Gina Lollobrigida, a neighbor, through binoculars."

According to Peter twelve years later, he made significant progress toward becoming a prototype Captain America by downing five quarts of Italian wine a day and being introduced to sex in a special style. At fifteen, in front of Saint Peter's, he was picked up by a serviceman's wife, who took him home with her "and balled me, and it blew my life out." The idea of dating nice girls in Omaha seemed remote after that.

Hank ran into more heavy going with his role as Pierre, playing opposite Audrey Hepburn's Natasha. "I knew I was physically wrong for Pierre, but I decided that, with the right kind of spectacles, some strategically placed padding, and my hair combed forward, I could pass. Then it seems that they didn't want a Pierre who looked like Pierre. One who looked like Rock Hudson was what they had in mind. They went into nervous shock when they saw my original makeup. The padding went immediately—over my anguished protests."

King Vidor, the director, took it all calmly, though Fonda fires at all targets when he is enraged. "You understand, don't you," he told Vidor, "that I can be a real son of a bitch?"

Vidor's answer was to arrange to pick up Hank every working morning so that they could spend forty-five minutes warming to each other while they drove to the set where six million dollars was in process of being spent. The tension eased until Hank burst into flames again over a scene in the script involving a Borzoi. "Understand, I'm not going to play with a dog."

Vidor quietly canceled out the dog.

Hank's quarrels with De Laurentiis centered on the unquestionable fact that Tolstoy's Pierre wore spectacles, and Hank, a good Tolstoyan, felt that spectacles were, therefore, necessary equipment. In that faraway era when eyeglasses were worn in movies only by grizzled character actors and coy secretaries who removed them before being indoctrinated in vertical kissing, De Laurentiis regarded spectacles as a box-office drag.

"I won about half the time," Fonda reported, "usually when he was nowhere near the set."

A flare-up threatened on the final day of shooting. In the last take, a sound engineer complained that Hank, mumbling his lines, was hard to record. "Will you speak up?" asked Vidor. Any implication that there are faults in the performances he creates sits poorly with Hank. But he let this pass. The satisfied director and the professionally disgruntled leading man dined that evening together.

At the table, Fonda attempted to explain a little of his philosophy. "I believe in truth in films. Being natural and realistic." He paused briefly. "We should reshoot it in Russian."

Something else happened during that Roman summer. Afdera Franchetti was introduced to Hank. He used to explain to friends later how to pronounce her name: "It's Af-*dear*-a, with the accent on dear." They thought there was a strong resemblance to Frances in her looks—the same slender neck, dark hair, fine shoulders, and handsome eyes. She was sometimes introduced as "Countess," sometimess as "Baroness," but that is not an Italian title. She was twenty-two years old, a Roman of the La Dolce Vita generation.

From what Peter said and the way he behaved, everyone at Westminster School concluded that he had enjoyed himself in Rome. He gave every sign of being content enough to be back, with the big adjustments required in his first year successfully concluded. Although he was still short of close friends among his classmates, more and more of the masters reached the conclusion that Fonda was a warmhearted, highly likable youngster.

The head of the Modern Language department was an expert hunter and fisherman as well as a linguist. Pete proudly showed him a magnificent split-bamboo rod that his father had bought for him in London. He kept it, unused, in a closet, until the master and the boy went fishing for trout upstream in the Farmington River.

"We didn't catch anything, but we had a great day, and at least the rod got christened," said the master afterward. "It was a pity that his father hadn't the time to do that with him."

Not all the boy's relations with the faculty were so

friendly. One of them, the aesthetic head of the English department, clearly disliked him. Pete responded in kind. The English master, proud and always immaculately turned out, walked with a limp, the aftereffects of polio. In the cruel vocabulary of schoolboys, he was nicknamed "The Gimp," but it was Pete who mocked him to his face and called him that when he knew the man could overhear him. Mr. La Roche was a disappointed actor, who at some time in his past had seemingly brushed against Hank— nobody was certain of the circumstances. He made it plain that he disapproved of father and son equally.

Pete was struggling to live up to what he believed was his father's code of perfectionism, and not always succeeding. The shadow of his father still meant Abe Lincoln and Tom Joad and Mister Roberts. Now and then, under the strain of emulating Hank, the boy broke down. The Seymours, he wept on one occasion, were trying to poison his mind against his father.

At Vassar, traditions were more adhesive. As a freshman —which was the approved description in those innocent days before Women's Liberation—Jane studied as hard as she had at Emma Willard, a liberal-arts course, including French and the history of music, two elective subjects. But as she remembers, she "just got by."

She had one old friend there in Brooke Hayward, who was considered exceptionally talented, irresistibly attractive, and talked of going on the stage. Jane formed some new friendships without particular difficulty, including one with Susan Stein, whose father was Jules Stein, the eye doctor who switched careers and became the sybaritical head of the Music Corporation of America. She considered it square to go to school dances; she did no dating, because she thought of herself as plain.

In her two Vassar years, however, she went to one dance at least—at Westminster—where she had kept in frequent contact with Pete. He fixed her up with a date with a sixth-former. She stayed overnight, and the bed she slept in is regarded nowadays with the reverence formerly reserved for the multitudinous places where George Washington laid his head. One faculty wife recalls that, after a sturdy dinner, Jane, anxious to keep her weight down, made herself vomit in the washroom by pushing a finger down her throat.

When her reputation as a professional actress and an uninhibited talker in press interviews was starting to glow, she amended the story of being something of a Vassar wallflower. "When I discovered boys liked me, I went wild. I went out all the time. I never studied." She left the calculated impression that sneaking off on illicit weekends became a habit of hers.

There was probably as much substance to that as to her claim, made simultaneously, that for the first twenty years of her life she was "trying to avoid acting." If there is any such creature as a born actress, it would seem to be Jane. She certainly didn't dodge taking part in a Vassar production of a Federico García Lorca play. (She played the role of a young Spanish girl who cuckolded her husband.)

Before she entered her freshman year, she took to the idea of going back to Omaha with Hank and making her stage debut before a paying audience with him at a benefit for his old stamping ground, the community playhouse. Another local girl, Dorothy McGuire, who was a big name in Hollywood by now, appeared at the benefit with the two Fondas in Clifford Odets' story of an alcoholic actor, *The Country Girl*. Like most other people, she recognized that a lot of Hank's talent and personal style had rubbed off on this ingenue who was on her way to college with a boy's haircut and her father's self-protective smile.

Her approach was a long way from the Stanislavsky method. In order to look upset, she had a stagehand give her a preliminary shaking, then push her out on the stage. To add a touch of extra realism, she pretended to herself that her father was dead. She didn't care for being an actress at all.

She used to fancy that being Hank's daughter somehow stultified her in discovering her own abilities and her identity as a human being. But at the end of her first year of college she sampled acting with him again. They retraced his footsteps to the Cape Playhouse in Dennis, Massachusetts, the theater that he had once slipped into, to stand in silence, watching a company rehearse, too shy to ask for a job. This time around, he was the advertised attraction, returning by invitation to star as Professor Tommy Turner in the James Thurber-Eliott Nugent play, *The Male Animal*, which was another milestone in Fonda's past. He had made the movie more than a dozen years ago. But sentimental memories did not figure large in his conversation.

Jane played a small part, as the young sister of a professor's wife, because, she explained, "I had nothing else to do." She was convinced, understandably, that the only reason she was in the play was her father.

There was occasional compensation. If he couldn't bring himself to gush over her performance, the look on Fonda's face told her his feelings. For cue for one of his entrances was Jane's slamming a door after she had raced downstairs in a rage. She went storming off one evening so impressively that he forgot his cue. She remembered him standing in the wings, "with that wonderful, silly grin he gets, simply enjoying the fact that I was enjoying his profession."

They were close that summer. She was secure under his wing; it was only later that she behaved as if she resented it. At eighteen, she would have been a freakish rarity if she hadn't found some satisfaction in recognizing that she was, for the present, a most important woman in her father's life.

After less than six years, his marriage with Susan was over. The ending was handled quietly, with taste and without drama: a trip to Reno, a sealed property agreement, a

May decree. In the ritualistic language of the law, he had caused the third Mrs. Fonda "intense mental pain." Some of that pain had been produced by days when he spoke scarcely a word to her. More had been caused by Hank's responses in Rome to the persistent attentions of Afdera. "I have had it," said Susan, a calm woman, soon after their return. "I'm leaving him." Amy remained with her mother. It was another instance where Jane knew more about family secrets than Peter, who had to sort out the details for himself.

The delayed crack-up came when he returned to Westminster for his third year. It could have been a standard study in child psychology: the hypersensitive boy coping with his problems until he is caught in the emotional storms of adolescence. Then the abrupt internal pressures of physical and mental change, upsetting the uneasy balance he had previously been able to achieve.

"I quit before the end of my junior year. It was more the fault of my psyche than the school. I couldn't make it under the circumstances of living in that community and of my family disintegrating. I started developing neuroses."

He looked about the same, only beginning to get a bit longer in the legs, still hyperactive in his efforts to find his fit somewhere in this tightly knit society of sportsmen and scholars. He had a doctor's prescription now for phenobarbitol to calm his nervousness and help him sleep. He picked up the pills from the school dispensary. Half the time, the boys on his corridor swiped his supply, so the dosages were uncertain.

The corridor fell under the charge of his old adversary, The Gimp, whose apartment could be entered from it. His old detractor lived alone there, his only companion an enormous, spoiled black cat, Mr. Prefect, who was regularly baited by Pete and the other boys. That was one cause of trouble. The apartment contained a refrigerator, where students were allowed to keep soft drinks. The master, something of a drinker himself, objected to being disturbed after he had gone to bed by Pete's wanting to quench his thirst. That spelled trouble, too.

The boy was inventive in finding methods of expressing himself. He wrote and mimeographed single-sheet newspapers, mildly scurrilous but lightened with humor. He drew cartoons of everyone around, which most of his subjects on the faculty regarded as highly talented. To the regret of the music director, who recognized a good tenor when he heard one, Pete quit the choir and put together something he christened The Wampus Players, a gathering of would-be actors organized more or less into a stock company, which was in keeping with what his father expected.

Faculty members asked him, "What's a wampus?"

"It's a mythical cat, very large like a dragon, and he doesn't do anything but eat fair maidens," Pete answered, his imagination ticking. The Wampus Players staged a rare performance in the dining hall of a forgotten work written, produced, and directed by their founder; most of the time they appeared only in advertisements in Pete's newspaper. (One staff member checked out their name in Webster's: a wampus is a wamus, and a wamus is a kind of cardigan.)

On a radio news bulletin Peter heard about his father's plans to marry again. Afdera was going to be the fourth Mrs. Fonda. Everybody in school got to hear about that, including The Gimp.

The next Sunday evening the master and the boy confronted each other in the corridor down which they both lived. The boy was upset to begin with, and, in retrospect, it was clear that the man had been drinking. He accused Peter of being late again in chapel.

"You think you can get away with it because you're Henry Fonda's son."

That was provocation. Peter refused to accept the rebuke. He began to protest, but he had to shout to make himself heard. "What's more, you're an atheist," yelled The Gimp.

"I'm closer to whatever God is than you can ever hope to be," screamed Peter.

By this time the whole corridor was listening. The boy, shaking with tension, and the man, lost to reason or restraint, flung insults at each other for what seemed to be hours. Then The Gimp returned to his favorite hate.

"Anybody who's been married all those times has got to be a son of a bitch."

It is likely that somewhere in the course of the endless, impossible ruckus Peter's memory blanked out. Once, talking about the events of that evening, he said, "He had crossed me on a personal level, man, so I slugged him, knocked him out cold." His father had to be defended, Peter said, and, equally important, what he saw as The Establishment had to be shown that there were limits to his tolerance.

But the knockout punch, which became woven into the legend of Captain America, was never delivered. It could not have been. The Gimp was a husky adult, Pete a trembling sixteen-year-old. What happened was that another master, new to the school and conscious of the boy's situation, broke in to end the uproar and escorted The Gimp back to his apartment.

When Henry Fonda learned about the slugging match in the corridor, he wrote again to the school, possibly the most telling of all the letters. He was calm, rational, just. He could not be proud, he said, of his record in marriage. Nevertheless, it was completely unfair for his son to be harassed because of it. He let it go at that, without calling down his wrath on the offending English master. But the incident was one of many that convinced the authorities of Westminster that The Gimp was unfit to teach there. Not much later he was dismissed.

Peter went down to New York to serve as his father's best man. Jane came from Vassar, and Hank's sister Jayne came from California, with her husband, John Schoentgen.

A New York State judge performed the ceremony before a handful of people in the house on East Seventy-fourth Street. Afdera, married for the first time at twenty-four, had to forego a honeymoon for the time being, because Hank had one more week of work on a picture he was making in New York.

Pete told him things were getting rough at school. Hank said, "You want me to take you out?" Peter said no; he'd try to make things work.

That proved to be a gallant, vain effort. The boy had needs that most of his masters recognized then as they do now in retrospect; but they lacked the means of reaching him, and he concluded that they resented him.

Toward the end, there was a degree of desperation in his attempts to win the regard of his schoolmates in much the same way that Hank apparently was universally admired. Organized outings into Hartford, fifteen miles away, provided an occasional treat for the students. One Sunday excursion took a busload of boys to a Harry Belafonte concert. They returned to the bus after the show, and Pete spotted a group of zoot-suited blacks strolling on the sidewalk.

He yelled some juvenile insult at them, in the desire to show off to his peers. Two or three of the blacks closed in on the bus, jeering. More of the boys joined in with new insults. Before the bus pulled away, some of its windows had been smashed in the start of a street brawl.

Trouble on this scale demanded an inquest among the Westminster staff. Who was to blame? What should the punishment be?

Ill health had compelled "Prof" Milliken to hand over the reins of the school to his former deputy, Pete Keyes, a Harvard man of diametrically different philosophy. A bit belatedly, Westminster was rapidly catching up with the times. The carrying of bricks and logs was no longer condoned as the penalty for wrongdoing. Sixth-formers had lost their privilege to paddle juniors; Peter in fact is remembered by the sixth-former who made him bend over to be swatted as the last boy ever to be paddled. The school was entering into a period of deep self-questioning as a prelude to major changes.

Probing into the causes of the bus incident went on for hours. The verdict reached by the factulty was that Peter was innocent; the school itself was guilty for not having indoctrinated its students in the rights of man, black and white. To make the punishment fit the crime, the masters decreed that the full day's holiday awarded during each term, which they looked forward to as much as the boys, should be given up. The reasons were explained in assembly.

"As a result of what Pete started in the bus, we really took a hard look at ourselves and began to make some progress," said one of the men involved.

Peter Fonda's adult memories of the event did not include that thought. "Then I got in a fight on a bus and they made me the scapegoat and I really flipped out . . ."

The final parting, the withdrawal of Pete from Westminster by agreement between the school and Hank, was as quiet as the wedding had been. He wasn't kicked out. Both sides agreed to a cease-fire. He felt he left with a certain amount of dignity.

He could think of no one else to turn to but Jane. He telephoned her at Vassar and told her he needed help. The following day she arrived in a station wagon and discovered him lurking in the shrubbery, talking to a dog. "Oh, wow," she exclaimed, according to Peter, "I think you're Holden Caulfield." He was not impressed with that comparison with J. D. Salinger's anguished protagonist in *The Catcher in the Rye*.

The newly married Fondas were on a delayed honeymoon in Europe. One of the highlights of the trip was a suggestion made to Hank, which did not work out, that he might add to the list of his movie portrayals of American heroes by playing the young Franklin D. Roosevelt, with Greer Garson as Eleanor, in Dore Schary's *Sunrise at Campobello*, a sentimentalized account of how the President-to-be caught polio in 1921.

In their father's absence, Jane put Peter on a train to Omaha, to stay with their Aunt Harriet, Mrs. Jack Peacock. Though Afdera was on record as wanting children, nobody who knew her regarded her as a motherly type. They called her charming, effervescent, a darling, a madcap, but home-making was not a specialty of hers.

As soon as he turned up at the Jack Peacocks, he was told that he should go back to school. "I'm not going any place, man; you're crazy," was his reply. He firmly believed that they regarded him as a confirmed liar. Frances had committed herself to a mental institution. "My aunt was afraid I would end up in one, too."

Without contact with Westminster, something had to be done to discover what Pete might amount to as a student. That made sense to him. He agreed, at length, to go to the University of Omaha in order to be tested. The dean of Liberal Arts, Dr. William Thompson, was also a psychologist. He ran every kind of test on Pete—scholastic achievement, intelligence, personality evaluation.

The boy thought some of the tests were meaningless, so he walked out of the examination room. But the results impressed Dr. Thompson. When Hank flew in from France, the two of them sat and talked on the sofa in the Peacocks' living room. "Your son," said the psychologist, "has an IQ of 160. He shouldn't go back to high school. He is equipped to be a college sophomore."

One requirement was missing: a high school graduation certificate. Close to the end of a school year, Pete could not be fitted into the public school system with any hope of graduating. The alternative was to enroll him in the only private school available, Brownell Hall, an Episcopalian establishment for girl boarders, founded in 1863. The misfit from Brunswick, Fay, and Westminster thought it was "really neat." He graduated without difficulty in a matter of months. Now that he could be fitted more conventionally onto the educational assembly line, he took entrance exams and went straight into the university, with Dr. Thompson keeping an eye on him, like many others, in his father's home town.

With the population count bouncing up toward half a million people, Omaha was still a small town at heart, homey, friendly, inquisitive. Crops and cattle set the tone and made most of the money, though new motels and new industries, like aerospace, were coming along fast. Hank was looked on as an institution, like the annual rodeo held at Ak-Sar-Ben Field on the corner of Sixty-third and Shirley. In Nebraska, he blends into the scenery.

"Daddy's more like an Omaha bookkeeper than a distinguished actor," his daughter said at the start of her career.

The town, conservative and staid, respected him and looked on his chequered married life as the kind of human weakness you probably had to expect in a fellow who had done so well for himself as a movie star. Jane, in subsequent years, when she got into politics, met no similar tolerance. She was identified in the minds of most townspeople as a ranting radical and was accordingly anathematized by them.

Pete fell somewhere between the two extremes. Omaha watched to see what he would make of himself and how things would work out for him. It was much in his favor that he lived with his Aunt Harriet and Uncle Jack, who was a highly regarded executive in a local department store. The social stratum of the Peacocks, with Aunt Harriet busy in respectable causes, gave Pete automatic credentials.

He appeared to be growing up along much the same lines as his father had, with the difference that there was money to spare in this generation. He wore an Ivy League haircut to satisfy Hank. The sweaters and slacks and jackets were casual but gentlemanly, like his father's.

It was an almost impenetrable disguise. Underneath it, the insecurity that came from existing in the older man's shadow continued. "When you are the son of a famous father, there is a great deal of resentment," Peter says. "I think I was resented by everyone." It might have been worse in Omaha than anywhere else. "There was a certain crowd always jeering at me."

A father's fame bothers daughters less than sons. What he is means less than what he does. Jane's portrait of herself at the time of Hank's marriage to Afdera has her sneaking off from Vassar for another unauthorized weekend and finding that her absence had been noticed.

"So I called up the house fellow, the professor who was like a don in the dormitory, and I was crying. But before I got a chance to say I was sorry, he said he understood my father had just remarried for the fourth time and that I was emotionally upset. And I wasn't. I'd just gone away with a boy for the weekend."

Two months after the marriage, at the end of her second year, she left Vassar for good in 1957. In a sense, she was homeless. Hank and her new stepmother were spending most of that summer in Europe. There would be nothing for her to do if she joined Peter in Omaha. In every sense, she was uprooted, nineteen years old, with no definable ambition except to get out and away.

She had one ability, picked up from her father, which she hadn't really worked at; it might be worth trying for lack of something better to do. From the time she was in kindergarten in Brentwood, she had liked to paint. The subjects she chose were similar to his—still lifes—things, not people.

She asked Hank if she might go to Paris and study painting. He left the choice up to her, in line with his belief that anyone's big decisions must be made alone, and she was old enough for that. In the motley set she mixed with in Manhattan, the rumor inevitably spread that she was going to Paris for an abortion—and France was perhaps the most difficult country in the western world to obtain such illicit medical attention.

With the stirred-up mixture of audacity and doubt that began to show in everything she did, she moved in with a French family. Eager to accomplish a lot in little time, she enrolled in two art schools simultaneously, the Académie Grande Chaumière and the Académie Julian. She was no better equipped for the experience than a chick pecking its way out of its shell.

Afraid that everyone was secretly criticizing her fumbling efforts to paint, she gradually gave up going to classes and, instead, looked for consolation in the bars and backstreet antique shops of the Left Bank. "After a month I was sleeping more and studying less."

Among the men of renown in France in 1957 was a freethinker who had long since dropped the Russian name he was born with because "Plemiannikow" was too difficult to pronounce, and he liked to be talked about. Roger Vadim had tried his hand at acting when he was sixteen, then at journalism three years later. Then he had switched from writing for newspapers to writing for the movies, and now here he was, with the first picture he had directed already a year old but still unreleased outside France because censors disapproved of it.

What lingered in their minds after a screening of *And God Created Woman* were views of the unadorned undulating derrière of a bouncy blonde known professionally as Brigitte Bardot, otherwise Madame Vadim, photographed mainly on location in blazing Mediterranean sunshine at St. Tropez. It should be recalled that, in the moralistic 1950s, the standards of Hoolywood censorship limited even the depth of a plunging neckline, as well as the duration of a screen kiss.

Vadim described himself as a naturalist whose "main stab has been at middle-class morality." Box-office receipts were interesting to him, too. His picture had made an instant superstar—the "sex kitten" in public-relations language—out of the hitherto unknown Bardot. The sheer volume of her flesh that was displayed made it impossible to assess her acting talents.

With an ex-journalist's eyes, ears, and nose for news, Vadim was not unhappy when the release of his film happened to coincide with rumors that his marriage was breaking up as a result of Bardot's relationship with the leading man. By this time he had found another protégée, a young Danish actress named Annette Stroyberg, almost a replica of Brigitte. They made a striking couple on their excursions around Paris, the lean, lupine director with the thick library glasses and the dazzling, obviously *enceinte* blonde. They also made tantalizing copy wherever newspapers were sold, from the rue des Capucines to Times Square.

Jane has told of their first meeting in Maxim's. "He was with Annette Stroyberg, who was very pregnant with — well, my stepdaughter, and I'd only heard the bad things about him. How he was a cynical, vicious, immoral, Svengali-type character. I was very aggressive because I'd only heard the legend."

In December, the Vadims' divorce was confirmed. On the following day, Annette gave birth to her daughter. Jane went home for Christmas.

Hank was back at work in the theater, going through agonies with a play in which he felt consistently cheated. He had been suffering with it for the past six months. So had everyone within range of his discontentment. He liked the script of *Two for the Seesaw* well enough to put up $20,000 to own 25 percent of the production. Its attraction lay partly in its story line about a middle-aging attorney from Omaha on the verge of being divorced by the wife he loves, who finds a new life with a girl from the Bronx. His contract guaranteed him $2,500 a week against 15 percent of gross receipts for the term of six months, and his life, as the star of the show, was insured for $225,000. But right from the start, when he read the script, he insisted that the role of Jerry Ryan, the man in this two-character play, was underwritten and needed some shoring up to avoid being swamped by the girl, Gittel Mosca.

The author, William Gibson, who in twenty years of trying had yet to have a play produced on Broadway, agreed. The job of adding dimension to Jerry Ryan began. Gibson hadn't really wanted Hank in the first place, on the grounds that he was "too straightforward" and perhaps too old. Gibson's original choice had been Richard Widmark. Later attempts were made to get hold of Jack Lemmon, Paul Newman, Richard Basehart, Jack Palance, Barry Nelson, Eli Wallach, Don Murray, Fritz Weaver, and one or two others. None of them proved to be available. As soon as Hank was signed, the rest of the necessary fund-raising was easy.

As Gibson related in his own disillusioned version of the behind-the-scenes crises that plagued every step of the road to Broadway, one businessman, who enthusiastically came in as a backer, said, "That star and that script, I got a hard-on for that show." With Fonda's name on the contract, the production was rapidly oversubscribed. *Two for the Seesaw* was one of the hottest properties in years.

On a trip back to New York in midsummer, Hank had invited Gibson and the unknown actress who was to play Gittel around to Fonda's house on East Seventy-fourth Street so that he could hear her read the part. He thought Anne Bancroft—whose name had worked its way up the list of candidates for leading lady, passing Gwen Verdon, Julie Harris, Kim Stanley, and Lee Grant en route—was perfect for the role.

"You couldn't ask for anyone better," said Hank at the end of a patient afternoon slumped on a sofa, wearing his horn-rimmed spectacles to read with. Anne Bancroft was accordingly put under contract at $550 a week, with a proviso that she could be fired after four out-of-town performances if she proved unsatisfactory.

Everyone concerned acknowledged that Hank, by accepting a role that a dozen other leading men had declined, had rescued the play from probable abandonment. The trouble came when he began to "baby up" to the role of Jerry and found there wasn't much to baby up to.

"I always know when it feels real to me," he consistently says, and Jerry Ryan puzzled him. "He has too many complexes," said the man who had reduced all his own complexes to a surface simplicity, as the sea smooths rocks into pebbles.

Gibson agreed that the Jerry Ryan role was deficient. In his inevitably partisan account, called *The Seesaw Log*, he concluded, "In my view Hank's style, which I respected, and that of the role, in those attributes where it had my respect, were not compatible; their marriage was one to which I had given a relucatant blessing on the brink."

He wrote and rewrote again; Hank and Jerry Ryan remained poles apart. Rehearsals began, at the standard scale of sixty-five dollars a week apiece for Fonda and Bancroft. He spent sleepless nights of worry, trying to make his endlessly rewritten lines his own, then endured days of thrashing things out with Gibson, who promised that Fonda would not be allowed onstage with a single line to speak unless he felt it was comfortable to deliver and true to the character.

Fonda, the instinctive, self-taught star, aged fifty-two, was odd man out when Arthur Penn, the soft-spoken young director who coincidentally was a friend of Gibson, got to working with Anne Bancroft. At twenty-six, she was a graduate of Lee Strasberg's Actors' Studio, whose gods are Sigmund Freud and that reluctant Bolshevik, Konstantin Stanislavsky. Penn spoke her language; Hank came from a different heritage.

In his book, an ounce of inspiration was worth a gallon of the soul-searching preparation taught by Strasberg as the essence of The Method, and he couldn't find much inspiration in Jerry. What Fonda had in abundance was stage presence or "star quality." The first time he walked on to the rehearsal stage, he literally dazzled the company.

"He stalks that stage like a stallion," murmured Arthur Penn. Gaby Rodgers, who understudied Anne, thought he was the most elegant man she had ever seen. But on the twenty-first day of rehearsals, he still felt his character was alien, no matter what Penn said to him. "I don't want to be *told* it's good, I have to *feel* it's good," he answered.

"It doesn't play, it doesn't *go*," he told Penn. "I know this as well as I know anything in my life. I wish I could show you how, boy."

By Thanksgiving Day they were continuing to rehearse. Gibson arrived bearing a bottle of Jack Daniel's as a gift for Hank. He found him sitting alone offstage. He received a "wan smile of thanks." At that rehearsal, held in private in a Forty-second Street theater before a crowd of other actors, "Hank seemed in a retreat of distaste, from the audience and from the role," as Gibson remembered. That is a special Fonda response to unpalatable situations on and off the stage. Directors who have worked with Jane recognize it in her, too.

One week later, *Two for the Seesaw* opened at the Shubert Theater in Washington, D.C. Hank passed up all invitations to dine with others in the company and stayed in his dressing room until the curtain went up. He played Jerry in such low key that he could scarcely be heard. When the curtain fell, he went back to his dressing room, to sit hunched up at his makeup table. By and large, the Washington critics liked what they saw, but they thought *Two for the Seesaw* needed more work.

Gibson took to his hotel room in a state of clinical anxiety for days of rewriting. "I saw no way out of our dilemma," he reported later. "Hank could not play what I wrote, and I could not write what he played." With Afdera, Hank was staying in a suite in the same hotel, struggling to learn a part that was changed for virtually each of twenty performances, trying to make his kind of sense of it, debating whether he was so miscast as to be trapped in a tedious flop. Gibson and he kept to their own separate quarters.

A review in *Variety* almost precipitated the end. It praised Anne Bancroft, while it criticized Fonda and the play. Hank wondered whether *Two for the Seesaw* should get get rid of him. The producer, Fred Coe, wondered whether Hank should get rid of *Two for the Seesaw*. "Thirty-nine angels danced on the point of this pin," sayd Gibson, "since if we separated from Hank we were liable for his contract, but if he separated from us we were not."

No separation took place, but Gibson sat in a Pullman car continuing to work on first-act rewrites when the company rode the train to Philadelphia. The play opened at the Forrest Theater on December 26. The reviews were definitely more enthusiastic, but Hank was still wrestling with Jerry Ryan and one time, at yet another rehearsal, looking as though he might do battle with Fred Coe.

"I had watched men more harrowed by daily misery," Gibson related, "but not outside of walls and responsibly functioning; I thought the price his soul was paying for this piece of entertainment was exorbitant for anything short of paradise, and his stamina in continuing was laudable."

A visitor to his dressing room asked Hank whether he felt more comfortable in his role. Not one moment onstage felt comfortable, he replied. Then what made it worthwhile? Was it money? No amount of money could make it worthwhile, said Hank.

This was the Christmas when Jane came home from France, recalled by her father, who didn't much care for what he heard about how she was spending her time there. He wasn't an easy man to fool. He had a shrewd idea about how things were with her in Paris.

IX

ON THE JANUARY morning a few hours before the opening of *Two for the Seesaw* on Broadway, William Gibson was still at work on the script, cutting lines from the third act. Hank, he reported, "was freezing me out." Unless the first-night audience at the Booth Theater took to the play, it would be dead, with Fonda's $20,000 gone down the drain along with every other backer's investment. The show was already $14,000 in the red.

Judging by the cheers and curtain calls when that opening-night performance ended, nobody had to worry, but what the newspaper critics had to say would be the determining factor. After taking his bows that night, Hank didn't bother to wait around or go to the party at the apartment of the producer's agent with the rest of the company. Instead, he went straight home to East Seventy-fourth Street, where Fred Coe telephoned him as soon as the first reviews came in.

"His most limpid and moving performance," said Brooks Atkinson in *The Times*, the first notice to arrive. "What he does not say in the dialogue, he says with the silent eloquence of a fine actor. . . . soft, shining acting."

The next morning, the line of ticket-buyers waiting in the cold at the box-office window stretched down the block.

The play was a smash hit that broke all records in the theater's forty-five years of history. Hank could scarcely care less. Three days later, he caught influenza and was out for a week.

"He would have no part of the praise," said Gibson, winding up his account of their battles, "or so I heard at second hand, respecting his wish that I not visit his makeup room—and the half year until his contract released him saw no dilution of his dissatisfaction." His share of income from the play paid him more than $4,000 a week.

Jane stayed at home with her father and stepmother, undecided over what she should make of herself. She had nowhere else to go. She had only one ambition forming inside, but she fought it down.

In New York and later in East Hampton, Long Island, Afdera flew at a social altitude that left some of Hank's friends gasping for breath.

"While they were married, however," one friend has said, "you'd think Fonda was having the best time of his life."

She engaged two Italian servants, lured away from ambassadorial employment. She had their house on East Seventy-fourth Street redecorated in fine Italian style, with frescoes around the living-room fireplace. House guests, usually her fellow countrymen, wandered in and out. Dinner guests flocked to the place, which turned up in photographs for *Vogue* as an example of what money can do to transform a home.

Leland Hayward went to one dinner party and related, "For dessert they had ice cream and chocolate sauce. There was dancing, and all of a sudden those nutty Italians began throwing ice cream and sauce on the walls. I thought Hank would commit murder. But he just stood there and smiled and enjoyed it."

She antagonized his old friends by her dominating possessiveness, her insistence on their doing what she wanted. Bored with the company at one New Year's Eve party, for example, she dragged him away well before midnight because she wanted to dance at El Morocco.

The size of the bills that arrived sometimes disturbed Fonda. "There's one thing that seems to drive him crazy," another regular guest said, "and that's spending too much money. She was probably spending a bloody fortune."

To fill in time and avoid making decisions about herself, Jane started to study French and Italian at the Berlitz School. From her bedroom window she could hear students practicing at the Mannes College of Music, a few doors up the street. One morning, to kill a few hours in each week, she enrolled there to study piano.

"But it was too frustrating. I wanted to jump in and start playing concertos instead of studying scales."

She took up painting again, working her way down the list of pastimes for a young woman of her social station, and went to classes at the Art Students League on West Fifty-seventh Street. But she ran into a problem that her father always avoided by insisting on teaching himself: the more she learned, the less she was satisfied with the result.

She resisted the growing urge to become an actress. The impulse to follow Hank had to be quelled somehow, she thought, or she would never be able to emerge from his shadow. She drew up mental lists of why she ought not to act as a career. It was too egotistical a way of life. It was self-centered and selfish. She was too insecure to have people watch her. She was too plain. Yet she turned up at friends' apartments at this time, gossiping excitedly about a "wonderful boy" she had met: "I want to marry him and have a family just like we had when we lived in California."

At every major turning point in her life, and she lists three to date, a curious phenomenon shows up in her habits. The change itself releases great bursts of energy in her. But its approach finds her like a girl in a Freudian fairy tale, asleep and haunted by bad dreams, weary of waiting for the magic to waken her. "I used to be tired all the time," she remembered, blaming that on lack of integration within herself.

Once she was riding in a car with Brooke Hayward and their families' friend, David O. Selznick. Brooke, a cool blonde with violet eyes, was already a model and something of a sensation in that business. Selznick thought she could go on to much bigger things as an actress.

"You're beautiful," he told her, "you're glamorous, you've got *star quality.* " Jane stored up her dismay. All she felt was awkward. But she longed to act. She would think about it and tremble.

To keep her mind off the subject that increasingly haunted her, she took on occasional jobs with or without pay. She worked briefly in the New York office of the *Paris Review,* which was more a nostalgic echo than the prestigious magazine it had been when Paris meant Hemingway, Dos Passos, and Gertrude Stein. But she was no writer. She became for a while a kind of Girl Friday to Warner Le Roy, whose father, Mervyn, had been one of the abundance of directors on *Mister Roberts.* Warner was developing a taste for directing in the theater, too.

With Jane, he'd drive out to Stamford, Connecticut, the next town up from Greenwich, to drop in on their friends the Logans at their house on Long Ridge Road. The encouragement she received from Mrs. Logan, a former actress and daughter of a playwright, Edward Harrigan, should have canceled out her reactions at hearing Selznick praise Brooke.

Nedda Logan looked at Jane one day. "I just can't help but say it—I don't know why you don't go on the stage. You're exactly made for it. You're so beautiful, and you speak so well. You've a bright brain. Everything about you makes me feel that you ought to be an actress." Logan agreed.

"It's the last thing in the world I'll ever do," Jane answered. "I promise you. It doesn't interest me whatsoever. I've had it up to here with my father and all of his friends. It just doesn't interest me." If "let's pretend" is the essence of acting, she was learning fast.

She stuck to her art classes. Confronting a stretched, blank canvas with a sable brush in her hand, she could be her own master with no need to please producers and directors, fellow actors and audiences. She didn't want to commit herself to anything more demanding than that. "An uptown beatnik," was the way one acquaintance described her, "not proficient in anything except the knowledge of where the parties were."

Her frame of mind had not changed the following summer, when she went to California with her father, who was riding the range again as a quick-on-the-trigger marshal in a "psychological Western" named *Warlock*. This put him back on the once despised Twentieth Century-Fox lot, but only on a single-picture contract.

He hadn't made a picture that pleased him in two years, not since *12 Angry Men*, which persists in his memory as one of his best. He liked Reginald Rose's television play about an all-male murder-trial jury well enough to try to find a studio to back a movie version of it. When he failed, he took the playwright in as coproducer and put up his own money.

12 Angry Men was shot in less than a month in New York for something more than $300,000. It earned respect from the critics immediately, but Hank imagined for years that it only just broke even at the box-office. Nevertheless, he was prouder of the movie than almost anything else he'd done in his career. For once, his pride was justly rewarded. Talking one day to his accountant, Charles Renthal, he mentioned that he had not profited by so much as a nickel from *12 Angry Men*. "What do you mean?" said the expert. "You've earned more from that than from any other picture you ever made."

Shooting it resulted in another friendship, with Sidney Lumet, chosen as its director though he hadn't previously made a a major movie. Largely as a favor to Lumet, Hank went into the young director's next picture. This was the one that had delayed the honeymoon with Afdera. *Stage Struck* saw him playing opposite Susan Strasberg, making her first movie after grabbing Broadway by the ears in *The Diary of Anne Frank*. Susan and Jane got to know each other. Another thread was spun on the loom.

In those days, Jane gave no hint that she would shortly be holding to politics with a passion. If she believed strongly in anything at all, she shared her father's left-wing liberalism, which had peaked out in the 1950s heyday of Joseph R. McCarthy, whom Hank detested. Now the witch-hunting Senator from Wisconsin had been dead for a year, and Fonda's political temper, which had him smashing a television set at the mention of the hated name, had cooled. None of the causes—American Indians, black liberation, Vietnam, women's rights—that later fired his daughter's soul had begun even to smolder in her.

Susan Strasberg, pale-skinned and intense, is the daughter of a couple who deserve some measure of immortality in the American theater for the controversy they have caused and the converts they have made to acting as a profession. Paula Strasberg, a drama coach, was the widely publicized molder of the career of Marilyn Monroe. Lee Strasberg, already recognized as the guru of the Stanislavsky Method, had been meditating on those lines when Hank first crossed his path nearly thirty years earlier. In Baltimore, where the University Players struggled to survive and Fonda was married to Sullavan, Strasberg was the director of a rival attraction, a production of the soul-searching Group Theater on its way to New York.

For the making of *Warlock*, the Fondas rented a beach house at Malibu, up the coast from Los Angeles. Their neighbors were the Strasbergs, who had also rented a place because Paula was coaching Monroe for *Some Like It Hot*. Jane and Susan, with little else to occupy them, sat on the yellow sand and talked.

Susan repeated what Nedda Logan had said. "Why aren't you an actress?"

This time the penny dropped. The options had run out for Jane. The fact that the suggestion came from someone in her own age group, not from her father's, may have helped. "And I finally thought, *Well, what the hell!* It was kind of like something to do."

Jane was "feeling sort of desperate." In a few more months she'd be twenty-one. At the end of the summer she would have to return to New York with Hank and Afedera. "None of the things I'd tried to do really satisfied me."

At Susan's suggestion, she telephoned Lee Strasberg for an appointment. Meeting the intense, soft-spoken impresario left her with the feeling that he was interested in her not because she was Hank's daughter, but strictly on her own account.

The techniques of The Method are very much Strasberg's own. He asked Jane to read nothing for him. The Stanislavsky technique judges traditional theater training as more of a burden than a help. Diction is infinitely less important than the internal boiling emotion the actor must feel in a role.

Strasberg probed her with questions. Why was she interested in the theater? What did she expect to achieve from it? Who was her favorite actress? Her responses were inconsequential. "The only thing that made me take you was your eyes," Strasberg told her afterward. "There was such a panic in the eyes." She believes he imagined that her interest was fitful and that she wouldn't last the course. But the first time she did an exercise for him, he told her, "You've got talent."

"That's all," she has recalled. "Somebody who was not a member of my family or a friend and who saw lots of actresses had to say, 'You've got talent,' and that was it. I went to bed excited about what I was doing, and I woke up and worked twice as hard as anybody else just so that nobody could say I was riding on my father's shirt-tails or apron or whatever. And it changed my life. Totally."

Sensations of panic are not uncommon among pupils on their introduction to The Method. One of their earlier tests is to be told to perform some act in public, in class, that they would normally only do in total privacy. When one of Hank's leading ladies was in her student days she accepted the challenge by simulating masturbation. Other young acolytes have gone through miming the routines of the toilet.

The avowed purpose of the exercise is to liberate the spirit, to destroy self-consciousness in the Method actor. Strasberg and other Method masters borrow heavily from Freudian analysis and teach introspection as part of the curriculum. They insist that the student must search for motivations inside himself, cross-examining his ego and dipping into his id.

"Creativeness," said Stanislavsky, "begins from that moment when in the soul and imagination of the actor there appears the magical, creative *if*, the imagined truth which the actor can believe as sincerely and with greater enthusiasm than he believes practical truth."

This was heady stuff, even as far back as Baltimore when Hank's generation was preoccupied with wondering where the next paycheck was coming from, while they speculated about what this guy in the Moscow Art Theater was all about. Strasberg had not deviated from what he regarded as the only true faith, though now he used a tape recorder at some sessions and his spoken instructions could be opaque.

Three weeks after their meeting Jane went back to New York and moved out of East Seventy-fourth Street. "I started studying with Lee, and I *flipped*. It was a whole new world."

She was wildly enthusiastic convert to the faith. "Talking to her," said an old friend, "was like having lunch with Billy Graham."

She tackled the business of learning to act at the same headlong pace that has marked her embarking on every other big cause she has found. It was the manner of a girl jumping off a diving board to teach herself to swim. The sensation of flying free liberated a flood of energy in her.

"I have never seen anyone involve herself so much," said Brooke. "She worked at it five days a week."

Between classes with Strasberg, which were held above the Capitol Theater on Broadway, she sped off to ballet and modern-dance lessons, took massages to ease her resulting aches, and debated undergoing professional psychoanalysis, which is not uncommon in students exposed to The Method.

"I figure this know-thyself business is very important for an actress," she said then. "Daddy's been married four times, and I don't think it's had any bad effects on me. But if I were analyzed, I might find out it had. And that would be useful to know, wouldn't it?"

The thought came straight from Strasberg, who as an amateur psychiatrist was probing to discover the "real" Jane Fonda under the layers produced by a secluded childhood, the death of her mother, the proper schooling, the impeccable good manners. He told her that she hid behind a mask of pretense. Unless she could peel it off, she would never amount to much as an actress.

As part of the breakaway from her father, she had to make herself financially independent. She had no knowledge of earning a living. Her twenty-second birthday was around the corner, and she fancied that she had been badly spoiled.

But money would be needed to pay the rent. With her Vassar friend Susan Stein, she found a little duplex apartment one block away from Hank's town house, a choice that carried with it a certain symbolism. They furnished it with antiques, borrowed from Jules Stein's opulent New York offices, where he ran Music Corporation of America, which included Hank among its clients. Two Siamese cats rounded out their establishment.

Applying proper Vassar standards to the situation, she and Susan agreed on exactly how they should coexist. "We lead separate lives and communicate in the bathroom every two weeks. Ideal roommate arrangement."

With no business experience or salable commercial skills, Jane took a leaf from Brooke's leather-bound portfolio of model shots and offered her services to the Ford Agency, one of the top three houses of its kind, with walk-up premises on Second Avenue. She wasn't precisely a tyro, because as an uptown socialite she had posed earlier that year for a fashion layout in *Town and Country*, a magazine Afdera was familiar with.

Eileen and Jerry Ford were happy to register her. "She struck us as a terribly nice, intelligent, unusually conscientious girl, who seemed to know exactly what she wanted," said Mrs. Ford, a top-flight model herself before she and her husband started the agency. "One of the things I remember she wanted was justice for American Indians. She talked about that now and then."

Assignments came swiftly as soon as the word spread that Jane Fonda was modeling at fifty dollars an hour. One reason, which she accepted as inevitable, was that photographers and their clients among magazine editors and advertising agencies were eager to get a look at her simply because she was Hank's daughter.

Fifty dollars was close to the top rate, earned by the highly Simonized glamour princesses like Suzy Parker. Jane lacked their often worldly affectations, but she made up for that with her air of direct, disarming honesty. At Condé Nast, for instance, she caused some fluttering when, in the course of changing into the clothes she was to be photographed in, she pulled off her sweater unconcernedly; she was among the pioneers of the bra-less look, but not without wavering. A year or so later she was talking self-consciously over the need to wear a padded bra. "I never liked my figure."

Within six months of working, she had achieved a grand slam of appearing simultaneously on the covers of four national magazines. Two others followed later in that brief, meteoric chapter.

The success she found as a model astonished her. She had always felt like an ugly duckling, awkward, overweight, with a face she would gladly have exchanged for another. The slim, graceful girls who floated in and out of the Ford Agency still impressed her as being infinitely superior to herself, but she *did* get a lot of bookings, so it must be that photographers were looking for more homely models than the Suzy Parkers and Dorian Greys.

When the first cover for which she had been photographed appeared on the July 1959 *Vogue*, she tried a private experiment to see what people who bought the magazine might think of the girl in the sleek sheath dress who seemed like a stranger to Jane. She took to haunting newsstands, watching the customers' faces. She was quite pleased with Irving Penn's photography. It made her look pretty. Six months later, the experience was repeated.

And then modeling ended as abruptly as it had begun. The Fords were sorry to see her go. Apart from her instant success, they were impressed by her impeccable good manners. "She was one of the very few girls to find time to write to us, thanking us for what we helped her do," said Eileen Ford.

The slowly increasing self-confidence she was somehow acquiring from Strasberg and his associates earned tangible dividends, though acting struck her as an alarmingly painful business, requiring you to behave in a way that, in other people's cases, sometimes qualified them for admission to a padded cell.

Mythology has it that she got her feet wet as a professional actress because Joshua Logan happened to spot her on the cover of a fashion magazine. Reality wasn't quite like that.

Nedda remained intrigued with Jane, even more so when she saw the lightning turnabout in her attitude toward acting. "You've got to find a part for her," she told her husband. "I started her. I made her do all this—"

"You didn't do any such thing," he said. "She just did it on her own."

Through his own company, he had a contract to make three pictures for Warner Brothers. He wanted a warm-up before he launched himself into the major production he was to undertake, *Fanny*, with Maurice Chevalier, Charles Boyer, and Leslie Caron. The studio handed him *Parrish*, the Mildred Savage novel about tobacco farming under cloth in the Connecticut River Valley, the region, incidentally, where Westminster School was located.

For the leads in *Parrish*, Logan had in mind two unknowns—his goddaughter Jane and a husky young man he had under contract for seven years, Warren Beatty. He also signed Jane to a five-year contract. When the script was finished, Josh had a change of heart; as producer and director, he didn't see how it could be successfully filmed. So he turned to another property owned by Warner Brothers. *Tall Story* was a play by Howard Lindsay and Russel Crouse, based on Howard Nemerov's novel, *The Homecoming Game*, which dealt with the days when it was a novelty for college basketball teams to be approached by gangsters to throw a match. He simply switched Jane and Warren into that story.

But the studio persuaded him that he had to have at least one more recognizable performer. He was offered Tony Perkins, well known to Logan who had once worked with his father, actor Osgood Perkins. "I grew very fond of Tony. The only thing I resent is that had I kept Warren

Beatty, I wouldn't have had to produce anymore—I could have just managed him."

Jane tested for the part of June Ryder, a college cheerleader, in an assortment of hairdos and makeups. When she saw the tests, she was in utter despair. "I look," she said, "like a squirrel with nuts packed into its cheeks." She wanted her puppy-plump face to be as lean as Marlene Dietrich's—or her father's.

"She went on a diet, and I don't think she ate for ten weeks," Logan recalls. "She was, from the very beginning, passionately involved, with her looks, with the way she acted, everything, just as if she'd been in the same mood all her growing years."

The picture was made in a hurry. It lacked all distinction, but it put Jane, instant professional, on public view at last. *Life* called Hank, who was in the middle of making a somewhat mysterious movie with Leslie Caron called, without a trace of irony, *The Man Who Understood Women*. No, the editors didn't want to put him on the cover; they wanted some baby snapshots of his daughter.

"My first reaction," she gushed in a subsequent interview, "was 'How *dare* they do that to him?' But he didn't mind. He was pleased. I bet if he'd been a famous *actress* he would have had some hostile reaction, like being jealous or something."

She leaped with both feet into the intoxicating chores of gossiping with reporters, who tended to ask the same standard questions that have been fired at young starlets since the time of Pearl White. Yes, she intended to get married, but only once. No, she had nobody in mind at the moment.

"I'd like to have a child now," she told one interviewer, "but I don't want a husband yet, so that's out. I think it's good to be a young mother. I was brought up by a very young stepmother, and it was wonderful."

No, money wasn't especially important to her. "I simply don't have this obsession with power or money or jewels, the stuff that causes trouble. One of my closest friends is the most mercenary girl I ever met. She absolutely *quivers* at the sight of diamonds. Not me. I make a lot of money right now, and I spend it foolishly—mostly on taxis, I guess. I loathe walking, but maybe if I found the right man I wouldn't even mind that."

California? She preferred New York. "I think you dream better dreams, you *feel* more, in a cold climate." Happiness? "It's a wonderful feeling when you finally find out where you're going. You're happier. You're more productive. You're *nicer*. Whether I'll make it is something else again, but at least I'm finally *channeled.*"

Now and then, she hinted at more serious things, which show up in the transcripts like intimations of the past and future. "I kept my own name because I'm proud of it, and I'm not afraid of being my father's daughter. But let's face it: if my name weren't Fonda, it would have taken me years longer. Contacts can get you there, but they won't keep you there. I'm planning to stay on my own."

She would talk briefly about her childhood as being happily spent with Peter in Brentwood. "It's scary, what's going to happen now. Hollywood can do funny things to people. Once you start playing the game as though it's for real, you're done for. But Daddy's always around. And the minute I start forgetting it's just a game, I guarantee he'll remind me."

Much of the time, to satisfy reporters, she talked about men, a favorite subject in press interviews. "Actors are so *boring.* It's very important for a young actress to have men around her. So many actresses," said the girl who had been one for six months, "tend to forget they're women, and most actors are so self-centered they don't have time to remind them."

Men and marriage, or its equivalent, continued to provide good interview copy for years. She made a point of being quotable in the interests of public relations. "Hollywood's wonderful—they pay you for making love," she said to the syndicated columnist, Earl Wilson. She outraged the puritanical Hedda Hopper by telling her that "marriage is obsolete."

In point of fact, she was as skittish as a new-born colt when it came to flesh contact. Tony Perkins remembers their meeting for the first time in Logan's apartment. "There was a photographer there, and he wanted publicity pictures of us necking on the divan. Well, Jane kind of turned pale. It was her first encounter with one of the absurdities of this business, and it was as if she said to herself, 'Well, are you up to it? Is it worth it?' You could see her draw a deep breath and say to herself, 'So okay. Is this what being an actress involves? Well, I guess it is. Let's go.' "

On the set, she was a study in concentration, deadly earnest in learning all she could about a new turn in her life.

Logan had nothing but praise for her work. "When she had to be funny, she was funny. When she had to be touching, she was. Tony Perkins was very good, too, though in *Tall Story* there wasn't anything really to be very good about. I'm not sure it was one whit better than *Parrish* would have been."

Since his enthusiasm for her soared, Perkins asked Logan, "Can we work out our scenes together without having to rehearse them in front of anybody else?" Josh gave him that opportunity to direct, and those scenes were photographed as Tony wanted them. Logan imagined that his leading man was having a wonderful time. Years later, in a television interview, Perkins named *Tall Story* as the movie he disliked the most because, "It was so slow; the scenes between Jane and I were endless."

Jane thought differently. It was impossible to escape the stereotyped feeling to which every actor and actress succumbs to some degree at the sight of his name in lights. It

happened to her on Forty-second Street. "JANE FONDA
—TALL STORY," it said on a moviehouse marquee. "I felt
proud," she reported simply.

If, as she said, she found actors boring, she had other
feelings about some of the members of Strasberg's circle.
She gave the strong impression that she was unsure of her
sexuality, contrary to her account of wild weekends spent
A.W.O.L. from Vassar and the parties she went to as an
"uptown beatnik." One of the constant companions she
sought out was a gentle young man who also worked with
Strasberg. Each wanted to prove something to the other.
Similar relationships are not uncommon among young actresses who know they must project sexiness in varying
degrees in the roles they play although they may have
abiding doubts about themselves as women.

After *Tall Story*, Logan's next job was to direct *Fanny*. He
had signed no one for the title role. Leslie Caron had reservations about an American studio making a French classic.
Audrey Hepburn, after agreeing to do the role, had become
pregnant. Josh, delighted with Jane, tested her for the part
of the winsome charmer of Marseilles.

"She played Fanny on the screen with a slight French
accent, just enough to take off the edge of her American,
and she was absolutely lovely," he recalls. "I very seriously
thought of her doing it, until I felt, 'We mustn't bring in
an American girl. We can use Charles Boyer, who's been
in this country a long time, and Chevalier, whom they're
going to dislike enough anyway because he's Chevalier. But
a purely American girl—the French might stab me in the
back.' They stabbed me in the back, in any event. I should
have let Jane do it."

Before *Fanny*, Logan had a few months to spare. He
spent it directing the Broadway production of Daniel Tara-
dash's play, *There Was a Little Girl*. It interested him principally for sociological reasons. It was based on the premise
that when a crime is committed, the victim unjustly

becomes associated in the public mind with the criminal. The "little girl" of the title was raped and then compelled to leave home because she had been identified, in a travesty of morality, as a sexual tramp, even by her family.

By current standards, the theme was respectable enough, but in 1960, the subject was considered shocking, notably by Hank. His views of propriety in the theater had led him to insist on having some of his lines in *Two for the Seesaw* well laundered before he spoke them.

David Merrick, who read *There Was a Little Girl* not as the producer but as a friend of Logan's, advised him to steer clear of it. "You know what they're going to say? 'Here's Logan going mad with sex again.' "

Three days before Jane enthusiastically accepted her godfather's invitation to play the lead, Hank called her, begging her not to take on the role. She detected that he wanted to protect her from a potential disaster, but this was a star role in a Broadway play. How could she refuse it? She went into rehearsal with no fear of failure.

She fell in love with what she was working at, the feeling of belonging, molding herself to the role of a weak-willed girl, doing precisely what she wanted to do.

Almost unanimously, the newspaper critics excoriated *There Was a Little Girl.* When the company opened in Boston, only *Variety's* reviewer had anything good to say, and he raved about both the plot and the players. With that taste of encouragement, they moved on to Philadelphia, where the critics hit them over the head again.

So Hank had an idea of the fate of the play when it limped into New York. A party was arranged for the whole company at Sardi's after the opening, where the ever-hopeful men and women who had put their time and talent into a flop waited for the morning newspapers. He advised Jane to go straight home, as he would have done.

"Sardi's is a great place not to be when your show has just been panned," he says. "But she insisted, so I went, too. She has to make her own mistakes."

When the first reviews arrived, everyone within range turned to stare at the two Fondas. "The play was slaughtered," said Hank. "Jane's eyes crossed a little when she read them. Then she smiled at me. I knew then she was a real professional."

He wasn't alone in that knowledge. Logan had resolved not to read any bad notices, but he did read the New York *Daily News*, which concluded that "with the budding talent she displayed, she might become the Sarah Bernhardt of 1990." At the end of the season, when she had scored again in a better play, she won the New York Drama Critics Circle Award as the year's most promising actress. By then she was in the toils of psychoanalysis. Hank learned of that from a newspaper article.

"You need it," he told her bluntly, "like a hole in the head."

The profession of acting is symbolized by two masks, one of tragedy, the other of comedy. They are interchangeable. The Fondas' delight in what Jane had achieved that year was marred by death of a kind that runs as a countercurrent in everything they have achieved.

Margaret Sullavan had not appeared on Broadway for four years. The girl with an overflowing sense of laughter had changed into a sometimes moody and depressed woman, fearful for her health. She pleaded illness as the reason for withdrawing from her previous play, *Janus*. Her old courage had disappeared, together with her previous fiery ambition, the day she was scheduled to star in a Studio One drama for CBS and Westinghouse.

Then she took on a new play by Ruth Goetz, *Sweet Love Remembered*, with a leading man, Kent Smith, whose days as an actor dated back to hers in the University Players. It was trying-out in New Haven, at the Schubert Theater, before its scheduled Broadway premiere at the Billy Rose. In New York her eldest child, Brooke, had made her debut as an actress at the Gate Theater three days earlier.

On New Year's Eve 1959, she had trouble with her lines and her interpretation of her part. In the Taft Hotel, New Haven, that night, she grew more depressed and nervous about her problem. At 2 A.M., a local doctor was called. He made another visit later and left her, as he thought, calmer and resting.

When her husband and the play's coproducer, Henry Margolis, went to enter her room, the door was locked. They called the assistant manager, but his pass key would not open the door because it was chained from the inside. The next move in the routine of emergency was for the assistant manager to bring on the hotel engineer with a hacksaw to cut through the chain.

The first Mrs. Fonda was still breathing when Kenneth Wagg reached her. Not all the sleeping pills that the doctor had left her had been swallowed. But those she had taken added up to too many. She was pronounced dead on arrival at Grace-New Haven Hospital. It was New Year's Day of the year in which she would have reached her forty-ninth birthday, a time that can be a difficult age for most women, perhaps unusually difficult if you have been so much of a woman as Peggy Sullavan, once called the finest actress of one theatrical era.

The coroner ruled that the cause was accidental. Her closest friends saw no reason to disbelieve him. In all her moods, she had loved life.

Her daughter Bridget, whom Peter Fonda had loved as a friend since the childhood they spent together, wanted to be an actress too, to feel the exultation of "let's pretend" that makes reality seem unendurable by comparison. At twenty-one, she had survived the breakup of her parents' marriage, the remarriages of both of them, her mother's death.

Her father had a new wife now that Nan Gross Hawks, known to her friends as "Slim," was no longer Mrs. Hayward. The present Mrs. Hayward was Pamela Digby

Churchill, formerly the wife of Sir Winston's son Randolph. It was Bridget's father who found her body one Monday afternoon in September 1960, in her three-room East Fifty-fourth Street apartment. She was wearing night clothes, the police carefully noted. The last words she wrote, in the pitiful, trite phrase that faithfully serves the situation, echoed those of another woman she had known as a child. "This is the best way out," they said. One more of fortune's children had found the stress of reality too much to bear.

Peter Fonda was in town, out that night to see a Broadway show. When he got back to East Seventy-fourth Street, Hank surprised him by inviting him to sit and have a drink. That puzzled Peter at first, then Hank told him what had happened. "Poor Leland!" said one father, thinking of the other. Bridget was dead from an overdose of sleeping pills. The young man who had loved her couldn't understand Hank's attitude. "Adults!" murmured Peter to himself in scorn.

Jane had been told a few hours earlier. She was in Boston in a tryout of her second play of that year that saw her named its most promising actress. She sat in her dressing room with a blinding migraine, under sedation, sobbing with grief.

The play's author, Arthur Laurents, asked her, "You're afraid you may kill yourself, too, aren't you?"

Though Jane has denied the story, he insists that her answer that day was "Yes."

X

HE WAS identifiable by the little black beret, which he wore even when dining out, and the cigarette holder, which he handled with a Continental flourish. His cheeks were lean and his manner patronizing. Hank was only one of the people who disliked and distrusted him for his influence over Jane.

Andreas Voutsinas dominated her, which was not difficult to do, though she was taller by a head than he. "I guess I'm a kind of slave type," she said of that earlier era. He worked at the Actors' Studio as an assistant to Strasberg, and he specialized in escorting young actresses as their mentor and molder of personality. Anne Bancroft was one of them before he met Jane; so was Sandra Church. Faye Dunaway was a later interest of his.

His background was polyglot and as alien to Omaha as anything readily imaginable. He was born a Greek in the Sudan thirty years earlier, though he had the ageless look of a featured player in an Eric Ambler script. He had spent school years in England, and his home those days was a cold-water flat on West Forty-sixth Street.

The apartment on West Fifty-fifth Street into which Jane had moved was sybaritic by comparison, furnished in high camp, with a ruffled awning over the bed, lace pillowcases, and animal pelts, including a brace of rugs, a leopard, and a tiger with his fangs showing, given her by Voutsinas. On one wall hung a photograph of her mother and grandmother, with Peter and herself as children.

As a staunch advocate of The Method, Voutsinas combined some of the functions of coach and mentor in their relationship. They were sharing the same analyst, as one of the ties that bind.

In Boston, at the time of Bridget's suicide, Jane telephoned him every night. He was to have been an assistant to Arthur Laurents, who was the director as well as the author of *Invitation to a March*, but Laurents found him abrasive. "He destroys every friendship," said Laurents, who had formerly counted him as a friend.

As a woman, she was as withdrawn as her father ever had been, given to sitting alone in a leopardskin-print robe in the tiny onstage dressing room needed for a quick costume change she made. As an actress, she was superbly professional. Within five minutes of their first rehearsal meeting, an older actress, possibly resentful of her youth and rocketing reputation, hit her hard across the cheek. As an invitation to a cat fight, blows of this nature are not rare in the pangs and passions of rehearsing. Jane said and did nothing.

She took direction without protest, even when the cold Fonda stare showed her contempt for anything she regarded as out of place. She accepted the skin contact and a kiss on the mouth from her stage mother as a necessary bit of business, seeming sometimes to enjoy it as some sort of release from pent-up tension. But in a scene she played in a swimsuit, it was clear that she hadn't overcome being ashamed of her own body.

Some of the rehearsal problems could be traced to irreconcilable conflict between The Method, exemplified in the telephoned coaching by Voutsinas, and the traditionalist approach of Laurents, who considers the Actors' Studio to be "one of the most destructive forces for actors in the history of the theater." Jane clung to The Method, which preaches that a performer acts for herself first and for the audience only coincidentally.

She identified strongly with the part of Norma Brown, a girl, Jane reasoned, who was brought to life by a kiss of love, but Laurents's interpretation of his character did not coincide with hers. In rehearsal, Jane thought the reality of Norma was lost, and she came out like a Hollywood ingenue, "a funny painted poster of a girl."

Hank was in the audience for the Broadway opening. He went backstage, ecstatic when the performance was over. "I want to thank you," he told Laurents, "for making my daughter an actress."

Helen Hayes was backstage, too. Her son by Charles MacArthur, Jamey, was another member of the cast. The photographers came up with one of the stock ideas of their trade: a group picture of two generations of the theater, father and daughter, mother and son. Jane, looking as bland as the head girl in a genteel finishing school, refused to pose.

The most promising young actress on Broadway continued to feel a sense of letdown with the role and her handling of it. After the first night, the enthusiasm was somehow dissipated. Nevertheless, she was always the first member of the cast to arrive at the stage door every night at least two hours ahead of time, and missed only one appearance in the run.

Hank thought the play and her performance were both great, which was undoubtedly an additional, pettish reason for her dissatisfaction with both. Without knowing it, she picked up one of his habits when he is working in the theater. Before curtain time he is apt to go into one of the boxes and take a look at the audience until he sees a friendly face. She followed him in doing exactly the same.

The most important male in her life remained Voutsinas,

who had ambitions for himself and Jane that did not coincide with what her father had in mind for her. "Svengali"
was one of the kinder descriptions of Andreas frequently
used by those by those who knew about the relationship.
Hank preferred not to discuss him at all.

"Why don't you marry a nice Yale boy?" he once asked
her. Voutsinas did not qualify in any respect as that kind
of husband.

He confessed to one reporter that he had fantasies of
emerging as what he chose to call "the power behind the
throne." But he quickly amended his remark. "I can't be
that much of a Svengali. I really can't, you know. And I'm
hurt, very hurt, by her father's rejection of me."

With or without his influence, Jane felt the urge to put
greater distance between herself and Hank and most of the
people she identified with him. That involved, among other
things, terminating her exclusive contract with Josh Logan, which gave him the right under the terms of a not-
unusual clause to loan her out to work at his discretion.

He had been approached from another source with an
offer to buy that contract at a profit to himself. "It would
have meant quite a lot of money to me," he said, "and I
always have been very happy to get money because I have
the same desire to spend it as most people have, only mine's
a little bit more aggravated."

His reply to the offer was, "I'm absolutely not going to
do it unless Jane approves."

By this time, she was receiving several invitations to
perform, though she was by no means a star. She answered
Logan by saying, "For God's sake don't sell me. Let me buy
myself out."

It cost her $100,000. "As it turns out, it would have meant
a tremendous amount to me to keep her and force her to
keep the contract," Logan said. "But I knew exactly how
she felt. I would have been terribly depressed to have been
sold myself. I'm glad I gave her back to herself."

The following January she auditioned for the Actors' Studio; until then she had taken part only in Strasberg's private classes. Her father's enthusiasm for Strasberg wasn't a great deal stronger than for Voutsinas, though Strasberg, possibly on the same Jesuitical principle that the worst sinner can be converted into the best Catholic, has praised the self-taught Fonda as an actor "capable of roles of the most enormous challenge."

Method actors tend to discuss endlessly their tensions and needs and motivations the way that reformed drinkers talk about alcoholism. Hank was not in the least like that. In their polarized years Jane said, "My father can't articulate the way he works. I mean, I used to come home from Lee's classes so full of what I was doing, and my father would say, 'Shut up; I don't want to hear about it.' "

She remembered doing one scene in class that satisfied her stern standards to the point where "it was like I was on fifty benzedrines." One her way home, she bumped into Hank, and she told him about it as they rode in a taxi together. "And I could see his curtain come down. He smiled, but I just didn't get through."

His recollection was as different as in the case of her childhood memory of movie stars in cowboy suits playing cards with her father around a table in the Brentwood farm. He talked about it to Al Aronowitz, a sensitive and perceptive writer, over a bottle of Scotch in Fonda's house. There were tears in Hank's eyes.

"Maybe," he said, "I'm—maybe I do things that I'm not aware of that mean something to other people. I don't know what she means by a curtain coming down. It may be that I was trying to hide my own emotion, and in her it's the curtain coming down."

The incident went back to a day when she was with a young man who was just beginning as an actor, Hank said. "He and I were talking about using an emotion, having to feel an emotion in the theater. And I likened my reactions to an amphibious plane. There's a section on the underpart of the hull," said the expert builder of model aircraft, that is called the step, and although the plane is very sluggish, slow in the water, as it picks up speed it gets out on that step. And I used to feel if I could get myself going, I could get up on that step, and then nothing could stop me. Then all I had to do was to hold back, hold the reins, because I was going, I was soaring."

The man who could not communicate was doing well. "Anyway, it was maybe a year, years later, and I found myself in a cab with Jane going downtown, and Jane said, 'You remember the story that you told about soaring?' And she said, 'I know what you mean. It happened to me today.' Well, I can get emotional right now remembering Jane tell it, and probably the curtain came down to hide my emotion. Because for my daughter to be telling me about it— she knew what it was like! Well, I wasn't going to let her see me go like this."

"Why not?" asked Aronowitz. "Don't you understand she wants to get to you?"

Hank overlooked any impertinence in the question. "Well, gosh," he said. "She gets to me."

"I know, but she wants to know she's getting to you. She's surely a demonstrative person."

"Well, I'm not."

Aronowitz persisted. "Well, you're demonstrative with me. Why should you be demonstrative with a stranger and not with your own daughter? I just hate to see her upset by it."

"You can't just . . ." He started to say something, but then he stopped. "Is she upset?" he asked.

She had begun her career as a kind of girl next door, which is what audiences expected of her, since Hank had, too often for his liking, been the boy and then the man next door. But Voutsinas encouraged her to seek out something meatier than ice-cream roles as an ingenue. The next job she took was in a Columbia movie, *Walk on the Wild Side*, the best feature of which was its theme music. As Kitty Twist, a bratty, foxy prostitute in a New Orleans brothel run by a Lesbian madam, she was as unbelievable as the plot.

But Voutsinas quite liked to see her in such roles. On his own account, he imported a kinky British play and staged it in the Westport Playhouse one summer, hoping to proceed with it to Broadway, but it faded away en route.

He spoke of himself and Jane now as "we." He said, "When we were doing *Walk on the Wild Side*, she did makeup tests. So she saw the makeup tests, and she said, 'I hate them.' She doesn't like her cheeks; she doesn't like her cheekbones."

Of himself and Jane, he said, "All her other relationships they had been too quick. So as fast as the match burns, it goes out. We burn together slowly." Hank burned more rapidly when Voutsinas turned up, uninvited and unexpected, to gatecrash Peter's wedding party.

In Omaha, Peter, with the IQ that had been checked out at 160 and a visible super-ego, had found the reality of three years of classroom lectures no more fascinating than the rest of his schooling. To please his father and his aunt and uncle, the Peacocks, however, he kept up the disguise of a conformist, from Ivy League suits to the matching, sincere smile.

Reminiscing a little later about his college days, he related how Aunt Harriet had urged him to date "a chick" whose father was prominent in Omaha society, which is decidedly conservative and proud of being so. "Well, the only chick I ever knocked up was this chick, and I got it on the first date."

He did not return to the Peabodys' until near dawn. His aunt, he said, did not complain, because he had been out with "a nice girl," who, it turned out, was pregnant. She had to be sent to Puerto Rico. Lacking the money, he sold a shotgun he had been given as a Christmas present to raise five hundred dollars. "I bought my freedom from her."

When he had grown a little older, he corrected one of the impressions left by that account. "But I have cousins and aunts and uncles who are very kind and good to me whom I don't see enough. My father's sister and brother-in-law were especially important in my life. They really helped me."

At the University of Omaha, he found something he had been lacking through all the previous years of growing up —close friendship or, more precisely, a close friend, a soul brother, in Eugene McDonald, nicknamed Stormy. Stormy was a fellow student, son of the late president of the Zenith Radio Corporation, heir to a $30 million fortune, under the guardianship of the courts.

"He became my brother," Peter said soon after he quit college. "He gave me my philosophy: Above all else, be true to yourself. Everybody who's been in contact with me knows Stormy."

Stormy remained at the university when Peter bought an old Ford out of the three hundred dollars he had saved and headed East to become an actor just as his father had. He was a year short of graduation when he joined a summer stock company.

He was already involved in acting without any pushing from Hank, who had gone to see his son play the lead in a university production of *Harvey*. He looked more like a young Byron than the disarming alcoholic with hallucinations about a giant rabbit. But his astonishing good looks fascinated half the women in the audience, and Hank thought he was "amazingly believable." He continued to talk about how effective Peter was for weeks.

The son's start was a close copy of the father's, but compressed into a tenth of the time, with no pressing problems of poverty and with powerful psychological undertones. With the summer-stock company in Fishkill, New York, he painted sets, worked the lights, handed out programs, performed bits in the repertoire. He has recounted that he used to hide naked, with a can of beer, behind the drier in a laundromat, waiting for his clothes. He was freaking out, he remembers. "I went around punching walls until my knuckles were bloody—but walls rather than people."

Any child of Henry Fonda has a certain curiosity value in the theater as a potentially salable commodity. If only out of friendship and respect for Hank, producers opened their doors to Peter, inviting him to audition for them, because they had already met him or knew about him through Hank.

A director who saw him has said, "Here was another Fonda suddenly, an excited young guy. But he wasn't as passionate, he wasn't as dedicated. It didn't matter as much to him as to Hank or Jane."

In the fall of that year, he read for a part in a play by James and William Goldman entitled *Blood, Sweat, and Stanley Poole*, an unconvincing trifle about life in the United States Marine Corps. He was turned down because the producers wanted Robert Morse, as a lot of producers did after *How to Succeed in Business Without Really Trying* made his name. The abiding sense of failure that haunted Peter rose to the surface again.

He telephoned Uncle Jack, who answered his SOS by telegraphing him the fare back to Omaha. When he arrived again at the Peacocks, Peter headed for Dr. Thompson, in search of balm for a wounded ego.

Six months later, he received a telephone call: the producers wanted him to fly to New York to read for the part a second time. This time, he clicked. At the tryout in Philadelphia, his path again crossed that of Logan, who had originally been discussed as director of the production. Josh, in his function as an amateur play doctor, had been asked to take a look at some performances and make some suggestions for sharpening the impact.

"Peter," he said, "looked almost as young as he does now. He was charming and effective and he made the play work. He wasn't outstanding, but there wasn't the chance to be outstanding. It wasn't a spectacular part, but it *was* the beginning."

The New York reviewers shared much the same opinion. "This is no doubt the very last morning," wrote one of them, "in which Peter Fonda will have to be identified as Henry Fonda's son." This was no *Mister Roberts*, but it was enough for Peter. He could stand on his own two feet, he thought, dispense with anyone who told him, "You are here because of who you are, not because of any talent." On his dressing-room wall, to remind him of a past he pretended to have no use for, he hung a group picture dating back to his Brunswick School days.

Three days after the opening he was married to a student from Sarah Lawrence whom he had been dating. Susan Brewer (the stepdaughter of Noah Dietrich, who in 1972 published a book about his tumultuous career as right-hand man to Howard Hughes) was a year younger than Peter, a patient, understanding girl. The best man was Stormy McDonald, the wedding was distinctly formal. The marriage was "probably the smartest thing I've done in my life."

Jane had her doubts about the whole thing. "It was a time when we weren't very close. Peter had very short hair and insisted on getting married in a big church ceremony. I didn't understand his life and he didn't understand my friends."

Man and wife experimented briefly with most of the trappings of upper-middle-class domesticity. He was trying to live according to the "straight" code—join a country club, register a silver pattern at Tiffany's. Hank's influence showed itself in little things, like the food faddishness that prompted Peter to make his own electric-blender breakfasts of bananas, eggs, milk, and chocolate flavoring. And he enthusiastically took up a kind of family tradition—flying kites. ("I knew my father was the best kite-flyer who ever lived," Hank was to write.)

There were a few individual whimsicalities, but they fell comfortably within the norms of a swinging socialite's life-style. He liked to wear cowboy boots with a dinner jacket, mingling the West with the bluebook. He enjoyed drag racing in his new silver Facel-Vega. He thought vaguely of following Jane at the Actors' Studio, but nothing came of that. Like Hank, he had no professional lessons.

Stanley Poole lasted for something over two months. Then young Mr. and Mrs. Fonda went to Hollywood, which Peter hadn't seen in years. He was a comparatively hot item, a kind of male ingenue, wanted for testing in the role of John F. Kennedy in the movie *PT–109*. It would appear that progress in his acting career could be plotted as a straight, climbing line, but nothing was ever so simple as that for the Fondas.

Peter's marriage was the only present one among all three of the family. Seven months earlier, the beautiful, effervescent Afdera had left for Rome. "The separation is completely friendly," said the joint announcement worked out by the attorneys. "It will give us a chance to work out certain problems of our marriage." She thought she was perhaps "too immature." Very soon, Hank was single again, which was a condition he never enjoyed for long.

The Fondas headed off in their separate directions like constellations flying apart in the old astronomical theory of an exploding universe. This was a period when Hank was telling Jane, "Jesus Christ, when are you going to straighten out?" Jane was saying of Peter, "I'm not talking to him; I don't know where he is, and I don't care." And Peter, with only a moment to recognize what he called sibling rivalry, was denouncing the first Hollywood movie he was pushed into, which he retitled *Tammy and the Schmuckface*; he claimed that he vomited when he saw it run. In an inane role as young Dr. Cheswick, all he had to do was look sincere, but it brought him $15,000 and helped support Susan and himself in a style that ran to a Jaguar XK–E, then in succession to a Mercedes 300SL Gull Wing, a Buick Riviera, two motorcycles, and a souped-up station wagon, which creamed the competition when it came to drag racing.

"Before acid," he said in his *Playboy* interview, "I was thinking about flying around in 320 Cessnas, traveling the world over like I was James Bond. Always trying to create an elegant, conservative, graceful fashion thing. Trying to emulate my father, whom I saw as an elegant, graceful, conservative man. That all went after I took LSD."

Meanwhile Jane, with Voutsinas as guide, had liberated herself into a new kind of bondage. George Cukor, famous as a "woman's director" of stars of such caliber as Katharine Hepburn and Greta Garbo, was interested in her for *The Chapman Report* when Irving Wallace's best-seller, patently stimulated by the Kinsey studies of American sexual habits, was converted into a screenplay.

In the hands of Voutsinas, she turned up to audition for Cukor gussied up in costume and face paint to look like a whore. She had in mind the part of a nymphomaniac. Cukor thought it was the best joke in years. He was impressed by Jane, but not by her mentor. He cast her as a frigid young widow of upper-middle-class background, a slightly spoiled WASP. The performance he evoked from her had undertones of Greenwich, Connecticut—a nervous, country-club smile, hunger for love hidden behind a façade of good manners. The only criticism Cukor had to make concerned something she hadn't learned yet in The Method, though her father knew about it all along: when you feel an emotion begin to soar, you have to hold it back to make it effective, "just like holding a horse."

"She has such an abundance of talent," her director said, "that she must learn to hold it in. She is an American original."

She talked increasingly as if she were all stainless steel

and self-assurance. "I'm going to fall in love," she burbled, "with every leading man—how can you help it?" She kept up her Method classes, finding it harder to do a scene now that she had more technique, exactly as it had been harder to paint when she had been taught how to handle pigments and brushes.

"I know there are people there who have far more talent than I do," she explained, with no boasting. "I know that I do have something else. I have star quality, I have a personality, I have a presence on the stage which makes me more important than they are, but in terms of acting, they have more. That's why it's so hard."

At home in her apartment she wore no lipstick ("I think it makes me look ugly"), chewed gum for tranquility, stayed up late baking cakes for friends, and walked in her sleep. Her nights were consistently filled with fearful dreams that analysis did nothing to cure. In them she found herself alone in an enormous, ice-cold house from which there was no way out. She saw pet dogs run over. She fancied she was being accused of going mad. She dreamed she had forgotten her lines. Sometimes she woke to discover that she had moved furniture. Once she awoke in the street, naked.

Voutsinas considered it was time for him personally to direct her in the theater. He came up with something called *The Fun Couple*, whose title was deceptive. With his special bent, he pushed its sexuality to a hard edge so that there was an odd atmosphere, like that in a hard-core girlie magazine. Three other rising talents made up the cast—Ben Piazza, Dyan Cannon, and Bradford Dillman. Jane appeared in a bikini as a further step toward liberation. But after the critics had finished with it, *The Fun Couple* mercifully lasted for only three performances.

That spelled almost the end of her affair with her father's first love, the theater. She didn't truly care for it, she decided. She had been mistaken in her original enthusiasm, when she had found that everything was at its best for her when she was on stage. "That's when I come alive," she'd said.

Before she gave up pure theater entirely she had one more play to do, an Actors' Studio revival of Eugene O'Neill's *Strange Interlude*. It gave her the chance to appear with one of the two actresses she most respected, Geraldine Page. (The other was Kim Stanley.)

The director, José Quintero, afterward wrote what could serve as a postscript to her romance with Broadway, which lasted three years almost to a day. "There are some people," he said, "who from the moment you meet them, you care about. Suddenly they have something to do with your life. You find yourself thinking about them at the strangest times and the oddest places. If they succeed, you succeed. If they have a failure, you have a failure. There are not many people like that. Jane Fonda is one of them."

He concluded, "With Jane we see life as it happens to her. We see it through her perspective. I think she is unafraid to see it all, and that's why I keep thinking once in a while (and I think it will become a chronic condition): What's next?"

She turned her back on the prospect crusty old John Chapman of the *News* had foreseen of her becoming "the Sarah Bernhardt of 1990," because working on a stage spelled discipline, not the freedom she had once imagined it would be.

"My experience on Broadway has been nothing short of disastrous," she said not long ago. She loved rehearsals and that feeling of a group of people working together toward a common goal in a dark theater while life went on outside. But playing a role over and over again left her feeling trapped. Movies gave her the freedom she liked. Making a picture was improvisational kind of work.

Some people close to Jane were quick to blame Voutsinas for her disillusionment and her departure, which did nothing to increase the popularity of the little man in the black beret.

At about this time, Hank went through a period of disillusionment with Broadway, too. Not with acting as such—that alliance had all the marks of a traditional marriage with vows of "until death do us part," and divorce was unthinkable. Not with plays, no matter how hard it was to find scripts in his constant and not always discerning search for parts that were right for him. But his teeth were set on edge by the response, or lack of it, among playgoers to a particular drama on which he put an especially high value.

One of the publishing successes of a previous season had been Lael Tucker's chilling account of the battle fought with cancer by her husband, the writer Charles Wertenbaker, which ended when he chose a Roman death. Garson Kanin wrote a play based on the book, *A Gift of Time*, and directed Olivia de Havilland and Hank in the key roles.

The last act saw Hank persuading her, as he lies dying, to bring him a razor and stay with him while he opens his wrists. The first-night audience watched in horror, touched only partly with admiration. Backstage afterward, John Springer heard Paul Newman in Hank's dressing room say, "It's just the God damnedest, greatest performance I've ever seen."

But the word spread that this was no more to be classified as popular entertainment than *King Lear*. Even Fonda devotees felt that his stage suicide was more than they could stomach. Audiences dwindled. *A Gift of Time* had to be rated a failure.

Hank had left Music Corporation of America and was represented by another agency, Ashley Famous, whose principals had a deserved reputation for being hard-nosed businessmen. He had insisted on going into *A Gift of Time* against their forecast that it was bound to flop. Their attitude, calmly stated, was, "We told you so." Now, as part of his contract, he had to make a picture that they would select for him.

Even a superstar enjoys only comparative freedom. Though Fonda had never been able to achieve any lasting equilibrium in his private affairs, he had worked out the means of balancing his cash needs with his psychical desires. He made movies for the money that enabled him to perform in the theater.

Ashley Famous steered him into what one critic called "a package of piety and prurience," a slice of hokum with a *Tobacco Road* flavor, entitled *Spencer's Mountain*. "The script," said Hank, "is old-fashioned corn. It will set movies back twenty-five years." But his contract gave him little choice.

He was in his agent's California office when he picked up a New York newspaper, turned to the Broadway news and noticed that Edward Albee's *Who's Afraid of Virginia Woolf?*" was opening that night.

"I loved those short plays of his," Hank remarked.

"Oh, Albee," said his agent. "He wanted you to do this play, but we turned it down."

Hank was somewhat shaken. "But why do you turn down plays for me without even letting me know? You know I'm always looking for a good one."

"We felt you should do this picture. And this play won't run. There's nothing to it except a husband and wife fighting with each other."

Praise for the Albee play rose higher than the Allied Chemical Tower on Times Square, first from the critics and then from Jimmy Stewart, Joshua Logan, and Jane. Each of them told Hank that they had pictured him in the role of the domestically embattled professor when they saw it.

John Springer shared that feeling. So did Edward Albee, who commented to him, "I had sent the play right to Fonda

—it's the first time I really had a star in mind—and I was so hurt when it was sent back without a word from him."

The first evening that Hank got home to New York after completing *Spencer's Mountain,* he went to see *Virginia Woolf.* "I sat there, sliding farther and farther down in my seat. I think I would have given up any role I've ever played —Tom Joad or Mister Roberts, any of them—to have had a chance at that part. And I couldn't even say, 'This should have been my part,' because up on that stage Arthur Hill was giving an absolutely perfect performance."

Fonda's name came up when a motion picture of the play was scheduled. Bette Davis would have appeared opposite him. But Elizabeth Taylor was chosen over Davis, and Richard Burton stepped into the part that permanently eluded Fonda.

When *Spencer's Mountain* was released, it lived up to his agent's expectations as a crowd-puller. *Variety* detected "depth, purposefulness and dignity" in Hank's performance. Which demonstrates, perhaps, how the quickness of an act deceives the eye.

For the better part of two years, all three Fondas jumped from one movie into another, spending most of their combined time in Hollywood. The careers of Jane and Peter were becalmed; Hank was playing roles that a less conscientious actor would walk through. Yet he always brought to them total credibility. No matter what they thought, and began to say publicly, about his shortcomings as a parent, both his children had to recognize his power as an actor, now that they knew more and more about his business.

"I really admired my father's acting," said Jane. "He's never bad, no matter what he's playing in."

Strasberg once asked Peter, in the usual ritual, who his favorite actor was. What came to mind was a mixture of Laurence Olivier and Lee J. Cobb. "If he had asked me that today," said Peter in his early Hollywood phase, "I'd say my father. I think he's the best actor I've ever seen."

Hank in a single year portrayed a candidate for the White House, then the President himself, then descended to appearing in a slyly suggestive movie made from a much more explicit book, *Sex and the Single Girl.* Jane, compared alternately with Sandra Dee and Marilyn Monroe, seemed to be in danger of being typecast as a Hollywood soap-opera heroine. Peter's fate apparently was to be cast either in flops or in movies like Robert Rossen's *Lilith*, where his part as a suicidal mental patient was so heavily cut as to be close to incomprehensible on the screen. He sank into a familiar state of fathomless depression, sure that his troubles were starting all over again.

But a door marked *exit* had opened up, in fact, for each young Fonda. For the second of his movies, Carl Foreman's abortive antiwar epic *The Victors*, Peter flew to London with his wife. At the fancy Carlton Tower Hotel, another actor in the cast persuaded him to try the first marijuana he ever smoked. Peter went up to his room, "and I told Susan we were going to smoke grass—no, it was *pot* then." He filled a little pipe with it.

"I told my old lady that I'd smoked it quite a few times and that it wasn't habit-forming," he said in *Playboy*. "But I was just a little bit afraid. The first time I'd heard about people smoking grass, it was in the context of dope addicts and weirdos who blew their minds. All the while, you understand, I was pouring down *gallons* of vodka. I'd started on wine, gone to Scotch and then to vodka, because all I wanted to do was to get drunk."

Susan was skeptical, but she believed in her husband, so she drew on the pipe when he passed it to her. But the smoke brought on a spasm of coughing. It hurt her throat, she said.

"No, it can't hurt your throat," he told her.

"I must have taken close to thirty hits trying to show my old lady how to smoke grass. The great teacher." It was useless. She couldn't hold the smoke without coughing.

204 : *James Brough*

"But I got *very* high. Giggled and laughed, jumped under the covers and got cold."

When she spoke to him, she sounded as if she was "talking behind herself." "It was a great hallucination, and I was digging it."

Then suddenly Peter, whose usual appetite is meager, got ravenously hungry. "I ordered up all this shit from that great hotel, and then I got very paranoid, which is the second thing I learned about grass. I started worrying that the waiter was going to smell it, that he'd know what had been happening. But the guy came in, laid the food down and split. I ate everything and had a ball."

In another hotel, this one in California, Jane also experienced a preview of her future, though it was not recognizable on that occasion. Vadim invited her to see him at the Beverly Hills Hotel to talk about a film for which he wanted her.

"But we had nothing to say to each other. I thought that all the charm and the softness were just an act to cover up for all the other stuff," she said. "One of the reasons for the flip-over was the discovery that he is so utterly different from his public image."

XI

HOLLYWOOD in its heyday was essentially an assembly-line process for manufacturing and marketing The Impossible Dream. For half a century, until television took over, the motion-picture industry supplied its customers with a comparatively harmless, though habit-forming, soporific: the flick, recommended in weekly dosages or more frequently if desired. The flicks contained the stuff that dreams were made on—stately mansions, effortless living, and above all, vicarious sexual frolicking with the most beautiful partners in the world.

All leading men were gods and the women goddesses, infinitely seductive with their firm breasts and languorous eyes and welcoming mouths, yet as intangible as rainbows. To true believers, it was sacrilege to mention that some of the heroes wore hairpieces, like Sinatra, or corsets, or, like Crosby, had their ears taped back. Only blasphemers would dare to speculate that it was soft focus photography and halo lighting that gave Dietrich her unearthly splendor, or that padding applied fore and aft rounded out the proportions of other female stars. Never did purer, platonic love exist than in the communion between the faithful sitting in dreaming darkness and the idols of the celluloid shrine.

Jane, who was in time to get a taste of Hollywood just

before the party died, has reported, "I did a movie where I did not want to wear falsies, and they told me I had to, because Jack Warner doesn't like flat-chested women. I mean, can you believe that? I said I wanted to wear a polka-dot dress, and they said Jack Warner doesn't like polka dots."

But since she didn't care to act in the theater any more, she had to play the Hollywood game, irrespective of what Strasberg and Voutsinas had drummed into her about searching your life for an experience similar to the one you are pretending as an actress. The girl-next-door roles hadn't established her as a definable personality for box-office merchandising. Neither had the tarts and prostitutes. The next thing to try was some boisterous sex, and the answer was *Cat Ballou*.

In that burlesque of every shoot-'em-up ever filmed since the reign of Bronco Bill, the titillating formula devised for her appearance mixed wide-eyed innocence and hot-lipped sex appeal, skin-clinging jeans and plunging spangles. Though it was Lee Marvin and not Jane who walked off with an Academy Award as a result of his role as Kid Shelleen, Jane was away to a galloping start as Hollywood's latest and hottest Impossible Dream, labeled as an American sex kitten.

"She somehow suggests that Alice in Wonderland has fallen among blackguards and rather enjoys it," said *Time*. "She's got the prettiest backside in Hollywood," said one magazine photographer invited to the set.

Unlike her father, who doesn't care to see or even hear himself on the sound track in movies, she had the habit of seeing every movie she made, but only once. That was another way of learning about herself, though she didn't care for her looks "except that I don't look at it as me; I look at it as a character that I'm playing."

What she saw in *Cat Ballou* was chronic overacting, a girlish lack of control, which pleased the moviegoing crowds but offended some of her longer-term admirers in the profession.

"I have never seen her father give too much ever on any score," said a director who knew them both. "There's no money you could pay him, there's no lure you could offer to make him do something more than he feels is right. Jane went overboard. When she was playing—and I'm sure it was done at the urging of her director, Elliot Silverstein— I had to turn my face away from the screen. Her accent was too much. Her playing was too much. I blushed."

She had a lot to learn, and about more things than acting. It was time for her to see if there were different patterns than those in Hollywood, where everyone was accustomed to being manipulated like a gold-plated puppet. "These are people," she said on another occasion, "who become famous overnight, and they know it can disappear overnight."

Perhaps she remembered something Arthur Laurents had told her on the day Bridget Hayward killed herself, when she was deathly afraid. "You've nothing to fear, Jane, because you're a survivor, stronger than people who give the impression of being stronger than you."

She flew to France, to make another movie there; she considered that European movies tended to be superior to American. Her first French picture had become something of a collectors' item of a specialized nature in the two years since it had been shot. Director René Clément worked without a script, but he had a telling title, *The Love Cage,* which was changed to the equally descriptive *Joy House.*

"I didn't speak very good French then," said its star, disarmingly, "and I never really understood much of what was going on. The only people who really dug that movie for some odd reason were junkies. They used to come up and give me a great big wink."

Her most ardent admirers wondered what was happening to her taste and her talent. Acid-tongued Judith Crist thought she was a "sick kid," alternately impersonating "the Madwoman of Chaillot, Baby Doll, and her father."

Vadim by now had ten pictures to his credit and a child by each of two of his leading ladies. Annette Stroyberg, mother of his daughter Nathalie, had succeeded Bardot as Madame Plemiannikow and starred in his fourth film, *Les Liaisons Dangereuses*. When that opened, the newspapers reported that Annette was enjoying a liaison of her own with a French guitarist, Sacha Distel, who had come to public attention as a boyfriend of Bardot's.

Stroyberg's marriage was as brief as Vadim's struggles to obtain censorship approval of the picture were long. When he arrived in New York for the delayed release in the United States of *Les Liaisons*, he had a new protégée as his companion. Catherine Deneuve fitted the prescription he believed in for his women: tall, cool, and blonde. *Paris Match* never tired of printing her photographs and then in recounting the circumstances of her giving birth to his son Christian, though neither she nor Vadim had any thought of marriage.

Vadim introduced laughter into Jane's tense, joyless life. She found him to be a man with a zest for whatever he did —reading, eating, making movies or love. He was utterly unlike anyone she had previously known. She did not expect him to be faithful to her. His capabilities were such that she never felt betrayed by him, "not even if he sleeps with another woman," as she said.

Meeting him brought many surprises for Jane Fonda. His appearance fell short of his reputation as a hunter of women, a twentieth-century Cellini. He was no domineering lady-killer, but a logical, precise intellectual, thickening a little at the waist now that he was closing in on forty. His smile showed teeth as strong as a stallion's; a derisive sense of humor lived in his wide-set Tartar's eyes. He was muscled like an athlete, an expert skier over snow or water, a hair-raising driver of fast automobiles. He was tolerant, amusing, understanding. Men who came within range of his charm could find him as persuasive as women did.

Sex—casual, experimental, overwhelming, or enduring —was a way of life for him, as well as the hallmark of his movies. It was as much a part of the climate of the set he mixed with as their favorite Left Bank cafes or the sunshine of St. Tropez. It was the first bond between Vadim and Jane.

The "sex kitten" label had already begun to stick to her. Publicity had identified her as "America's Brigitte Bardot." Under the direction of Vadim, who nicknamed her "Kiki," she cornered the U.S. market. The next step in the emancipation of Jane Fonda was liberation from her clothes, starting with *Circle of Love*, a lackluster remake of a much more distinguished earlier picture, *La Ronde*. Its principal contribution to her career was a seventy-foot billboard that rose over Broadway, depicting her sprawling naked on a crumpled bed. It didn't offend her sense of propriety, but it outraged her sense of justice. She had authorized nothing like this, so she threatened to sue, and the more revealing sections of the poster were papered over.

It all made wonderful publicity, as did the news stories, which coincided with the picture's release, of Vadim's latest romance.

The girl who not long ago had been repelled by her own face and ashamed of her body, had no objection to being considered a symbol of sex. "I didn't even expect people to treat me as a person who thinks."

As "Kiki" she cultivated the symbolism, with her long hair dyed blonde. She dressed for the part in brief skirts and Courrèges boots. She undressed happily for photographers, to demonstrate to newspaper and magazine readers that even her shape was different, with an inch or so added in the Jack Warner zone. She was, in her own phrase, "Jane Fonda, the doll"—in the nursery, not the pin-up, sense. Another impossible dream was coming true.

Contact with Peter was all but broken off. He remained a believer in American institutions, including the movie business, despite the producers' limited belief in him as a box-office draw. He was a registered Republican, a conservative in thought and word, but not in deed.

"We could only be close in a far-out, surreal sort of way," he said on one occasion. "We put feelers out, and I recognized her and she me."

He was still uptight, attempting to act out in reality the parts his agent usually found for him, a prototype of Rotarian America, "the ultimate David Eisenhower," in his own phrase. The accessories were a fur coat bought for Susan; a house in Beverly Hills; having four sycamore trees cut down because they dropped leaves on his cars; madly competitive tennis playing until he permanently damaged his right ankle trying to beat an opponent; habitual drinking.

He also carried a gun, "and I probably wanted to kill somebody—myself, I guess."

The desire grew stronger after a visit to Tucson, Arizona, to visit Stormy. While he was there, the young man who had given Peter his philosophy, "Be true to yourself," was found dead in his apartment with his wrists slashed and a bullet in his head. Enough marijuana to roll fifty cigarettes was turned up by police searchers in the apartment, too.

The coroner's jury ruled that Peter must submit to a lie-detector test to determine whether he had criminal knowledge of how his friend's life had ended so bizarrely, with such relentless determination. The headlines screamed the Fonda name for days, until the process of law decided that the death may have been "a homicide in the presence of a person or persons unknown."

Frances; Margaret Sullavan; Bridget Hayward; Stormy. Three years after the visit to Tucson, Peter Fonda said, "There's never a day that I don't think about my best friend putting a bullet in his head. There's hardly a day I don't think about my mother cutting her throat. There's hardly a day that I don't realize this girl whom I was in love with, and who was almost like my sister, took pills and did herself in. And all the other people I knew who tried to do themselves in. I have no sympathy any more. Compassion. But no sympathy."

He had gone back to marijuana himself after the first turn-on in London. He found that regular smoking calmed him down, and he felt an urgent need for internal quietude. He had no patience for other routes to tranquility that were available and increasingly popular—meditation under a guru's guidance or interminable sessions on an analyst's couch. But he had to escape somehow, he realized, from the self-doubt and hatred that flourished inside him.

"Sometimes grass will quiet your mind down a bit," he explained in *Playboy*. "That doesn't mean grass is necessarily the way to do it, but I'm just saying it's an example of a way to get past some of the daily abrasion of living that can hang you up."

Seven months after Stormy died, he climbed into his station wagon with two friends and a St. Bernard dog named Basil. At his house he left his wife and their baby daughter, Bridget. The car headed East out of Beverly Hills into the Mohave desert. One of the two men had recommended that Peter should take a trip on LSD.

He was careful to point out for publication later that acid was not an illegal drug at the time. "It was pure, non-chromosome-breaking, nonhabit-forming, nondangerous. So I dropped 500 micrograms and never came back. That's what I like to say, 'cause then people say, 'See, see, I told you, he never came back.' I was looking to get my head straight. And it helped."

Parked in the desert, he remembered to feed the dog. The first part of the trip was compounded principally of horror. He felt isolated and full of pain, as if in fever. He bit into an oatmeal cookie, and its coarse texture looked like writhing worms and tasted like them in his mouth. He found nothing wrong with that. Then he ate a plum, and that was alive, too.

After that, he'd had enough to eat. He got to his feet and wandered, with no sense of identity. The sky looked like a magnificently colored Tiffany lampshade. From somewhere in the lampshade he could feel waves rippling through the air like heat. He looked up in bewilderment and saw that the source was not the sun but a plane flashing high in the sky, and he was seeing its sound. The dog chased a toad under a bush. When Peter followed, he saw a monster roaring and shooting flames out at him. Hours passed; somehow he reached a house that was not his own.

At one point, he remembered climbing onto a shelf in the linen closet of that house and squeezing himself in to hide there, afraid. "I was thinking of my mother and I was thinking of her womb, and I didn't want to be in there. And then I saw my little daughter Bridget, who just popped out of my stomach and looked at me. When I got out of the closet, I stopped being scared."

The terror eased into contemplation. He thought about his father and the family's past relationships one with the other, father and son, father and mother, son and daughter. The past always seemed radioactive to him, setting Geiger counters clicking if he got close to it.

Suddenly he burst through that and began feeling related to the world and everything in it, free from guilt, about his father, mother, and Jane. The past, he convinced himself, was dead and unmourned.

The methods his children had chosen as roads to liberation, sexuality for one, drugs for the other, served to enrage Fonda, for whom the slavery of perfectionism was an iron cage. The lines of melancholy deepened on his face. He began to wear a perceptible look of middle age as he passed his sixtieth birthday.

"I knew those two children were going to be rebellious if their old man was successful at something and they decided to do the same thing," he said. "I had to hold my breath sometimes and not let it hurt too much."

One of his few consolations was a hit play. The critics dismissed it as trivial and banal, like too many of the vehicles he appeared in. But it bore a distinct relationship to his own situation and helped to brighten his mood. *Generation*, by William Goodhart was a comedy about a theme on which he had every right to regard himself as a specialist: the generation gap. The subject had a fleeting significance in those dawning days of the Age of Aquarius, before hard rock, communal living, the pill, and amphetamines finally melded to produce a youth culture and a virtually unbridgeable divide.

In *Generation*, he had a complete disguise for his actual role as a parent. He played not "the agelessly active lover who promises youthful ardor plus maturity," as one reviewer neatly expressed it, but the understanding father of a headstrong girl in urgent need of marriage to an undesirable son-in-law. Audiences who had boycotted *A Gift of Time* hurried to see it because it was a lot of laughs and a perfect vehicle for Fonda at this point in time.

"He is a testament," one critic glowed, "not to drama but to those dreams of human perfection into which no conflict is ever allowed to enter." The irony was not lost on Hank or either of his children.

But he had another consolation to turn to—Shirlee. From the time of their introduction three years earlier ("Now who's that gorgeous man?" she had said when he walked into the party) they had been going together in California and New York. He had been careful about the relationship. She went home every night from his rented house at Malibu.

Shirlee Mae Adams came closer to meeting the needs of the agelessly active man that Fonda had grown to be than any other woman he had known. She had the extraverted friendliness and the open pixie smile of an archetypical airline hostess, which had been her previous job. She was easygoing, attentive, uncomplicated, and neither Peter nor Jane approved of her and what she meant to their father.

Shirlee enjoyed sharing in good times, but she hadn't Margaret Sullavan's flaring temperament. She delighted in material things like high-style clothes, but she lacked Frances's intense preoccupation with money. She wasn't introspective like Susan or as socially ambitious as Afdera. She found Hank, she said, a "warm, sweet man."

She paid serious attention to insignificant subjects like vitamins, dieting (a glass of hot water and lemon every morning), and yoga ("I don't do the spiritual part or the meditation—just the basic stretch," she has said). She gave credit to exercising for adding two inches to her height, bringing her within five inches of Hank's. She was devoted to health and to him. Her ambition, of course, was to be the fifth Mrs. Fonda.

He was in no hurry to marry again. It is a truism among marriage counselors and matrimonial attorneys that every divorce increases the odds that a husband or wife will seek the same end to a later married partnership. Hank could not for the life of him understand how he had been into and out of marriage so often. He didn't want to go on repeating his mistakes. Perhaps four times was more than enough.

"I disapprove completely of people who keep getting married and divorced," he once said over dinner. "I'm a staid Midwesterner, not that kind of person at all—and yet I obviously am. I have to stop when I think about it and say, 'Hey, that's you, man!' "

He was appalled by Jane's outspokenness about living with Vadim, whom he could only look upon as yet another Svengali in her path, debauched, cynical, and vicious. She talked of marriage as being something out of date in the brave new world, an archaic institution that made no sense. She loved Vadim, and that was more than enough.

When it was over, she used the feelings she had found in herself through being in love with Vadim as a yardstick for the future. The man who caused such painful ecstacy might change, she reasoned, but the feeling remained a phenomenon of living.

"Daughter?" said Hank during the early years of her enchantment, "I don't have a daughter."

"His duplicity," said Peter, "blew our minds."

She was a resident of France, but she made pictures in the United States too. That was where the money could be found, and she earned at nine times the rate of Vadim, who needs eighteen months to complete a movie. At the average Hollywood pace she could appear in four or five. She played a Texas trollop in *The Chase* for Columbia and a part-time concubine in *Any Wednesday* for Warner Brothers. There was never a shortage of job offers from producers eager to cash in on her publicity value as a symbol of free-flying sex, who had to keep on talking compulsively for publication about her chosen way of living.

The trouble lay in the roles themselves. *The Chase* emerged as a half-baked "message" picture, full of good intentions and stereotyped characters, in which she was miscast. *Any Wednesday* was a coy little sex comedy with a soppy ending, in which she looked wholesome and cried a lot.

Not surprisingly, she preferred appearing under the sensual direction of her lover in *The Game Is Over*. As usual, it called for her to take off her clothes, but she had never looked as beautiful in the lenses of any other cameras. He held nothing back, nor did she.

"You have to be relaxed, free. Pornography," she said, always ready with a pat definition, "begins when things become self-conscious. But the set was clear and closed, and I knew Vadim would protect me in the cutting room. Months later, we discovered that a photographer had hidden in the rafters and taken pictures, which he sold to

Playboy. It rocked me, it really did. It's a simple matter of breaking and entering and invasion of privacy."

The scene in question featured a Turkish bath, awash in opulent color. "For all of ten seconds, you saw my breasts," said Jane. But the consequent magazine spread of her was a more permanent souvenir ("Our water nymphette emerges from pool, wrapping herself in a warm robe.") that sold like balloons at a fireman's parade. She sued the publishers for $9.5 million dollars—and lost.

The Game ran into the customary problems which Vadim had with censorship, this time in Italy, but all the smoke couldn't hide the fact that this was his best picture to date and, without a doubt, her best acting job, a milestone that left the antics of *Cat Ballou* and everything else she had done in the past a long way down the road. Under its original title, *La Curée,* as in Zola's original novel, it was a full-sized hit in Europe.

Jane took professional pride in doing her own French-language dubbing. "You feel a certain kind of freedom," she said, employing the word that may mean more to her than any other. "The way you feel when you learn to speak a foreign language and find you can say things you wouldn't dare to say in English."

If her stepdaughter hadn't been around, it is probable that one of the things not to be dared in either English or French would have been the decision to marry after two years of denouncing the idea. She and Vadim took Nathalie with them on one trip to California. Annette Stroyberg's daughter had grown into a pensive, lissom little girl, closely resembling her mother, but with her father's slanting eyes.

"You know how they are," said Jane. "Kids used to say to her, 'Oh, your mommy and daddy aren't married, are they?' and there was all that nonsense with hotels and things like that. It was just easier to be married, that's all."

Their decision eased much of the tension with Hank,

whether or not his feelings on the question had been considered. He was frankly disgusted with them. It was important to him, as a man as well as an actor seeking roles, to be identified with what one director, Joseph L. Mankiewicz, has called "that middle-class American morality that is Henry Fonda." He was righteously indignant when Vadim and Jane rented a place in the same community, Malibu, where he was living.

"What are you trying to do to me?" was a question he had asked Jane.

In her view, marriage was plain silly. "It just doesn't make sense to me. That people form couples seems perfectly natural. Marriage is something else again, something superfluous, like the human appendix. I'm sure that in the future, like that organ, it will be eliminated, because it certainly doesn't protect anything as far as the couple is concerned. We're all fickle. Why have the added burden of marriage? Maybe women do need the security. I don't know. But two days before the wedding I went into a complete panic, and I wanted to call the whole thing off."

On a sizzling August day, they took a planeload of friends and relatives to Las Vegas. They were married on the twenty-first floor of the Dunes Hotel. It could not be called a sentimental occasion. Hank was conspicuously absent. Vadim's mother, a tiny, gray-haired professional photographer, missed the ceremony because she spent the day peering through her spectacles at the crazy gambling city and snapping pictures of what she saw.

A hastily hired orchestra of women violinists, swaying in sheath-fitted gowns of blue sequins, played the wedding music. Vadim had forgotten to buy a ring, which was a bitter disappointment to the seventy-year-old judge who was to make them man and wife.

"That's the best part of the ceremony," he complained.

Christian Marquand, an intimate friend of Vadim's for whom Catherine Deneuve's son was named, lent them his finger ring. It was so loose on Jane that she had to hold her finger upright in a Gallic gesture to keep it from slipping off.

When the undulating musicians had played their final saccharine chords, the wedding party went downstairs to gamble. Other patrons of the Dunes stopped by to stare and now and then to insult the bride and groom because her hair wasn't combed and he hadn't a tie to wear.

"I thought it rude and in bad taste," commented Jane, in whom conventional instincts persisted.

The show they watched that night was a striptease musical version of the French Revolution, performed to the beat of Ravel's *Bolero*. As its climax, a number of showgirls, naked but for G-strings, submitted to the guillotine. M. and Mme. Plemiannikov continued to try their luck at the gaming tables through the night until morning came. They flew back to the coast without having gone to bed at all.

Besides forgetting a ring, Vadim neglected to register their marriage with the French consul in Los Angeles. The oversight meant that, as residents of France, they remained legally single in that country. Nearly two years after their trip to Las Vegas they presented themselves at the town hall of Marchefroy, near the village where they lived, and were married all over again by the mayor, who was also the local gas man.

"I got married to Jane," Vadim said, "because I was lazy. People used to ask me, 'Why don't you marry Jane?' So as not to have to explain so much, we got married. Now everyone asks, 'Why did you marry Jane?' "

Her brother, more closely in tune with her, felt that he knew her side of the answer. "Vadim is so like my father. I think my sister married my father. Vadim is kinder, though, because he's more open."

Certainly Hank warmed up somewhat to the man now that he was his son-in-law, interested, like him, in such innocent pastimes as chess and fishing, even though their ideas on what constituted morality never coincided. The member of the family whom Vadim was unsure of was Peter. "I think your brother hates me," he once told his new wife. Peter did not agree with that. Vadim's problem, he thought, was that he suspected Peter, unjustifiably, of making "value judgments" about him.

Peter took his first trip on acid one month after the Las Vegas marriage. According to his telling, he took ten more in a brief span of time, and he credited them for his transformation as a personality. "After LSD, I have seen the worst and I've seen the best, and I know where I am on this planet."

Analyzing himself in a matter of weeks, where Jane spent five years in professional analysis, he discovered that he loved her, just as he could now experience the stirring of love for his father, though he was convinced that Hank did not return the feeling.

"I felt frantically drawn to her," Peter remembered on a later occasion, "as if awakened from a nightmare of war and wanting to contact buddies in the trench with me to assure me that we were really there and assure her that I had insight into her childhood. I wanted her to know that we hadn't been failures when we were little and we shouldn't feel guilty with hangups."

He recognized her as a mind close to his own, and he wanted to be with her so that they could share all the available time in the world talking about their separate lives and everything that had happened to them, so that the great gaps that existed in their past might be filled.

"We came out of the same hole," he said. "We should never be strangers." It was, in his judgment, "a union that's indissolvable," to the obvious discomfort of Vadim.

"I don't get into it with him," said Peter, bluntly. The relationship, as he saw it, was between himself and Jane. "Vadim is left out of it."

Three weeks before Christmas, during the run of *Genera-*

tion, Hank and Shirlee drove out from Manhattan to Hempstead Town Hall on Long Island. The usual twenty-four-hour waiting period was waived at his special request, and the license was issued that morning. On December 3, 1965, in the chambers of Judge Edwin R. Lynde, a state supreme court justice, in Mineola, they were married. The bride, sleek in a white brocade dress with a buttoned-down back, looked as well turned out as any leading lady Hank had appeared with in his thirty-seven years as a professional actor, starting four years before Shirlee was born. Their good friends George Peppard and Elizabeth Ashley flew from Los Angeles to serve as best man and maid of honor.

"In the ten years I have been officiating at wedding ceremonies," said the judge in closing, "no couple I have married has broken apart. I don't expect you to."

When the third Mrs. Fonda heard of the event, she said, "Henry is a very moral person. Otherwise, why would he marry all those girls?"

Shirlee had her own kind of answer ready. "I'm the oldest woman he's ever married," she grinned. "I'm thirty-three."

Jane, who was going through what she subsequently called a "ruff, ruff" period in press interviews, thought that her father should undergo psychoanalysis. "Anyone who marries five times," she said, "must be a very unhappy person."

XII

AFTER his self-exploration trips on LSD, the personality of Peter Fonda underwent a rapid change. Within a matter of months, in looks as well as in philosophy and personality, he was a completely different human being. The clean-cut, right-thinking, square young actor going nowhere in particular had been replaced, just as it happens in a lap dissolve on a movie screen, by a long-haired rebel wearing funky spectacles, talking a blue streak to anybody who would listen, smoking grass "every day, or at least every night," on his own testimony. He would have needed to be a bomb-throwing nihilist to get much more remote from Hank's image of middle-class American morality.

Where his father was appalled, one Hollywood company was intrigued. To the bosses of American International Pictures, he looked like a natural candidate for another in the fifteen-year-old series of low-budget, quickie movies they were planning for the special audience they had staked out for themselves, the youth market. AIP plots usually had to do with golden boys and long-haired girls merrymaking on the beach (*How to Stuff a Wild Bikini*) or grotesque monsters rampaging through the drive-ins (*The Beast With 1,000,000 Eyes*). This time Roger Corman, producer and director, had a different idea to exploit—California motorcycle gangs in hot pursuit of sex and violence.

The Wild Angels had as its source of what could loosely be called inspiration the swastika-stained Hell's Angels, whose members, paid off as "bodyguards" with free beer, beat a bystander to death with sawn-off billiard cues at one California rock concert of The Rolling Stones. Peter didn't look exactly like an Angel, "but I had a good reason for being there because it was an anti-Establishment film."

He was hired for ten thousand dollars to portray the leather-jacketed leading man, named Heavenly Blues, in this gaudy melodrama of gang rapes, boozing, pot-puffing, and a particularly repellent orgy conducted in a church where a flag bearing Hitler's crooked cross covered the altar.

It turned out to be exactly what a considerable segment of the youth market had been conditioned to enjoy, bringing in total box-office income of roughly ten million dollars and boosting the reputation of Peter as the pre-eminent underground star of the new generation of moviegoers. Two million posters of him astride his juggernaut totaled up to the biggest seller in that booming by-product business. He did his own motorcycle stunting, and, by his own word, was "stoned the whole time."

American International started pumping out lurid press publicity about its new picture with the new hippy star who was the symbol, the releases declared, of alienated youth. Apparently, the Los Angeles police believed every word of it. Peter received a telephone call in the middle of an August night, advising him that the house of a friend of his, who had helped him as a secretary, had been raided, and marijuana had been found growing in the backyard. Peter got hold of an attorney for him.

A day or so later, the lawyer called Peter. "*You're* going to be busted," he warned. In the raided house, police had discovered a guitar case with Fonda's name on it. As the newspapers picked up the story from the police, it was

Peter's house that had been investigated. The charge against him was a felony: possession of narcotics.

Hank had completed the run of *Generation* and was in the throes of another Western on location in Arizona with Shirlee. He flew into Los Angeles to appear at Peter's side in the Los Angeles courtroom, a patrician in a business suit, the only departure from convention being the beard he had grown to play some of his scenes as a kind of anti-hero lawman in a picture whose title had the weird, coincidental fit, *Welcome to Hound Time.* Peter, ignoring his lawyer's advice, wore one of his sharper, double-breasted suits, long hair, and his tinted *Wild Angels* glasses.

"I am here," Hank told the judge and jury, "to give moral support or any other support to my son."

The jury was instructed that the charges must be proved "beyond a reasonable doubt and to a moral certainty" for Peter to be found guilty. For acquittal, the jury's decision would have to be unanimous. Two women voted against him. Perhaps in the circumstances the charges might be dropped as a favor.

The outcome of the case remained undecided, while lawyers worked behind the scenes—when he was arrested again. Sunset Strip, running between Hollywood and Beverly Hills, had once been a tourist landmark of fancy stores, fancier restaurants, and the fanciest people. Now it was suffering from the erosion of the youth culture, with hippies, as etymologists recall them, milling over the sidewalks. Marijuana scented the air on windless nights.

One November evening, the police sailed in with billies to break up a crowd outside the Fifth Estate coffeehouse there. As a riot, it was a campfire by comparison with the flames and fury that had devastated Watts the previous year. But tension between any nonconformist segments of the population and Los Angeles' law enforcers continued. Police reaction to "incidents" was conditioned by memories of the thirty-five dead, the nearly nine hundred casualties, the thousands of arrests in the disaster of the black ghetto suburb of Watts.

Peter was an easy target, with the funky shades and collar-length hair, mingling in with the crowd. He had come, his press agent proved in order to satisfy the police at three-forty-five the following morning, to shoot a documentary film about angry youth. He was arrested as a loiterer, jailed, but not booked.

"I've marched on Washington," Peter recalled some time afterward, "and it's usually all very courteous there, but I've also been banged around and kicked in the balls by cops when I was out on Sunset Strip at the wrong time."

Violent rioting had exploded into a seemingly permanent manifestation of American dissent. In the country whose birth pangs included street massacres in Boston and elsewhere, the scale of demonstrations had escalated alarmingly now. There was only a nucleus of consolidation in most of the early irruptions, beginning with the Alabama bus boycotts led ten years earlier by Martin Luther King. Experience of race riots in Harlem and northern cities, and in protest marches on Washington, had produced a new generation in America of seasoned organizers and willing followers. They ranged in degree of intensity from liberal-minded clergymen outraged by American policy in Vietnam to the nihilistic Weathermen, dedicated to bombing and generalized terror. They included students battling the draft; itinerant singers like Joan Baez, protesting any form of violence; yippies like Abbie Hoffman, set on overturning capitalist society; increasingly militant blacks, disillusioned with broken promises of change in their economic condition. Against the war, against the draft, against oppression, against law and order as it existed—the crowds marched and milled through streets and college campuses.

To a resident of France like Jane, what was happening in the United States seemed almost unreal, too remote to have much bearing on day-to-day living. Vadim had no overwhelming interest in politics. Other than sympathy for the plight of American Indians, she hadn't any particular cause that she held dear. She had never tried to raise money or solicit signatures for anything or anybody. At Vassar, she had stayed away from the Washington marches and the student drives to register black voters in the South when some of her friends joined in. After Vassar, she had been too busy with her internal drive to act to get involved with public affairs.

Home to the Vadims was a half-ruined farmhouse, 134 years old, near the village of La Fontaine Richard, 35 miles west of Paris. Jane bought it as some kind of remembrance of her California childhood and set about transforming the place into a livable house, with a built-in family of Italian servants. Six acres of flat farmland were bulldozed into a reasonable facsimile of rolling landscape not unlike the hills that her father used to plow.

She had fifty full-grown trees trucked in to add interest to the scenery. "They don't cost as much as an evening dress," she said in justification of this Marie Antoinette touch, "and they last a lifetime." She offset some of the expense by invading empty houses close by and walking off with plants from their gardens.

One feature of the restoration job was a huge master bedroom separated from its adjoining bathroom by a glass wall "so no one gets lonely." The Vadims filled the house and yard with pets; at one count there were seven dogs, eight cats, rabbits, ponies, and a flurry of laying hens. As part of the furnishings, she paid five thousand dollars for a Lichtenstein rug.

"I must say," the proud housewife mused, "that, with the dogs and a husband who flicks his cigarettes on the floor, it is really asking for it."

Vadim, after taking flying lessons, was talking about buying a plane. At St. Tropez, where they had a summer

place on a private headland leading down to the Mediterranean, he drove a status-laden powerboat. In both homes
she played hostess to a constant flow of visitors and house-
guests, more often than not the men and women who peo-
pled Vadim's past. Vadim's Russian mother was usually on
hand. Bardot, Stroyberg, and Catherine Deneuve wandered in and out, sometimes leaving Jane to mother their
children, Christian and Nathalie.

The new Madame Vadim confessed to being scared to
death of Bardot. "She's a real phenomenon. She can be in
a room filled with powerful personalities, but you are still
constantly aware that she is there." Occasionally in the
town she was mistaken for the first Madame Vadim. "I
mean, I just find that puzzling, I don't know how people
can make that mistake."

She and her husband talked and talked to their visitors
—about themselves, marriage, sex, morality, anything but
politics.

"All the women I've married or lived with," Vadim said,
"had three things in common: they were actresses, they
were beautiful, and they dyed their hair blonde."

"Look, I know there is a pattern that repeats itself with
Vadim and women," she said on a different occasion, "but
it's not something he works at. It's just the way he is. He
has his friends and his way of life here, and we are constantly running into people who knew him then, but
you're married to someone like Vadim and you were jealous of his past, you couldn't go on living, could you?"

"I am asking a lot from life when I am living with a
woman," he said at St. Tropez. "What is important for me
is to trust, and to trust is not to protect a woman too much
and never to put her in situations where she has no tempta-
tions to face. To protect your wife too much is to be like
a stingy man with money. It is a sick thing. In life, beauty
must be seen, and it is a terrible conception that if the
beauty exists in your wife, it must be hidden. I would not

be jealous if my wife was naked in our garden and she was seen by someone for whom I have respect, someone who would appreciate her beauty on a normal, intelligent level. I would not mind a bit. If a man has an intelligent wife, he will not hide her, will he? I do not have the slightest sense of sin so far as sex and the body are concerned. Why should I pretend that I do for the sake of narrow, stupid, bourgeois thinking?"

"I guess," she said, "I'm a kind of slave type. I seem to function very well when someone puts me in a framework, and Vadim always knows exactly where he's going. His marriages, you know, don't end because he's impossible to live with. He's a very understanding, easygoing, intelligent sort of person, the complete opposite of everything you hear about him before you know him. He has the ability to make a woman bloom. He brings out qualities in her that may have been there already but were never going to come out without Vadim to help them along. He seems to be attracted to complicated, impossible people, myself included, but he is never the one who makes the difficulties."

With a Scotch in his hand, sitting on the terrace of the villa at St. Tropez, he said, "You change a little at adolescence. Sometimes that adolescence lasts a very long time, but you never really learn anything really new after you are twenty, except perhaps in a relationship with a woman. I think that Jane is sensitive and intelligent and evolved enough to understand that, which is why, at the moment, we are very happy."

Jane told someone else, "For me to say I'm not happy would be ungrateful. I've got everything anyone could ask for, but I'm pretty moody. I have ups and downs. I worry a lot. I'm not the most stable person in the world." She thought she was "just not as nice a person as he." At that time, she was pregnant.

"I think," she said, "that it would be nice if you could have babies by all the men that you love and respect. There are a few of Vadim's friends that I would love to have babies with, but the trouble is that it takes too long. Christian Marquand now, who is Vadim's best friend, said to me once, 'I'd like to have a baby by you,' and it would be wonderful to have a son of Christian's, but I mean, nine months. If a pregnancy lasted two months, say, it would be different, but I don't think I could consecrate nine months to anything that wasn't Vadim's."

She had posed naked for him in *Barbarella*, the third movie she made under his direction and the thirteenth in his career. But she did that, she said in justification, because the last of twenty-one costumes hadn't arrived when it came time to shoot the titles for his creation, which was loosely derived from Jean-Claude Forest's book and comic strip, combining pseudo-space science and sex spiced with sado-masochism.

"I don't think of it as an erotic film," said Jane, whose screen duties included stripteasing her way out of her "space armor" and joining in a high-camp "futuristic copulation" scene. "It's just funny and free and nice. You know, Vadim only has me completely nude behind the opening titles. He said, 'Everybody will be waiting for that, so why don't we get it over with right away and get on with the picture?' That's how he thinks about it all."

When she saw the first result she felt that too much of her showed through the lettering, so to satisfy her he had the titling done over again. According to the torrent of publicity that preceded *Barbarella*, she was supposed to be "a kind of sexual Alice in Wonderland." The critics, who praised her for lending style to trash, thought she looked more like Dorothy in a corrupted *Wizard of Oz*.

She thought of her father to play a cameo role as the President of Earth. Hank's reaction, a classic of its kind, was to ask, "Will I have to take my clothes off?" The answer was that he would not, but he pleaded that other commitments prevented him from taking up the invitation.

What with the gadgetry and Vadim's unhurried working pace, *Barbarella* was two years in the making in Rome. Among those engaged in its production was Voutsinas, employed as a dialogue coach. When the Vadims flew back to France, they needed an extra jet to carry all their pets.

"Jane has survived more bad movies than any actress should be able to in a lifetime," Hank has said.

She obviously was not making any great strides forward, and she had to defend herself. "If I have anything as an actress, I have variety. Why not go out on a limb and do something like *Barbarella?* It's fun, it's something new and different. Maybe making the picture wasn't as rewarding to me in the acting sense, day by day, but I like taking a chance like that. . . . I would never have done *Barbarella* with anyone else but Vadim. He convinced me that it was right for me, and I'm very glad he did."

Peter, tongue in cheek, allowed that he wanted her for the role of Crass Commercialism in a picture he claimed to be planning entitled *The Yin and the Yang.* It was his first and last suggestion along those lines, and she heard no more about it.

The only picture he and Jane made together was decidedly peculiar, but not as kinky as that. They played two cousins, Wilhelm and Frederique, in the segment of *Spirits of the Dead* that Vadim directed; two other segments each had a different director. This being an American International production, there were generous displays of Jane's physique, hints of perversion and a love-hate relationship between Frederique and a horse who was really her dead cousin and lover, Wilhelm, with the whole fantasy dressed up in pseudo-Renaissance clothes that reminded some moviegoers of a drag ball. Voutsinas turned up, gorgeously costumed, in a minor role.

When one or two American reviewers questioned the motive of putting Jane and Peter into this bit of falderal, she was moved to make an indignant and not quite coherent reply: "It was not our intention to 'titillate' this way, and in Europe, at least, no one took it like that. Not that I am against incest, but our style is more direct. When the time comes for incest, we will do it head-on and leave the titillating for others."

Originally, neither she nor Vadim wanted a child. She fancied that she didn't even like children, that she would never be able to bear a normal, healthy child. She wasn't interested in motherhood as such. Yet having a baby proved to be one of the two "most violently important things in my life," the other being her decision to become an actress.

"I was thirty, and I thought, 'Well, if I'm ever going to do it, I'd better try now or before I know it, I'll be forty, and it will be a lot harder.' But all those things they tell you about motherhood taking over are absolutely true."

When she first learned that she was pregnant, she was terrified. "I didn't want anyone to know it. I felt so vulnerable. I realized how I had always, strangely enough, rejected femininity because it represented to me vulnerability and a lot of things that scared me. During the process of becoming a mother, I completely overcame this. I became so proud and so aware that I would give and die, and it didn't matter, that I was an *animal*."

As her belly grew bigger, she felt herself change as a personality, becoming more feminine, less agitated. After some months had gone by she caught mumps, and her doctor talked about an abortion. But she was past the first trimester, so she refused to consider it and spent weeks at the farmhouse in bed to protect the child, at peace with the world, comfortably conscious of her part in the whole life cycle.

"At the same time that I was pregnant, all of the animals were whelping and foaling. The dogs were giving birth, and the cats were giving birth, and the rabbits and the chickens. We were all kind of all together. It was really kind of marvelous, and it was a very peaceful, beautiful period for me. I just realized that I am a female animal. I just came to terms with myself and my body and my fellow women. Truly, my relationships with women have changed since then and consequently with everyone."

In and out of the house as usual that summer, Bardot told her with every mark of confidence that the baby would be a girl, born on Brigitte's birthday, September 28. Jane wanted a boy, but in her habitual nightmares, she dreamed that her baby would be born a ten-year-old blonde, looking exactly like Bardot.

She passed the weeks of idleness in studying child psychology and nutrition, avid to learn as much as she could in preparation for the birth. "I developed an awareness of what a child meant and physically what it was. I developed this relationship with this being in me, and I guess it was the first time that I had ever accepted myself as a female human being."

The Vadims spent some time at St. Tropez. Jane was up and about again, very pregnant, very poised. "If I weren't married to Vadim," she said, "I'd be very sad not to have his baby. He has such extraordinary children, you know."

He was relaxed about her condition and her swollen shape. "I am sure," he told his friends, "that it is really full of water and there are seven little red fishes swimming around in there. I am so certain that I am preparing an aquarium for them instead of a nursery."

He joked, "One night of pleasure and nine months of waiting for seven little fishes."

"He has been through all this pregnancy thing before," Jane explained, "but he forgets. It's just as though it's the first time. You know, he has even had *cravings.*"

At heart, she was uncertain of his true feelings about their baby, who arrived precisely as Bardot had predicted, a girl, born on September 28, 1968. "What a nice gesture of friendship," said Brigitte's telegram to Jane in a Paris clinic.

The baby was named for another friend, greatly admired

by Jane. Vanessa Redgrave, the lanky English actress and political activist, has been something of a model for much of Jane's career. They are within a few months of being the same age. "If I were a man," Jane has said, "that's the girl I'd want to marry."

Two years earlier, Vanessa had been voted best actress at the Cannes Film Festival for her movie *Morgan!*—and she had sung Fidel Castro's freedom song, "Guantanamera," at a London poetry festival. She had been in and out of prison as an agitator in ban-the-bomb protests at the time she was starring in Shakespeare on the London stage.

"Vanessa," said Jane, "is a beautiful name. It belongs to a person I admire, and it goes well in French and English." The headline in one French newspaper celebrated the event: "VV BORN ON BB'S BIRTHDAY."

She savored the sensations of childbirth and stored them in her mind. "The pleasure and pain were so extraordinary I tried to hang on to every memory, every mood, but there were constant new ones." A kind of bitterness came with postpartum depression. Brooke Hayward put it into words in a letter: "There is that sad quality. No matter how many children you have, it will never be the same."

Jane and her baby shared the same bed, in accordance with French hospital practice. She felt one of the most important decisions she ever made was to breast-feed Vanessa. "I hate those actresses who say they can't nurse their babies because it ruins their breasts."

She had one brief nightmare in which she fought the clinic doctors because they refused to let Vadim stay with her. Actually, there was no such problem. One morning, he slipped into bed with her when she appeared to be sleeping and what she saw ended her fears about his feelings. She watched him hold their baby on his chest, his rough brown hands in sharp contrast with her little pale ones. As he lay there, tears trickled down his cheeks onto the head of Vanessa.

She had never felt more elated over anything. "There was a grin on my face that I couldn't wipe off. Vadim said I'd stay that way the rest of my life." By the time she went home from the clinic, she was talking about having more children. "I missed being pregnant. I was jealous of women who were."

She was given only one month to nurse her baby before she had to report for work again. She bitterly resented being compelled to switch to formula-feeding and refused to allow photographs of herself giving Vanessa a bottle. The idea of a breast pump as a necessary part of the switch was repulsive to her.

"They took away what belonged naturally to her," she complained. At less than six weeks old, Vanessa was fed wheat germ, blackstrap molasses, liver, brains, and fish. She gained one pound in ten days. "I'm a nut on health foods," said Jane: fertile eggs, no chemical fertilizers, no polished rice or white flour.

Hank found nothing to argue about in that, nor with her desire to start teaching Vanessa to swim when she was six months old. On a visit to see his granddaughter, he wanted to know, "Have you taken care of her swimming lessons yet? You must, you know." This was something of a family tradition. Jane had been taught as a baby.

He was reminded of another bit of the past when Jane said, "I wish I could freeze her at this age, she's so beautiful." He had felt exactly the same when his own daughter was three years old.

Perhaps it wasn't too much for him to hope that the family, which had pulled apart for so long, might soon be made whole again, not in the conventional fashion he once dreamed of, but at least without visible fissures. The cursing of their childhood by his children had lasted long enough. Perhaps the public squabbling could be ended.

This had been an impressive year for him. Marriage with

Shirlee was working out fine; he hadn't been happier with any other wife. One of the favorite masks he wore nowadays was that of the stoical patrician. So many years had passed since he was the starveling from Nebraska that it seemed like a natural fit. The movies of his which he most admired, like *The Grapes of Wrath* and *12 Angry Men*, were being shown and cheered at film festivals.

That spring, he had been honored at a New York dinner of the quietly influential Holland Society, the first actor in its history to be recognized in this manner. It was especially satisfying for the descendant of struggling farmers from Italy by way of the Netherlands to join a group that once included Franklin Delano Roosevelt and his father, James Roosevelt, before him.

Of the people standing in line to greet him that night— Myrna Loy, Lauren Bacall, Leland Hayward, and dozens more—the sight of one man brought tears to Fonda's eyes. John Steinbeck had been in seclusion in his shingled cottage at Sag Harbor on the far end of Long Island for months, seriously ill. When he heard of the Holland Society's plan to honor Hank, he told his wife Elaine, "I must go. I wouldn't miss it for the world."

By some mysterious chemistry, Hank had become the public personification of what his friend stood for. When Steinbeck sat down to write, he pictured Hank in his mind. Even Elaine saw them in some respects as one and the same man. When the time came for Fonda to do a television special of Steinbeck's *Travels With Charley*, only his feet and hands showed on the screen, his flat, expressive drawl sounded nothing like the author's voice, yet she felt somehow that her husband himself was there, resurrected, narrating his story, and not their good friend.

Steinbeck once told Hank, "When I was writing *Sweet Thursday* I had you always in mind as the prototype of Doc." Doc was another friend, a marine biologist, Ed Ricketts. When Richard Rodgers and Oscar Hammerstein were in the process of converting the book into a Broadway musical named *Pipe Dream*, Hank took singing lessons for a year so that he might be cast as the leading man.

"I was praying that he might not learn to sing too well," Steinbeck once reminisced, "because I remembered that Walter Huston, who couldn't sing, did "September Song" better than anyone else has done it since."

Steinbeck's prayer was granted. When Hank auditioned for Rodgers, he was rejected. "And I think that one of my sharp bitternesses," Steinbeck told Hank, "is that due to circumstances personality-wise and otherwise beyond our control you did not play it when it finally came up. I think it might have been a different story if you had."

On the night of the Holland Society dinner, Steinbeck dressed in white tie, tails, and his Nobel Prize medallion. Into his dress shirt he put the pearl studs that Elaine had given him to wear in Stockholm for that presentation. An inveterate, highly skilled tinkerer at the end of every working day, he had made a little leather box for them, inscribed in Latin: *Vanity of vanities, all is vanity.*

The dinner for Hank was Steinbeck's last appearance in public. After it was over, Fonda told him, "I was so overwhelmed to see you last night, I just couldn't communicate. . . . You made the evening for me." Before the close of the year, Steinbeck was dead of a massive heart attack. Nat Benchley telephoned the news to Hank, who was filming in California. He got himself written out of the next day's shooting and flew East for the funeral at the St. James' Episcopal Church on Madison Avenue.

At the service, he read from Steinbeck's favorites, Robert Louis Stevenson and Sir Thomas Malory, who next to the Bible most influenced Steinbeck's prose. And he read a J. M. Synge translation from a well-thumbed book his friend had bought in Dublin in 1911.

If the birds are making lamentation, or the green banks are moved by a little wind of summer, or you can hear the waters making a stir by the shores that are green and flowery. That's where I do be stretched out thinking of love, writing my songs, and herself that Heaven shows me though hidden in the earth I set my eyes on, and hear the way that she feels my sighs and makes an answer to me.

"Alas," I hear her say, "why are you using yourself up before the time is come, and pouring out a stream of tears so sad and doleful. You'd right to be glad rather, for in dying I won days that have no ending, and when you saw me shutting my eyes, I was opening them on the light that is eternal."

Hank spent a few minutes with Elaine, then flew back that evening to work again. As a remembrance of John Steinbeck, she gave Hank the pearl studs in the little leather box her husband made.

In tears, he thanked her. "I much prefer the box," he said.

He had earned friendship from many people. He had handled success with no danger of being spoiled by it. He had kept his own brand of integrity without bending to any man or woman alive. And it looked as though he could learn to come to terms with his children. He had done a little self-analysis, too, without benefit of LSD or a psychiatrist.

He was a grandfather three times over. Peter's son Justin was a year older than Vanessa, and Peter was hoping to establish himself in a special slot of his own in another movie, *The Trip*. It's a solid rule of life in Hollywood that one hit must be followed quick as a flash by another aimed at the same market. After motorcycle gangs, how about LSD? American International was ready and willing.

Jack Nicholson, who shot into movie stardom soon afterward, wrote the script. Peter read it at home one night and was moved to tears by its sheer inventiveness and imagination. Susan shared his excitement when he read her extracts.

"I don't believe it," he told her. "I don't believe I'm really going to have a chance, that *I* get to be in this movie. This is going to be the greatest film ever made in America."

Almost everyone he knew advised him against going into it. Making a drug picture after his own involvement and publicity would be a stupid move, they said. But he kept telling himself that he must do it. "This'll be the first time you can make a movie and won't have to compromise once. It's got LSD in it, and that's all it needs."

He signed a contract for $25,000 and 5 percent of any profits. His friend Dennis Hopper was another member of the cast. Susan Strasberg was the female lead in a role that called for her to join in the fashion and take off her clothes. "The naked scenes were my idea," Peter claimed, considering himself something of an expert on acid.

The producer and director was again Roger Corman. Peter believed that he, too, would not compromise in making *The Trip.* "You can only make something good if you don't have to worry about making money," Peter told him. "The ones who won't go see it because it's an AIP dope film will have to see it because it's a *great* movie. And if you make an exploitation film, you're still gonna make money."

Fonda and Nicholson both began to feel uneasy when, after contracts had been signed, the studio talked about clarifying the script. Peter's confidence was only partly restored when Corman, leaving for Europe to embark on another picture before final editing was completed, let him and Dennis Hopper shoot the desert sequence for *The Trip.*

"I told him I had the equipment, but I didn't, man. I had to go out and rent it." There was no question of taking LSD to stretch his mind while he was filming. "I did it straight because I wanted to see if I knew how to act."

He had doubts about the finished product, which was far from being the film he had originally imagined. But he felt sure that it would make money, since it had cost less than half a million dollars to produce.

"Can you imagine what's gonna happen like in Texas, man, when those kids in that drive-in get to that first nude love scene?" he asked one magazine interviewer. He started dreaming about buying a $250,000 boat. "Now I figure 5 percent of *The Trip* means I get $50,000 for every million they make in profit. . . ."

Honesty compelled him to say publicly that American International had wrecked the picture. He went on saying that on his travels, paid for by AIP, to promote it. The newspaper and television reviewers didn't know whom to blame for the flurry of flesh and kaleidoscopic lights they saw on the screen. "Listen to the sound of love," the advertising and promotion trumpeted. "Feel purple . . . Taste green . . . Touch the scream that crawls up the wall."

The young generation decided it didn't care to. The picture bombed. The dream of the sixty-five-foot yacht disappeared. "By signing a contract and trusting AIP to make a beautiful flick, I had put my balls on the table—and they got lopped right off."

Peter was soured again, worse than ever, on Hollywood. He thought about going back into summer stock, gypsying around the country, though that would have been hard on Susan and their two children. He daydreamed about making some funky European films and investing the profits in a farm on Madagascar, to sit there "growing grass and getting high for the rest of my life."

Toward the end of the tour supposedly promoting *The Trip*, he sat in a Toronto hotel room, depressed and dispirited, working his way through some bottles of imported beer, taking a sleeping pill because the hotel was noisy with conventioners. "I was a little bit loaded," he told *Playboy*, and I looked at a picture that had been left on the table for me to sign for somebody's cousin. It was a photograph from *The Wild Angels* of me and actor Bruce Dern on a chop. I looked at the photo for a while and then thought about what it would look like if, instead of two guys on one cycle, I had each of the guys on a bike."

Peter Fonda had just taken the first step toward making himself a millionaire. It is certain that nobody was going to be more surprised than Hank.

Jane was in the habit of telling people, "Vadim and I are closer," as a result of Vanessa, but it was not so. It wasn't simple, domestic differences that began to separate them, like Jane's having to take the baby pictures because he consistently forgot about them. Or the necessity of getting up at six o'clock every working day, coming home from the studio to a houseful of people, leaving them talking when she went to bed, waving good-bye to them the following morning because they were still there as she left for work again.

"The baby hasn't changed our life," she kept saying, but that was not true. Even her approach to newspapers was different. "Everything I read is in terms of my daughter. For example, will they find a way to clear away diseases of old age by the time she's thirty? I'm hoping when she grows up I won't be doting or overly possessive."

Jane got back into physical shape in no time at all. She had gained more weight than she wanted to. "When I was pregnant, they could sit me on a couch and I'd stay there for twenty-four hours." Now she made time most days to go to ballet classes again. She hated doing exercises as such because they froze her, but she could go into ballet feeling exhausted and depressed and leave relaxed and at ease.

"When you are acting," she explained, "you do a hell of a lot of sitting on your ass and waiting."

The most important change was in her interior feeling, which came when she was carrying Vanessa. "I began to feel a unity with people. I began to love *people.*"

She started reading about Vietnam and watching news of the war on French television. She talked to French activists, to American deserters, to members of the Vietcong visiting Paris. She was fascinated and stirred by a movie she saw of the 1963 March on Washington, with 200,000 men and women from all walks of life demonstrating to support black Americans' struggle for civil rights.

She was reaching out for a way to put it all together in

her head. In these early stages of change that entailed relating it to the subject with which she'd been identified as Madame Vadim—sexuality in motion pictures.

She fancied that one day a major Hollywood studio would make movies showing copulation, and it would not be sexy, though it might be boring, funny, or beautiful. It would put an end to shame. The human body would be accepted for what it was, and the world could progress to more important matters.

She didn't personally plan on pioneering as an actress in this direction because she was "too shy," said the woman who had already cut her long hair, let it grow out its natural brown, and washed it at home. She had given up dressing to look sexy in black leather boots and miniskirts; slacks and sweaters were her choice. "I think it's sexier when people are saying it with their eyes, fully clothed," she said.

Like her brother, she was set for change, but on a totally different road. As a family, the Fondas were still out of step.

XIII

IT WAS NOT the picture she had initially hoped for, "saying something about the war," but it had some telling points to make about a different kind of conflict, the exploitation of desperate people. That had a strong appeal to Jane in the new climate of her thinking. *They Shoot Horses, Don't They?* fitted well into a lot of thinking. She was glad to sign for it at $400,000 and a percentage of its earnings.

Then, because she was far from being the iron-willed radical that she was often taken for, she started to worry over whether she had made the right choice. Like every other performer in movies, she knew the value of a quickly recognizable image and the importance of never alienating too big a proportion of the audience. She had been identified for years as a sex kitten, or possibly a sex cliché. Now she undertook to play a flat-chested, skinny drab, a girl in a marathon dance contest of the 1930s who expected little from life except death.

"I look so scruffy in the part," said the one-time "Kiki," "that I'll probably never get another."

Looking back, with the political perspectives that she acquired in the months to come almost as fast as you can put on makeup, she was satisfied with the movie's message: that in our violently competitive society, people are ready to do anything in order to win.

In spite of her increasingly bold talk about her own turmoil and affairs in general, she was painfully uncertain of herself. "I worry a lot," she admitted, "about Vadim and me, or if I'll ever be hired again."

She found it difficult for two people to share one life. One day she startled a woman journalist, a German, who had come to interview her. "How are you today?" said the writer by way of an opening.

"I've been thinking about getting a divorce," replied Jane, who didn't believe in evasion.

The German quickly offered her sympathy. "No," Jane said, "we'll still live together. I've been thinking it might be good for our relationship." She thought of a neighbor they once had in Malibu, a widow who sat in a window all day and shouted at the Vadims, "You'll be punished, you're living in sin."

They were back at Malibu while she made *Horses*, with Vanessa installed in a room that her mother was slightly apologetic about because "it looks like a circus." It was filled with pictures, gaily colored toys and mobiles, and a radio was kept playing. "That's why she's so alert," her mother explained.

She devoted much of her free time to planning how Vanessa might be brought up, taught to read and learn languages before she was five years old. In addition to books on child psychology, she dug into the Horace McCoy novel on which the new movie was based, burrowing her way into the part. On the set, Sidney Pollack, a former actor and dramatic coach who was directing, regarded her as an expert on the subject of the marathon dance craze.

"She was completely involved and totally professional," he recalled. "She carried a copy of the book around with her, and because she had strong opinions about it, she was slow to be persuaded if she disagreed with somebody else's interpretation of a point or a scene. That was so much more exciting than working with a puppet. She had a kind of remote quality. There was no socializing at the end of the day, no need to send her flowers or give her the 'Good morning, dear,' treatment. She wanted none of that." Vadim arrived most days to take her home when work was done.

Then to concentrate on her part and to escape the distractions of living at home, she moved onto the set in a trailer with Vanessa and a nurse. Some nights she slept in a portable dressing room on the set itself, as secluded as a walled nun.

"I do much more giving than Jane," Vadim told reporters later. "In a way, in our relationship, she is the man and I am the woman."

In *Horses* her previous professional incarnations as the chick next door, the unhappy hooker, and the sex bonbon were killed and buried. Her performance as Gloria, the girl from Texas who finishes with her brains blown out, won her an Academy Award nomination and the New York Film Critics' vote as best actress of 1969.

She arrived with Vadim at Sardi's on West Forty-fourth Street to join those critics in a quiet Sunday buffet held in her honor. A little later, she took a few minutes to talk about a moral question implied in the movie; with echoes of the devastation of her mother's death: Has anyone the right to help end someone else's life?

"The one, ultimate, final choice you have is to take your own life, which is a very important choice. Everyone should have the right to do that."

When the movie was finished and Vanessa was one year old, an old need arose in her to put herself "into a position of extreme loneliness." She wanted time again to put things together in her thinking. The most remote place she could conceive of was India, remote culturally and physically, a place she had never seen. She went there alone, and she was overwhelmed by the experience.

She started off staying in first-class hotels, but not for

long. The contrast of going outside into the marketplaces, where child beggars carried dead babies, was too sharp. The poverty, the sounds, the smells, the teeming mass of people tore at her.

With her insatiable drive to learn, to absorb and understand, she spent her days meeting Indians at all levels and of all castes. She was invited into their homes. She was taught how to bargain in the marketplaces.

After India she made the difficult journey north to Sikkim, the mountain state tucked away in the Himalayas and met American hippies there. More than ten thousand of them, by official count, were living in India then, to escape from Western civilization, to search for what they fancied to be truth and tranquility. From Bombay and Calcutta they spread north to the foothills of the northern mountains or as far as Katmandu, spurred by the guru faddism that the Beatles and Mia Farrow, among others, helped propagate.

At first, local people welcomed these flower children, principally as objects of curiosity, because they were white, partly because they had dollars to spend. But in Indian culture an unwashed body is anathema, and bathing was unimportant to most hippies. Puritanical Indians were shocked by the sight of nudity, by drug addiction, by the lewdness of the public copulation that sometimes occurred. When their funds ran out, some of the intruders took on jobs, which Indians felt was unfair competition, or turned to prostitution. Jane despised them for polluting the country and for their blindness to the incredible problems India was facing. And the fact that she was there herself made her equally guilty.

The self-education in reality was making rapid progress. In politics, she was taking her first uncertain steps leftward from liberalism.

She felt, uneasily, that she could have gone on that kind of a dropout trip, but she suddenly understood "the incredible irresponsibility" of doing any such thing. She asked herself, "What am I doing over here?" So she came back.

She flew from Bombay to Los Angeles and arrived at night in Beverly Hills. When she woke in the morning, India still seemed to be the reality and the manicured American suburb the dream, with its aloof, pastel-colored mansions, exotic trees, lawn sprinklers whirling, status automobiles idling through the quiet streets.

In this strange halfway zone between two worlds, she picked up a copy of *Ramparts*. On the cover of that magazine there was a picture of an Indian, a pitiful American Indian girl, stirring sympathy in Jane for the militants who seized the island of Alcatraz in San Francisco Bay to dramatize the plight of their race at the hands of white men. She read the article, "Red Power," which the picture illustrated but could not believe what she read. She telephoned the author, Peter Collier, and asked him to take her to Alcatraz.

The visit she made can only be regarded as the first and most important link in a chain of events that transformed Jane Fonda. It was also the first step on a long, unfinished journey of discovery of this country, of the cabalistic world of revolutionary politics, and of herself. In every instance, she insisted on seeing for herself. What she saw drove her farther and farther leftward.

Of course, she was far from being the first WASP to be deeply stirred by the fate of Indians, victimized by what started in the last century as a policy of deliberate genocide and still treated as an inferior race. But the impact in her case overwhelmed her. Her personal life was disjointed. Her marriage was coming to an end in spirit, though not in legal fact, since she saw no reason for divorce. Her career was in a period of transition, giving her no assurance yet that audiences would accept her as a serious actress and not just the girl with the prettiest backside in Hollywood.

She was convinced that she had been physically and intellectually asleep during her years with Vadim, as she had been before she met Strasberg. Now she was revitalized and bursting with pent-up energies. She needed a cause to throw herself into with her particular combination of passion and single-mindedness. Instead of one cause, she rapidly found a dozen and more.

Her Alcatraz trip made newspaper headlines, but the questions that reporters tossed at her caught her at a disadvantage. She didn't know enough to provide answers that satisfied either them or herself. She found herself carried away by emotion instead of fact.

She needed to go off with her suitcases of books, lock herself up and read until her knowledge caught up with her instincts.

She had few illusions about her vulnerability. It was easy to make her look ridiculous in interviews on many subjects. She could not defend herself. She had to flesh out her feelings with knowledge.

One of the determining books for her was *Our Brother's Keeper*, by Edgar Cohn, of the *Citizen's Advocate* in Washington; "very scholarly, fascinating and depressing," she thought, in its look at the situation of Indians in America today. Again, it aroused in her the desire to see for herself so that she could make up her mind. She chose the State of Washington as the place to begin.

"All you have to do is go to any of these places and just scratch the surface," she said as a convert to the cause of equal rights for the original Americans. Washington Indians had been joined in legal battle with the State government over fishing rights for years.

Jane realized that she needed to return permanently to America to find out, aside from being a white liberal who gave money to worthwhile causes, what she could do to implement what she felt.

She decided to take two months off, not to lock herself up and read, but to explore the United States, searching, between Los Angeles and New York.

The idea of how a motion-picture actress goes on her travels has been implanted in the imaginations of us all by Hollywood. We picture her swaddled in perfume and furs, rings flashing on her fingers, bracelets jangling on her wrists. In our mass fantasies, she is attended by at least two maids, a uniformed chauffeur, a personal hairdresser, and a large dog, usually a Borzoi. She rides either in a block-long limousine, preferably a Duesenberg, with a dozen pieces of Vuitton luggage, or in the entire first-class section of a jet. That's what we were taught to believe by movie-studio publicity departments from the days of Pola Negri down to the time of Marilyn Monroe. Television has not done much to dent the image.

The travel style of Jane Fonda was either disillusioning or encouraging, depending on which way you look at it: "I have never been someone who dresses particularly fancily." She wears blue jeans, an Army-Navy surplus jacket, and Army boots if she's going to be any place where there's snow. She doesn't wear makeup."

As a companion on her journey, she chose a dear friend from the era of her life that had been spent in France. She had met Elisabeth Vailland, widowed now, when her husband, a writer, was working with Vadim. Both the Vaillands were members of the Communist Party. They would stop by at the Vadims' Paris home in the evenings, "sometimes with workers," and Jane would talk for hours at a time with them.

Elisabeth was half Russian, half Italian. Everyone needed someone like Elisabeth in his life, Jane thought. Elisabeth had never been to America before and did not speak English.

Shortly before they set out, Jane went as a guest to a party given in his Hollywood home by Mike Nichols, one-time partner of Elaine May in a television comedy act, who became what the motion-picture industry calls a "hot ticket" by making *Catch 22* and then *Carnal Knowledge*. Antonioni, the Italian director, was there, too, along with a young man named Fred Gardner, who had worked as a writer on *Zabriskie Point*, which Antonioni had directed.

Speaking of Gardner some time later, Jane said, "I didn't know who he was, but I was mentioning that I had decided to make a trip across the United States. He said, 'Why don't you visit some GI coffeehouses?' I said, 'What is a GI coffeehouse?' I didn't know."

Fred Gardner is an author and activist against the Vietnam war. It was his thought that GIs needed places "where they could be treated as human beings, enjoy their own music and culture, and meet together away from the eyes of 'lifers.' " Coffeehouses were the answer, to be opened in Army towns as havens from harassment by the brass and centers of organized protest within the Army.

With the help of some sympathizers, Gardner opened the first of them in Columbia, South Carolina, in the fall of 1967, to attract the 23,000 soldiers stationed at nearby Fort Jackson. The town police took to making regular calls, sometimes every hour.

Three organizers of the coffeehouses were arrested and charged with conducting a public nuisance, fined $10,000, and initially sentenced to six years' imprisonment apiece. But within a year at least half a dozen similar havens of dissent had been opened—there are currently twenty-six of them throughout the country and at bases in Germany and Japan, including one called the Shelter Half in Tacoma, Washington.

Fred Gardner told Jane Fonda about coffeehouses, to have her feel that maybe this was something she could get her heart into. She had been working in Paris with deserters, helping them get work permits, homes, help and medical care. So far as she knew, a GI Movement meant deserting.

She told Gardner, "Well, now, this sounds very interesting, because I'm very against the war, and I am very in favor of protests and petitions and demonstrations. But I know there is some area which I haven't found yet, in which I know I can be very useful." She asked for his telephone number.

The two women drove north up the coast of California into Washington. Vanessa, one year old, stayed in her father's charge. Before Jane could turn her attention to coffeehouses, there was another piece of business she wanted to attend to, the original cause that awakened her, the plight of American Indians. She called on the leaders of a forthcoming demonstration and joined in when a group of young Indians staged a protest demonstration at Fort Lawton. Their announced intention was to take over the base, which is a satellite of Fort Lewis, as a "native cultural center." The attempt ended in a minor skirmish, and she was ceremoniously expelled from the place. She and Madame Vailland went on to visit the Shelter Half coffeehouse, a thorn in the flanks of the Fort Lewis brass.

It is an important general rule in any active political group, reformist, radical, or revolutionary, that a recruit needs to be bloodied to pull him into the ranks as a qualified activist. Sympathizers are converted into participants by taking on a job, any job, that calls on their time or their courage. The task may be as safe as addressing envelopes or as hazardous as marching through Alabama turned out to be in the 1960s. In conventional politics, your name goes on the active list if you donate a dollar to the cause. In radical politics you need to do more than that: you must give something of yourself. It's as ritualistic in many ways as a boy in primitive society going out on his first hunt and coming back a warrior.

At the Shelter Half, Jane Fonda was asked to go to Fort Lewis and hand out antiwar leaflets. This was of necessity a job for civilians because Army regulations make it a court-martial offense for a serviceman. She said no. "I'm not ready yet to do that."

Fort Lewis was an open base. The coffeehouse was briefly declared "off limits" at one point by the Army, but the order was rescinded after complaints were stirred up among Congressmen and the public. She went to the base with a plain invitation for every GI who cared to listen: "Would you like to come and talk with me at the coffeehouse this evening?"

As the printed words of the supporters say, a coffeehouse is many things. "It's a place to hear your music, sip a good cup of coffee, and eat wholesome food. . . . Its warm, relaxed atmosphere contrasts sharply with the bars and B-girls of army-town strips." But it is also "a center for dialogues on the war and on other social issues of concern to all Americans—racial justice, sexual equality, the rights of farm workers to a union."

It seems likely that, in the Army's view, the first of those enticements are more than canceled out by the last. Anyway, good coffee, wholesome food or not, Jane Fonda was arrested twenty minutes after she showed up. MPs closed in on her in the middle of her role as herald and hostess. Spic and span in sharply pressed olive drab, the forces of good order and military discipline escorted her to the office of the Provost Marshal. By her account, she was kept "waiting around for three or four hours."

Face to face at last with the officer, she was insistent on what she must be allowed to do. "I have the right to make a phone call to my lawyer. May I please exercise that right?"

"You are a civilian and this is a military base. You have no rights here."

She knew better. Righteous anger was a quality she inherited from her father. It was time to confront the Provost Marshal with a different kind of challenge and make him realize what the Declaration of Independence and the Bill of Rights and the Fourteenth Amendment really stood for. In a cold rage, she stretched herself on the floor, quickly and smoothly with the ease of her years of ballet classes.

"Get up, Miss Fonda," the officer commanded.

"I will not move," she said, with her long, thin fingers clenched, "until you let me call a lawyer. And if you don't let me call a lawyer, you're going to be in such *trouble*—"

She won her point. Permission was granted. That was her first act of civil disobedience. She felt that she had a certain flair for it. When you know you're right . . . "anybody in this country who gets arrested for doing something that they know is right will never be the same again. I think that does more to radicalize than anything else."

She was given an expulsion paper stating that she had broken Army regulations. As a result she was barred forever from the base. If she came back she was subject to six months in jail and/or a five-hundred-dollar fine.

That was in March 1970. Her personal war with the United States Army was now declared. Before the end of May she had been arrested on three more military bases across the country as a full-blooded fighter in the Movement. The Army put her on its list of those people on whom it keeps undercover watch as troublemakers. The radicalization of Jane meant that there was no possible turning back to the liberalism she had previously called her own.

In a real sense, the Army molded her, in much less time and with every bit of the same efficiency that it employs to take a young draftee and turn him into a fighting man. It was part of the process that the leaders of any serious-minded radical organization can always count on. Being arrested for what you believe to be unjust reasons is the best recruiting device they ever had.

The final radicalization of Jane Fonda took place on the journey as she continued wandering in the little rented car through Nevada, Idaho, Colorado, Utah, and elsewhere. She left Los Angeles a left-wing liberal. She arrived in New York a rebel activist. What she saw on the way and the people she was introduced to made her eager to commit herself.

"As a revolutionary woman," she said, "I'm ready to support all struggles that are radical."

She accepted the commitment as a vow of poverty. She soon began trying to sell everything in her wardrobe except her work clothes of slacks and sweaters. She got rid of the $1,000-a-month house she had rented in Malibu. She accustomed herself to go tourist-class whenever she traveled, with all she needed in one bag, "and that's more than enough." She walked on picket lines. She gave away her money to the point where she was almost permanently broke, living, as one friend put it, "in sackcloth and ashes." As soon as Vanessa was old enough, she often traveled with her mother. At a later date Jane sold the farmhouse at La Fontaine Richard so that, with the proceeds, Vadim could pay off his French taxes.

She was prepared to do battle for any number of causes —for striking lettuce workers in California, for welfare clients demanding fair treatment, for the Young Lords, for GI rights, for women's liberation.

None of these things was foreign to Hank's way of thinking. What made it impossible for him to see eye-to-eye with the daughter he praised so highly as an actress was a basic change in her philosophy. In politics, she had shared his approach, as she had been brought up to do.

"It was doing everything one could to have the right people elected, the people who were opposed to wars, the people who would try to help the poor and oppressed in this country," she said. "Not something that he necessarily talked about, but something that he did. By his example, it was something that we were brought up feeling."

The big change in her was the end of that feeling that you could work within the American system of party politics. Change from being a liberal. Change from thinking you could take the bad guys out of office and put in the good guys. She thought that was important, but she no longer thought it made much difference, and she was sorry.

Newspaper readers scarcely had time to adjust to the idea of a former sex kitten speaking up for Indians and getting herself arrested by the Army before they caught other views of her, which many citizens found much more alarming. Backing Black Panthers carried her over into hostile territory. As most people saw it, the Panthers had declared guerrilla war on white America. They believed in and practiced violence in their efforts to overturn established society. They carried guns and weren't slow to use them on the police or, if the police were to be believed, on each other.

How did she come to get involved with the Panthers? Out of curiosity, is the simple answer. The Indians' cause was nothing like enough to satisfy her hunger for something bigger than herself. She read about the Panthers in newspapers and in the leftist magazines she had taken to buying, notably about the arrests of Panther leaders in their running battles with the law.

She contacted the Panthers. People were saying, "You can't do that. It's going to ruin your career. You're going to get killed." She confessed to being frightened, but she wanted to discover the facts, so she talked to Panther leaders in Los Angeles. It was the first time she had met blacks who were going to the root problem of the system and not saying that black capitalism would change anything, but would only end up exploiting blacks.

She didn't completely understand Panther ideas, which derived from Karl Marx's thinking on the inevitability of war between the classes of society and the need to establish a dictatorship of working people until class has been abolished. She had not read *Das Kapital* and other standard classics of Communist theory.

But if she was muddled in her approach to problems of social wrongs and rights, she admired the Panthers' clear-cut discipline. The free meals they served to black poor and white poor alike in city ghettoes appealed to her sentiment.

She accepted their argument that the arrest of Huey Newton, Bobby Seale, and other Panther leaders represented persecution by the police. She was indignant that they were often denied their right to legal defense.

With characteristic passion—or ignorant recklessness, according to her growing army of critics—she plunged into the Panthers' cause. She gave up her time, her money, and, to a considerable degree, her personal safety. Before the year was out, she was committed heart and soul to the Panthers, identified by J. Edgar Hoover as the black militants' chief fund-raiser, a familiar figure in jeans and sweater at many of their rallies, under surveillance by the FBI.

She saw the continuing armed conflicts with police exclusively in Panther terms. "The Panthers are truly not racists. Those who kill them are racist." Of course, she liked the Panthers. Of course, she totally supported them. Fighting for the Panthers was not violence, in her view, but self-defense.

When Huey Newton, the Panther leader, was released from prison, she became for a while his constant companion, and she made no effort to defend herself against malicious whispers that she was his mistress.

On the whole subject of violence, she stood on shaking ground. "I think violence is a foolish tactic," she would say at one point, then rationalize that the idea of the Panthers being violent was pure propaganda.

Though no formal announcement had been made, she had left Vadim. Except when talking to people she trusted, that fact was left blurred. "It was hard to shake hands and say goodbye, but it was absolutely essential."

The ending was as unconventional as the beginning had been. They would continue to be friends. She would be delighted to see him and go out with him. They would share love and custody of Vanessa. Neither of them thought about divorce, "unless Vadim wants to get married again one day."

It had not been easy to win his understanding of what she was doing and why she was doing it. He had been caught by surprise, like everybody else who knew her, and he was as much hurt as she was. He would have understood better if she had left him for another lover, not for a multitude of causes, some of them remote to him.

"Except that he approves of what I'm doing," she said. "He doesn't agree with it all. It's very difficult for a Frenchman. I mean, for example, I will talk to him about the fact that a Black Panther's bail for a particular crime will be $100,000,000 whereas a white man's or any other black man's bail for a particular crime will be $10,000, and he'll say, 'What are you talking about? In France, nobody has bail.' Or you talk about a no-knock warrant. He said, 'You don't ever have to knock to come into a home in France.' So it's very hard to explain some of these things."

He was concerned about the physical danger she ran into at Panther rallies and elsewhere, now that she was a vulnerable target, frankly detested by some law officers as well as readers of newspaper reports, which were not always objective.

When she followed up on her promise—she seldom makes promises lightly—Gardner suggested how she could take a cram course, teaching herself in the least amount of time as much as possible about what is loosely known as the GI Movement.

This operation, usually referred to with a capital "M," is a fairly tightly knit, but understandably low-profile, network of resistance to the war and what its members regard as military persecution of resisters within all the armed forces. It includes fifty raucous underground newspapers, bookstores, advice services, and what are guardedly called "Movement centers" in the United States and overseas.

Movement organizers in a recent report stated, "Perhaps more than any other single development in the GI Movement, the birth of GI coffeehouses has aided the growth of organized protest in the military."

Finding out more about them was one of Jane's objectives when she rented a car and set off with Elisabeth Vailland across America.

"But he knows he can't stop me from doing anything. I know, and he's told me, that if anything happens and I need his help, he will be there."

Hank, who had taken a long time to warm to his son-in-law, began to feel sympathy for him. Vadim, he said, "is as fed up as I am."

Her father wasn't completely out of sympathy for Jane. He could see a lot of his own thinking reflected in hers. "I was fighting for civil rights before Jane could spell it. I'm not so much in disagreement with her sentiments as I am with the way in which she does things. But it's her bag, and I must say she's totally committed."

That ranked as important with this man who prided himself on being able to spot phoniness from a mile away. "For her, there's nothing insincere or phony about it." But he thought, along with virtually all his friends, that she was being used. A little later, she agreed that, on occasion, she really had been ripped off.

XIV

PETER probably understood her better than anyone. Her ceaseless, selfless work for Indians and Panthers and the other causes that came along could be explained by some of his long-standing thoughts about her. "She always went for the runt of the litter," he once said, "out of a natural affection, not just pity."

"Jane and I are easy prey for people who want to pull us down; we're targets." That was another thought. And a third: "She has got a career and family, and it's not important if she stays with Vadim or not."

But Peter didn't share her enthusiasm for Panthers, whom he looked on as black racists. Racism, to him, was what he called "spiritual pollution." The only solution was to stop thinking in terms of black and white. "My personal belief," he told *Playboy*, "is that armed revolution by black people is not the answer. I totally reject that notion," though blacks had real grievances that had to be redressed.

The Panthers were reactionaries, in his opinion. "They're out there reacting against something, not acting *for* something. It's too late for black identity, or white identity, or green identity. That's all past." The only possible identity for everyone was human identity, with no relationship to skin color.

"This doesn't mean," he said, "I don't have compassion for the Panthers, of course, even if I don't agree with them. I know very well that the Man's down on them. Smacks a wee bit of harassment to me when you got a hundred cops shooting at six Panthers at five in the morning. But this is a tough area to get into, because I'm a Beverly Hills, uptown white. I suppose my views would seem more valid if I were living in the ghetto."

He talked as Hollywood's existential heir, a man of influence and affluence, a dark horse who had won the race, thanks to the legend that had sprung to life in his imagination. *Easy Rider*, his apocalyptic vision of two loners on motorcycles, with money in their pockets from dope-peddling, crossing America to retire in Florida, was making millions around the world. Peter had gained the credentials to be listened to in the business.

The plot, including the blood-drenched murder of the two riders at its climax, had come into his mind sharp and clear as he fantasized, sipping beers in a lonely Toronto hotel room. "It's *right*," he told himself, "because we've got all the things that backers want. We go for dope, we go for motorcycles, we go riding across the country, we'll even get some sex here and there—but we can do all these things really honestly."

The only person he felt would latch onto the idea was Dennis Hopper, a fellow actor and outcast who had married Brooke Hayward. Hopper was known for his gall as well as for acting talent. As a brash fifteen-year-old, he had been barred from the Columbia Pictures lot for offending Harry Cohn, and he had retained a special brand of well fortified *chutzpah*.

Hank never cared for him. When *Easy Rider*'s success brought Hopper to the Oscars hand-out celebrations, Hank carefully spelled out his opinions: "Any man who insists on wearing his cowboy hat to the Academy Awards ceremonies and keeps it on at the dinner table afterward ought to be spanked."

Hopper and Peter had quarreled after their work together filming desert scenes for *The Trip*. But the job he had done then convinced Peter that he was the director he wanted for *Easy Rider*. Hopper had sworn never to talk to Peter again, but that was forgotten once he had heard him outline his new idea.

"Man, wow, Jesus, I'm glad you called me," he said and came up instantly with the thought that the two motorcycle riders should make their money by smuggling cocaine. Most of the twelve-page outline was devised between the two of them as they walked around the tennis court of Peter's house on Lime Orchard Road. The primary motivation was to make money.

"I kept thinking about this seventeen-year-old coming up to a couple of friends saying, 'Hey, man, you got to see this flick. These guys, they smuggle coke across the border and then they get on these chops, these wild, far-out bikes, and then they ride, and they get high—I mean, *really* get high—and at the end of the movie, well, they just get shot. Like *that*, man, just because they're there at the wrong time."

Another motive, to be combined with the first, was "to show the beauty of the anarchy of the individual versus the decrepit anarchy of society." As time went on, though, Peter had some second thoughts about the existential hero he created, Captain America, otherwise known as Wyatt, and his faithful sidekick, Billy.

"I promise you that when you base your life solely on economics, as Wyatt and Billy did in *Easy Rider*, you blow your life right out the window."

With the concept bubbling in his head, Peter took off to see Jane when she was making *Barbarella*. On the set he met Terry Southern, one of the eight scenarists credited with writing Vadim's science-fiction fantasy, whose fame as an author originated with *Candy*. Southern offered to let his name be used as a coauthor for *Easy Rider* to help Peter raise production money, though his contribution as a writer didn't warrant that degree of credit.

The next step was to form a company, Pando, named for Peter and Dennis, with a house rule that barred the word "star." Jack Nicholson signed on as another professional actor in the cast. Billy Hayward, once the little boy who followed Peter in school, joined in as coproducer; he had held Hollywood jobs before, including working in the cutting room on *Camelot*.

With 16mm cameras, a shoestring budget, and their families in tow, the moviemakers set off to gypsy across America, starting in New Orleans. An old friend from the past caught up with them when they were shooting in the desert outside of Hollywood. Joshua Logan was the company's guest and Peter, tanned and bearded, the host, who introduced his two children, Bridget and Justin, aged five and two respectively, to their "great-godfather." Everybody's family had unpaid roles in the sequences they were filming, a hippie commune where Captain America and Billy come to call and pass the grass around.

The veteran producer and director was impressed. "Here were all these people I had known as babies with their babies now. As I saw it, I thought, 'I guess there's a public for this kind of thing,' but I didn't know *what* they were doing. I didn't understand it at all, but I was fascinated."

Hayward invited Logan to see Dennis Hopper's first rough cut of the finished picture, which ran four and a half hours. After the first reels, Josh fell asleep. At this reaction from their first audience, Peter was crushed. But the film was recut, and total costs amounted to a piddling $375,000 of Columbia Pictures' money; that studio had bankrolled the film's making and given Peter 22 percent of the profits.

At the Cannes International Film Festival *Easy Rider* was

given a standing ovation. In New York, it broke house records from the day it opened. It became one of the biggest draws in Columbia's history from Tokyo to Helsinki. Nobody could have been more delighted than Hank. So far as he was concerned, money wasn't the main consideration.

"When I told him it had been sold to Columbia," Peter reminisced, "Pa says to me on the phone, 'Well, boy, it doesn't make any difference whether it's sold or not, the fact that's important is *you* did it.' It opens up a whole new can of peas."

Now that he could afford it, he had tried to recapture the happier days of childhood in a tangible way by buying the farmhouse where he and Jane had played together. Hank had sold it for $90,000 after the death of Frances. When Peter wanted it back as his own, he offered the new woman owner $450,000.

"She said she could get $1,000,000, and she actually sold it for $950,000. Now there are seventeen houses standing on that land."

Another thing he wanted to do, now that he accepted the fact that he had a certain influence on at least some sections of the population, was "to preach to people." His thoughts were distinctly his own, as hostile in some fundamental respects to the New Left as to the old Right.

He was considering a plan to make a full-length documentary on pollution. His definition of pollution covered a list ranging from DDT to racism, white, black, and Chinese. It would be a long-odds risk if he couldn't get a major movie company to finance it and distribute it, and he'd had more than enough experience to recognize that probability.

But pollution, physical in the poisoning of air and water, mental in the poisoning of minds by prejudice, was a subject that preoccupied much of his thinking. He told *Playboy:* "I've got two hostages to fortune, as Jack Kennedy said— my two children. Not only do they have to grow up surrounded by an atmosphere of hate and misunderstanding, but they are also growing up in an atmosphere so polluted it may poison them to death."

He calculated that he might well have to put up the money to shoot the picture, then if it couldn't be distributed to moviehouses he'd sell it for television. He reasoned, "I want to reach as many people as I can with this one. I really want to shake people's minds. If it makes money, too, that'll be fine, but the main thing is that I want maybe fifty million people to see it and discuss it, and I want to create an economic interest in ecology within the movie industry."

On a totally different level, he wanted to buy a boat. That was one more reason why the easy money from *Easy Rider* was important. Owning a boat was an old ambition. When he was going through the pangs of putting his individuality together inside his head, sailing was a great help. Controlling a boat against winds and tide wasn't unlike beating a course through heavy weather toward a port you could identify as home.

He envisioned a sailboat big enough to sail around the world in with his wife, Susan, and family. Something close to seventy feet of hull, with an auxiliary engine and cabin space to take some friends along as company and crew. What he had in mind would have to cost $200,000 or more. Hawaii would be a good spot to set sail for as a start.

It would inevitably be expensive, but so was just about everything else. "Whatever you do, there's a lot of dues to pay. Man, there's been a lot of bad Karma in my life and what I've been through."

His plans for the boat were already common gossip in the village life of the movie business, where one man's success is another man's envy, and setting people up and cutting them down is sport for almost everybody. Peter Fonda's radical cool and Dennis Hopper's roaring egotism antagonized some fellow professionals of his own generation, as well as a multitude in his father's age group.

"Let's face it," said one member of Peter's age group, "they gave the youth what they wanted to hear—knocks at the Establishment. And now they're getting rich like the Establishment they knock. If they were really honest in what they believe, they'd drive down to Watts and pass that money out."

That may have been what Jane would have done, but brother and sister would have no quarrel about it. Where the United States Army was a decisive influence in radicalizing Jane, Peter Fonda was another. He rated himself as "partly" responsible. "We've talked a lot in the past couple of years about the state of this country and what we can do to change it," he said at this time.

So there was one more consideration to be included in his assessment of his future: how to hold on to the precious and very special relationship he had always had with her, whether they were together or separated by circumstances beyond their control.

"My past is radioactive," he once remarked, "and if I get close to it, Geiger counters start clicking. I identify her as one of the minds I'm close to. We stood and fell together, as if we were involved in a nuclear explosion. By listening to each other talk, we reaffirmed reality and found our place."

He was ready to talk about the change in himself and share his thoughts as usual with Jane "to assure her that we hadn't been failures when we were little, that we weren't guilty for what happened."

He said, "I grew up with one question: 'What did we do to cause everybody to dislike us so much?' How come everybody didn't just love us? I asked what did those two little innocent kids do to get fucked up so much?"

"He did many things, or allowed many things to happen, that caused problems in our lives," he said of his father. "The worst thing I could say about my whole life was, 'Nobody told me anything.' I didn't know anything—why we should say 'Negroes' when other people said 'niggers'; why some people love Jews and others are anti-Semitic. I didn't know my mother committed suicide until years later when I read it in a magazine. Pa never tried to explain.

"He depicted great American honesty, yet he had no way of telling us about his life. We weren't part of it. Wherever he was we'd spend Christmas and summer vacations. Spain, Italy, France—the world became our backyard. But while we were there, never sharing, we weren't let in.

"We longed for the relationship he had with his pals—John Wayne, Ward Bond, John Ford, John Hodiak, Richard Rodgers, Oscar Hammerstein, Josh Logan, Leland Hayward. It never happened. We couldn't talk to him staring across the dining-room table.

"Imagine being the kids of a person as incredible as Henry Fonda in visage, value, status, and symbol. If you're with him consistently and don't get in, you can only blame yourself. You feel guilty about things you may have done.

"He rationalized his lack of attention to us by saying we weren't worthy of his attention. Jane once said, 'You and me, when we're happy, we feel really guilty.'

"She started lashing out at him in the press first, then I started lashing out at him. When she was doing it, he'd call me and ask, 'What's she trying to do?' But both of us said the same things, though not at the same time.

"It's all changed now. Pa is a much mellowed man. His life has changed, and so has ours. I'm reconciled to him. I come to his defense. He's a generous, kind man, and I love him dearly. I forgive him.

"He no longer sees his kids as failures. She's trying to fulfill something, be recognized, do something right. I'm ready to do anything as long as I can make a life for myself. Maybe I'd be happier being a taxidriver."

Some months before this time, before the sheer scale of his *Easy Rider* started to disclose itself, Peter wrote Jane a letter. In it he told her of the changes he saw in himself and in Hank, of what was happening in America and something of his feelings about her.

"I assume a fantasy life for her," he explained after he had written it. "It's an ideal situation for her, where she has such a superego that she can walk through things as strong as a lion. If she can be cool and understand the workings of life, what all the games really mean, she can be unaffected by them, she can fulfill herself. The best I would want for her is to reach fullness all the time without self-deceit or self-deception."

On each of the letter's three pages, he pressed his thumbprint. It was the first time he had ever written to her.

XV

WHEREVER she traveled to make a speech, picket a store, attend a rally, march in a demonstration, she was conscious of being watched and sometimes photographed by men with a different interest in her from that of the newsmen, who always rated her as good copy. Half a dozen separate government agencies kept files on her now as a potentially dangerous rebel. Her involvement with GI rights and the antiwar wing of that amorphous, loosely knit thing called the Movement meant that undercover Army agents watched her, as well as the FBI. State troopers and local police watched her when she arrived in town. But, though by this time she was getting used to being picked up on bases by military police for stirring up trouble, she was enraged to find that United States Customs, which is a branch of the Treasury Department, had her under surveillance, too.

On the plane down from Canada to Cleveland she had worked as usual, boning up on her notes and reading the dozen and one subjects precious to her heart, taut and unrelaxed. This had been an assignment for an organization called Vietnam Veterans Against the War. Some North Vietnamese had visited Windsor, Ontario, for a conference by closed-circuit television with members of the American group gathered in Detroit. The Americans crossed the border at the close of the affair to dine with the Vietnamese.

At Cleveland Airport, waiting for Customs inspection, she was asked to leave the line. She made no objection at first, but after a minute or so, her curiosity overcame her fatigue. Weren't her rights as a citizen, which she holds so dear, being tampered with? She went back to the Customs inspector. "Listen, your job is to open my bag, not to make me step out of line."

"Shut up!" was his response, according to her account. When he finally examined her luggage, he took out her address book, glanced through it, and kept it for photographing. Then he found the plastic vials with which she habitually travels, marked "B L D."

Vitamins, yeast, and similar nonprescription food concentrates are important to her diet, keeping her weight down. "I like to feel close to the bone," she explains. In her restless urge to change the world, she sleeps sporadically, between two and eight hours a night. She considered it a very healthy thing to stop eating from time to time. She had more energy if she didn't eat too much.

The inspector grabbed the vials and read aloud the identifying letters. "Yes, BLD," she snapped. "Not LSD. BLD means breakfast and lunch and dinner."

"We will have them analyzed," he said.

In this situation, as in so many others, she was easy prey. She had gone through a phase where she made a point of smoking marijuana at press interviews and praising its virtues. "I am a shy person. I had a hard time communicating with people. I had a hard time relaxing, and it enabled me to let go."

Customs men took the tapes she was carrying, of GIs talking about violation of their rights. They confiscated her lecture notes and research material, to be photographed. She was allowed to telephone her attorney, Mark Lane of Boston, who first captured public attention by insisting that John F. Kennedy was assassinated by conspirators, not simply by Lee Harvey Oswald. Then she was held in an office for three and a half hours.

She was beside herself with anger. The look on her face was one that Hank had come to recognize and almost fear. "She preaches revolution," he said on another occasion. "Sometimes when she talks to me, her eyes widen almost like a madwoman's, and she screams about the injustices in American life. You can't reason with her. She won't believe a word I or anyone else says."

Mark Lane kept attempting to call her back, but "they wouldn't let me talk with him." To let him know that she was still detained in the office, she sang the "Marseillaise" at the top of her lungs. Police had arrived in the room now. She was undergoing a menstrual period, but one policeman blocked her way to the bathroom, as she related the incident. When she pushed him, he called another as a witness.

"Did you see that? You're under arrest for assault and battery." In evidence, he said she had kicked him in the shins. She was handcuffed for twenty minutes until a policewoman came with a sanitary pad. The woman stripped her and searched her handbag. In it, she found an old bottle with Dexedrine pills, prescribed by a doctor to help fight sleep.

Jane was driven to jail. "Here's another Commie," she heard the police say. It remained a mystery who released the story to the newspapers, but the headlines were plain enough, and misleading, too: "JANE FONDA ARRESTED ON PILL-SMUGGLING CHARGE."

"Now they are trying to discredit me by saying I use dope," she commented.

No charges stuck. Federal tests showed the pills to be exactly what she had said they were. When what was left in the vials was offered back to her, she refused to take them. "I am sorry," she said, in her best Vassar manner, "but I cannot accept such distrust on anybody's part." She took possession of her tapes again only after she insisted on having them played aloud in the presence of FBI men, so that they would have to listen to the recorded voices of GIs denouncing the war. A Fonda invariably tries to find some way to turn defeat into a victory.

The war in Vietnam, which has wracked a generation of Americans with doubt, inevitably divided the Fondas. There never was any question about who was a dove among them and who a hawk; by the standards of the Pentagon, they were all doves of one species or another, opposed to the massive bombing of North Vietnam. To the amazement of anyone who believed that attitudes harden like arteries with the years, Hank showed the greatest flexibility in his thinking.

He started as a firm believer in the need for U.S. troops in that country when the Johnson Administration was escalating the number of them up to the half-million mark. He accepted a United Service Organizations invitation to take a conducted tour of American bases. When he came back, he said, "Before I went, I wasn't anti-Vietnam, although I'm anti-card-burning and flag-burning, and I think a lot of the unwashed who go into those parades are protesting for the sake of protest. But I was apathetic. Well, my eyes were opened. I discovered it was my morale and America's morale that needed strengthening, not the troops'."

He was opposed to organized demonstrations against the war, like the marches on Washington, which Peter had joined in and which Jane had watched, fascinated, on film in Paris. "Every time there's a parade or peace rally in this country," Hank said, "it will make the war last that much longer, because it doesn't escape the attention of Ho Chi Minh."

He still regarded himself as a liberal. "I don't feel I'm a hawk because I'm pro-involvement in Vietnam, and I don't agree that we should bomb the hell out of them. But you can't be there and come away and not at least feel, well, obviously we should be there and that the job is being done and it's a good job."

At the time—this was July 1967—he had high hopes that his family could be made whole again. "As for those things Jane said about me, you can discard them. She said a lot of things that she wishes she was dead instead. She could cut her tongue out. She was trying to be a rebel and break away. As a parent, you just have to not pay any attention to it. You just have to keep your fingers crossed."

The next year, U.S. forces in Vietnam exceeded half a million; nearly fifteen thousand of them were killed and more than forty-six thousand wounded. The cost of the American presence there in that year alone reached $26,-839,000,000. The Vietcong's Tet offensive rocked American opinion, which had grown accustomed to hearing nothing but optimism from Washington and General William Westmoreland about the certainty of "victory." The discontent of Americans drove Lyndon Johnson to withdraw from the Presidential race.

Hank was among the millions whose views were changed by events. In the elections, he supported and helped what he described as "peace candidates," which included John V. Tunney of California. His enthusiasm for Hubert Humphrey, a previous voice of optimism about "steady progress" in the war, as a contender for the White House, didn't come close to what he later felt about George McGovern.

His growing opposition to the American involvement fell a long way short of Jane's. "I don't believe in the Vietnam war," he said, "but I do believe you have to express yourself by working within the system."

He had one experience that hardened his hostility to many of the things his daughter advocated. He made an appearance at a fund-raising rally for peace candidates at Madison Square Garden, New York. A group of what he believed to be Black Panthers jumped up on the stage with him, a woman among them, shouting, "Bazooka the mothers in the streets!"

"Jane checked it out and said they were not Panthers," he said gently, "but when I saw that woman pacing the stage, screaming obscenities and demanding revolution, I could see Jane doing the same thing."

He clung to some old dreams. "I hope Jane will come to her senses. We love her so much. I haven't given up on her. Someday, she'll find out all these people have been misleading her. I hope she doesn't wait too long."

He also continued to believe and act as a liberal, a creed that to more and more people of his children's generation seemed outdated in the world they wished to see. But it wasn't the young generation that bared its teeth at him. On one television show he read extracts from a speech by Abraham Lincoln, interspersed with lines from Martin Luther King, part of a program with memories of his adolescence in Omaha in the company of George Billings that is one of Hank's standbys. In the mail he received after that TV appearance was one letter calling him "a Commie bastard." Another threatened his life.

Similar insults and the same threat were commonplace to Jane. She presented a much more reachable target when she added public lectures to students and other groups to her working schedule. The purpose was to raise funds for Vietnam Veterans Against the War. She got into that almost by accident.

She had never spoken in public before. "People think actresses do that easily, and it's not easy at all; we're used to hiding behind masks," she said. She was in Santa Fe, New Mexico, when President Nixon announced the invasion of Cambodia. She called the University of New Mexico and asked if she could please speak there.

This was May 4, 1970, the day of nightmare when a thirteen-second burst of National Guard gunfire killed four

Kent State University students and wounded nine more, when young Americans in uniform clashed head-on with young Americans with long hair, and a generation of college students felt overwhelmingly that the future had darkened for everyone. For her appearance on the campus at Santa Fe, Jane found a thousand people crowding the hall. She felt that she could talk about the country the United States was entering in an extension of the war because she had met people who had been there and knew Prince Sihanouk, its head of state. She talked for a half-hour, and then turned the meeting into a debate. "My rap has gotten better since then," she says.

Now that she had discovered a new ability in herself, talking to audiences face to face, she had to exercise it. In the tourist sections of half the airlines of America she covered more territory than most traveling salesmen, trying to make converts to the Movement or, if not converts, contributors of funds. Every cause she spoke for fitted together with the one great challenge that she was convinced America faced. Some days she gave two separate talks to students, usually avoiding any formal introduction, simply walking to the lectern and jumping into her subject.

She chose an apostle's role, setting out to convert the maximum number of people to her belief that they must fight for political power. Her critics jeered, "You're a beneficiary of the capitalist system. How can you talk the way you do?" She agreed that she was indeed in a favored position, but went right on with her chosen mission.

As well as handing over most of her own earnings, she soon could raise thousands of dollars from sympathetic audiences in lecture halls or in sympathizers' living rooms for the Panthers, for Vietnam Veterans, for virtually anything the Movement worked for. But there was something paradoxical about her success, and it took her a long time to adjust to it. As a big-name celebrity, she was the candle that drew the moths. Yet she rejected all the material things associated with that kind of fame.

She was stunned by the resentment she found among women who expected a movie star to look like Marlene Dietrich in her prime. They accused her of slumming when she showed up at gatherings with her urchin-cut hair hastily combed, wearing her work clothes instead of some high-fashion outfit. She accused them in return of being fat and bored.

Later on, many dozens of public and private appearances later on, when she had thought harder about this personal problem, she was less critical. White, middle-class liberals prepared to give money were important. "You shouldn't put them down for what they are," she said. "They can help, too. They're part of the Movement, too. You can't write anyone off like that."

But she continued to fight off the attention she got simply because of the fact that she was a movie star. "What society has done is to say certain people are up on a pedestal, certain people have made it, are special. And what that is, is an incredible putdown to other people. And what the star system represents is a typical sickness in our society—competition, competition, success-oriented. And that's why, when people ask me for an autograph, I try to explain that no one person's name or relic of them or signature of them should be more important than anyone else's."

When she ran out of money, she had to go back into the only paying job she knew. Once again Vadim and a nurse took over the care of Vanessa while her mother flew to New York to play Bree Daniel, a high-class call girl threatened by a psychotic killer, in *Klute*.

The idea of the picture attracted her, though she had some reservations about the working out of the plot. She would have liked every movie to be heavy on politics, but that was impossible. It was hard enough to get any worthwhile picture. She would settle for a movie that would at least say *something*.

She went into preparation in her habitual Method manner, walking the East Side streets of Manhattan with girls like the one she was to portray, getting to know their trade, making friends of some of them. "What's your idea of the easiest kind of money?" she asked one.

"In and out in five minutes," was the calm reply.

When the picture was finished, she realized there were two turns of the plot that dissatisfied her, though she had been "too immature politically" to analyze the reasons. Bree Daniel, unlucky in a stage career, is in the hands of a woman psychoanalyst.

"Why do I still want to trick?" the girl asks the doctor.

"What is the difference?" the analyst answers. "You're successful as a call girl. You're not successful as an actress."

On reflection, Jane thought that she should have fought against that sequence. As a long-term patient of psycho-analysis, she disbelieved firmly in individual solutions to problems, to be found by talking about your bad dreams to psychiatrists. She was convinced that the problems of women, sexual or psychological, were social problems, to be tackled by changing society. The other "message" in *Klute* that she found fault with was its ending, which could be summed up as, "If you meet the right man, you can settle down and be a happy woman."

In a sense, however, she did meet the right man for the situation as a result of *Klute*. Donald Sutherland, her lead-ing man, played a detective "looking like a bloodhound," as one reviewer noticed. But without exception the critics admired Jane.

"Even those who put her down for stepping out of her safe role as a screen star cannot deny her considerable talent," one of them wrote. "She turns in the most impres-sive performance of her checkered career and by far the best piece of work done by any actress this year." Members of the Academy of Dramatic Arts and Sciences agreed with that.

In an almost symbolic gesture of blank ignorance about what motivated Jane, a national fashion magazine seized the opportunity to invite her to pose again, draped in furs, for some pages by photographer Richard Avedon. "Please thank them," she said in a state close to bewilderment. "I'm flattered, but it's too far removed from what I believe in and am involved in. . . ."

She talked to Donald Sutherland, a creative actor in better roles, about the journey she took with Elisabeth Vailland that had completely altered her. In the months that had gone by, she'd thought hard about its impact on her, and she could explain why it was so significant to her personal history.

She was convinced that the struggle to change society was her special struggle. The *system*, as she called it, was responsible for people going hungry, for illiteracy and lack of medical care. The system led to people being framed for crimes they did not commit, shot for resisting arrest, jailed for political reasons. And it was the same system that had messed up her life as an upper-class white, created the situation where she was treated by men not as a human being but as a sex object. She had only just started to find fulfillment in her life, expressing in her chosen work those things that she felt were important.

Her desire for knowledge of the Movement was like a thirst for sea water; the craving grew with every taste of it. Before *Klute*, she had arranged a cram course for herself with Mark Lane and other contacts on her ever-lengthening list of political affiliations. She had to understand the true intentions and purposes of the GI coffeehouses, which had captured her interest from the moment she heard about them at Mike Nichols' Hollywood party. She read books, watched documentary films of life in North Vietnam, and talked to disaffected U.S. soldiers by the dozens.

At first she imagined that the purpose of the GI Movement was inciting soldiers to desert. She regarded desertion as bravery, but it was an act without an encore. The deserter was simply replaced by another soldier. What she learned in her cram course "literally blew my mind." Most members of minority groups, she learned, as well as a growing number of others in the armed forces did not want to fight in the Indonesian wars.

Then she discovered, in the process of being arrested by MPs, that Army regulations covering the Constitutional rights of soldiers were often violated, including the right to sign petitions to Congress and take part in off-duty demonstrations under certain conditions. One job the coffeehouses did was to spread the word about GI rights. A serviceman learned what his rights were and how he could exercise them—legal ways to avoid or delay being shipped to Vietnam. He might apply for recognition as a conscientious objector. Or he could emerge as such a skilled political organizer that the armed forces would want to discharge him.

She heard about the "Vietnam syndrome," a tolerance for violence that turned troops into killers without conscience and produced the horrors of My Lai. She talked with soldiers who had thrown war prisoners out of helicopters because their offices said that was the only way to force them to talk. One serviceman, she said, told her that his company used prisoners for bayonet practice. She heard of a psychiatric case who traded the testicles of Vietnamese he had killed in exchange for transistor radios, which he then sold to his comrades.

Her instinct for the theater told her that the best way to arouse her audiences, to turn them on the fastest, was to talk about atrocities. The reaction from those she spoke to was usually to say, "It can't be true. You're out of your mind." Or the white liberals, from whom she felt increasingly alienated, would exclaim, "We don't do that; we're Americans." That simply fed her determination to make them understand that the commitment of atrocities was not limited to Hitler's Nazis.

Among the white liberals she tackled was her father,

whom she consistently tried to win over to her point of view in all its changes through the years. She went through the list with him, not forgetting her story of Fort Holabird, Maryland, "where they're trained to torture the prisoners." "The fantastic human being," as she's described him, could not bring himself to believe her. Too much of his life had been spent wearing a mask that was a composite of American heroes for him to accept such claims as reality.

His response, she said afterward, was what she had come to expect from other men of good will like him: "You don't know what you're talking about. We don't do that; we're Americans. And even if the soldiers did it, they wouldn't talk about it."

She told him that psychologists' experience showed that once a man involved in atrocities began to unburden himself of guilt, he was impelled to talk and keep talking. "If you can prove that it's true," she quoted Hank as saying, "I will lead a march to Nixon and confront him."

She took a group of Army veterans to his house so that they could give him their firsthand accounts of what they had done in Vietnam. He heard them out in silence, clearly disturbed. Then, according to Jane, he said sadly, "I don't see what I can do besides what I am already doing, that is, campaigning for the peace candidates." That he certainly did, up to appearing on national television to raise campaign funds for McGovern after his first favorite, Edmund Muskie, retired from the race for President in 1972.

Jane did more. She scheduled some of her time to collect money to open, with Mark Lane, an office in Washington, D.C., "to collect affidavits and documents from all over the world concerning violations of GIs' rights." She set about finding the funds for the Winter Soldier Investigation, climaxed by a public hearing in a crowded Detroit hall of soldiers' accounts, often told in tears, of what they had done and seen in the war, the mutilations, the ravaging of Vietnamese women.

And on the set of *Klute,* she mentioned to Donald Sutherland still another campaign that had sprung into her mind. He was the leading man in her life as well as in two of her pictures, sharing her opinions in politics and in man-and-woman relationships. Why not put together a comedy troupe, in which they would appear, to tour military bases with a sizzling antiwar stage show?

Sutherland was enthusiastic. With a handful of dimes, she started making phone-booth calls to get the wheels rolling. Jules Feiffer, delineator of the damned in cartoons and plays, liked the idea. Mike Nichols joined in, and Elliott Gould. So did Dick Gregory, the black comedian who waged a write-in campaign as a Presidential candidate in 1968. Rock groups, singers, writers, and poets volunteered their help. Dr. Howard B. Levy, discharged as an Army captain and jailed for refusing to train soldiers headed for Vietnam, gave his support.

At a news conference at a downtown Manhattan hotel, Jane announced her latest involvement, this plan for expressing the things she felt in work as an entertainer. In a voice that has never quite lost its private-school accents, she explained, "It's been very disconcerting for many of us in Hollywood to see that Bob Hope, Martha Raye, and other companies of their political ilk have cornered the market and are the only entertainers allowed to speak to soldiers in this country and Vietnam. A lot of us who have different points of view about the war and what's happening to this country have decided the time has come to speak to the forgotten soldiers. They are the majority of the soldiers. They want peace and freedom, but they are isolated in the military world, and they need our support."

The troupe of traveling players had come up with a bold plan. Like any group of entertainers, they would need an official invitation from the commanding officer to perform on any base. They decided to put the Army to the test by trying for such an invitation from Lieutenant General

John Tolson, commander of Fort Bragg, North Carolina. If they obtained it, they would enjoy the added satisfaction of having the Army pay for their antiwar propaganda; their room, board, and travel expenses would automatically be reimbursed under a standard Pentagon policy toward civilian entertainers. They sent a script of the show to General Tolson.

To nobody's surprise, their request was turned down. Their skits, said the brass, would be "detrimental to morale." Of course, the troupe had alternative arrangements ready. Jane talked about filing a lawsuit against the Pentagon to seek permission for them to appear at any base with their expenses paid. The show itself—"funny, professional, and an enormous hit," in one reporter's judgment —played at Haymarket Square, the GI coffeehouse in Fayetteville.

It was a revue with no stars. Among other bits, Jane performed a burlesque of Pat Nixon in a mobcap, and the audience of GIs whistled as though she were Barbarella. Sutherland did a battle "sportscast" as if from Vietnam. ("Nixon would have liked to be here at this great game today to throw out the first grenade.") Dick Gregory covered a dozen and one subjects, including Army intelligence agents. ("When you see a man in the audience wearing a beard with a price tag hanging on it, it's a dead giveaway. But the real clincher is to look down and notice a spit-shine on the sandals.")

For one scene, Jane put on a top hat and did a soft-shoe dance to the music of "Carolina" while she sang:

> Nothing could be finer
> Than to be in Indochina,
> —Making money.
> Asia is a hobby
> When you're in the China Lobby,
> —Life is sunny . . .

Afterward, she summed up what she thought was being achieved. "When the time comes for these guys to make a decision, will they allow themselves to be used in riot control? Will they allow themselves to be used to break strikes? Or will they kill people in Vietnam? When the time comes for them to take an active position, they know that they will not be doing it as isolated, vulnerable individuals. It will be a collective. That's the most important thing we could have done. Because, after all, we didn't tell them anything they didn't know."

For months ahead, the show, named "FTA" for public reference, toured GI coffeehouses, a thorn in the Army's flank, while attorneys pushed for carte-blanche permission to take it onto bases, with the Pentagon picking up the tab. Sometimes Vanessa, a miniature of her mother, traveled with her and Liz Morrow, the woman who takes care of her when Jane isn't available. The highlight of every show came when, invariably, the watching crowds stood up and joined in singing the title song, "Fuck the Army," which represented the sentiments of everyone in the cast. Hank, who always insisted on cleaning up any scripts he worked with, could only shudder.

For Jane Fonda it was a necessary, minor part of the job that she saw as the foremost task of everyone who wants to change the world—ending the war in Vietnam. It was important for her to, win an Oscar, as she did for *Klute*, because that gave her an extra credential with millions of Americans.

"The Oscar is what working people relate to when they think of people in movies. That's what the masses of people in America, who think I'm a freak and who think that people who support the Panthers and speak out against the war are all some kind of monsters, relate to. It's important for those of us who speak out for social change to get that kind of acclaim. It means that we're legitimatized in the eyes of those working people, those people whom we have to reach and make understand that our cause is legitimate, too."

For months before she won her gilt statuette, she had somehow given the impression that she had already visited Vietnam to witness the horrors of war. Statistics and anecdotes about it filled her mind as a result of her cram-course studies, and they poured in a torrent from her tongue in public speeches and on television shows. "There were guys who had come back from Nam who were sent into training with open wounds," she would claim. Or she would take aim at a whole row of her chosen targets, talking so fast that the words were blurred.

"From the beginning of the war until April 1971, five point eight million civilians, one third of the population of the southern part of Vietnam, have been killed, injured, or made homeless. . . . While the bombs and artillery are committing one kind of genocide in the rural areas, the cultural underpinnings of society in southern Vietnam are being torn to shreds by the introduction of the American market system of material values. In other words, cultural genocide, the turning of the southern part of Vietnam into a transistorized, television-watching, Honda motorbike-riding consumer society amenable to the exploitation of American industry. . . . The extent of the chauvinism and racism of American playboy-type cultural standards can be measured by the thousands of operations performed on Vietnamese women to change their eyes, noses, chins, and breasts in order to look more 'American.' . . ."

The Movement arranged for the woman who had just been acclaimed the world's best motion-picture actress to see the country she had talked about so often and the people, the North Vietnamese, she had praised so much. She had prepared herself for this climactic trip by learning a few words of the intimidating language, by boning up on the country's history and arts.

She was clearly prepared to approve of what she was shown, and she did, wholeheartedly. She dressed up in peasant clothes and posed for photographers, grinning under a straw hat with the little-girl face that still occasionally shows in her hollowed cheeks and tired eyes. She talked with American prisoners-of-war. She saw the damage that American bombs had done to the country's tenuous dike system and told about it in a tape-recorded interview broadcast over Hanoi radio.

An outcry for her impeachment rose among Americans who were sick and tired of Jane, the New Left, and her whole disturbing generation. She drew an official rebuke from the State Department in Washington, D.C. Letters of protest filled columns of newspapers and magazines across the United States. One outraged Congressman demanded her immediate arrest for treason, then, finding the law on the question to be unsatisfactory, talked about the need for new legislation to take care of the likes of her. The House of Representatives Internal Security Committee did its best to oblige him. Hank refused to be drawn into the donnybrook. The storm passed over, at least temporarily, when other antiwar activists who followed her to Hanoi succeeded in obtaining the token release of three U.S. pilots from captivity as prisoners-of-war.

Jane remained unperturbed by the uproar. It was no more nor less than what she expected. Perhaps she was reminded by a conversation she had on the eve of an "FTA" show in Killeen, Texas, not long before she went to Hanoi. A hunky, crop-haired, aging policeman started to talk to her. "Let me say this, Miss Fonda. I think we're on opposite sides of the pole."

"Not as much as you think, perhaps."

"I've followed your exploits in Fort Lewis and everywhere, and I think you're an American. I think you should say what you feel, as long as you don't hurt this country."

She turned the cool Fonda eyes on his. "I bet that if you and I knew each other well we could agree on more than you think. On what we both want."

"What do you want, Miss Fonda?"

"I want people to be able to determine their own lives. I want people to control their lives. I want all people to be able to get an education, to get good medical care."

"Doesn't everyone want that?" asked the cop. "May I ask you a question, Miss Fonda?" She nodded. "How does your father feel about this, because to my generation he's an idol?"

She paused. Then, "My father thinks that to change things you just have to put the right people in office."

"Do you talk to your father a lot about this?"

She shook her head. "No. He doesn't like to talk about these things. It scares him."

For herself, as a woman, before and after the cries of "treason," she gloried in the fact that she was free, finally, from restraint, from fear, from guilt. She has explained her feeling in these words:

"One knows that one is free if you don't have to pretend that you don't mind what you're doing, or mind who you're living with, or that you really don't mind getting up and going to an office, doing something you don't really like to do.

"You know you're free when every morning you wake up and you know that whatever you do during the day is going to be something you have decided you want to do because it fulfills you in some way and serves a function that you feel is important. Having been someone who was not always free, all I can say is that there's no other way to live.

"There is no reason why anyone in the world cannot be in that situation. Most people become dependent on money, on possessions. It's incredible how many people's homes and physical surroundings become extremely important. Because the relationships aren't important. And so, whereas someone can easily imagine leaving the spouse, it's very difficult for them to imagine selling the furniture and moving out of the house. Well, that's terrifying and it's inexcusable.

"We have only one of these things which we call lives, in which we walk around and breathe and everything like that, and then it's all over so far as I'm concerned."

For her father, she says she has love and respect now that she is no longer dominated by the sheer fact of his being. She accepts, sadly, that they can probably never be close face to face, *corps à corps*, as the French say, but perhaps that possibility was only the dream of a lonesome child in dark distress.

Peter has found it no easier. He, too, speaks of his love for Hank, and "today we communicate." They share less time together than the son would like, but they hold a lot of opinions in common. "He got older and I got wiser, or I got older and he got wiser," Peter says. "I'm not sure which happened. . . ."

Politically, they are working Democrats, left of center. The father would echo the son when he says, "All we've got to do is get the government back to the Constitution, Bill of Rights and Declaration of Independence, and for that I don't believe an armed revolution is necessary."

After throwing some of his *Easy Rider* income into writing, directing, and acting in *The Hired Hand*, a high-styled Western that reviewers liked more than audiences did, Peter Fonda took off for Hawaii with his family in the boat he had dreamed about for years, paid for with $225,000 cash. On his father's advice, he changed his mind at the last minute and, instead of trying to go it alone, picked up a captain for the ten-thousand-mile Pacific crossing.

That was communication between the two of them of a kind that the father once imagined would be impossible.

Not long after they had sailed home, the marriage of Peter and Susan Fonda, which Hank hoped was as solid as a rock, came to an end. In his consternation, he could accept some of the blame as his. The "let's pretend" world of the theater is heavily populated with men and women with little knowledge of what shared love means, because they had no example of it set by their parents.

Then in January 1973, Jane flew to Santo Domingo for a twenty-four-hour divorce from Vadim. She traveled under an assumed name, as part of the discreet arrangements made by her attorneys. Publicity is something that all three of the fabulous Fondas try to avoid sometimes. Three days later, Hank and Peter joined a hundred or so other guests, some of them Vietnamese, who packed into her Laurel Canyon home in Los Angeles to see her married to thirty-three-year-old Tom Hayden, antiwar activist and a defendant in the conspiracy trial of the "Chicago Seven," a follower of the same gospel as Jane.

They decided on marriage when they made a tour of American cities before the Presidential election the previous fall. They agreed not to talk publicly about their plans because the speeches they made about the peace movement were more important.

"Our engagement is a very private thing," Jane said, "and must not interfere with the campaign. Of course, we are in love. When we are together we behave just like any other couple who are getting married. But there is a healthy distinction between our private life and our public life."

Those remarks were made in answer to a publicity agent's bewildered statement that he had never seen them hold hands or kiss. "They spend their time trying to convert people who do not share their point of view—which is most of us."

Hank reported that he had grown to know Tom Hayden "and admire him very much. I'm very happy that Jane plans to marry him. I think she'll be happy with a man like him."

At the wedding there were Irish jigs to be danced and lilting Vietnamese ballads to be sung, but the vows exchanged were formal enough, and the minister was a full-fledged Episcopal clergyman. The principal contribution to publicity, however, came from the Bishop of California, who promptly suspended the officiating priest for neglecting to obtain the necessary permission to remarry a divorcée. Within a month or so, Jane was noticeably pregnant.

The remote father, the nagging perfectionist, the unseduceable actor, the much-married moralist has changed more slowly than his children, but he has changed, and because he is Fonda, the change continues in his probing mind.

"The kids don't have the dedication we used to have," he says. "In some ways, though, I understand why Peter doesn't take my advice and doesn't believe old-timers. It seems as if a lot of the advice I gave him was wrong. Old-timers are cautious. The kids are daring, and they're getting away with it."

The poor boy from Nebraska is definitely the senior patrician now, something of a clubman, a mingler in society. The urge to act, he recognizes, is rooted in neuroticism. "I am not neurotic," he insists, "but I think you become an actor because there are these complexes about you that aren't average or normal, and these aren't the easiest things to live with. You can be easily upset, or short-tempered, or lack patience."

The urge to act still dominates him—for its rewards in money, the reputation of his peers, and personal fulfillment —but the mask has worn thinner with the years. More of the man shows through now, reflective, detached, with few illusions.

"Frankly, I've never really dealt with problems at all.

They keep happening to me. Eventually, if you sit there long enough, they just fall off. I can't deal with problems, and that's the truth. The only thing I could tell anybody is to go on with your life and not let things destroy you. Somehow you do survive these upsets. The name of the game, I guess, is survival."

Can anyone say more than that?

Index